CRIT
FOR TR

"The *Travelers' Tales* series is quite remarkable."
                —Jan Morris, author of *Journeys*, *Locations*, and *Hong Kong*

"For the thoughtful traveler, these books are an invaluable resource.
There's nothing like them on the market."
                —Pico Iyer, author of *Video Night in Kathmandu*

"The *Travelers' Tales* series should become required reading for anyone
visiting a foreign country who wants to truly step off the tourist track
and experience another culture, another place, first hand."
                —Nancy Paradis, *St. Petersburg Times*

"...*Travelers' Tales* is a valuable addition to any pre-departure reading list."
                —Tony Wheeler, publisher, Lonely Planet Publications

"I can't think of a better way to get comfortable with a destination than
by delving into *Travelers' Tales*...before reading a guidebook, before
seeing a travel agent. The series helps visitors refine their interests and
readies them to communicate with the peoples they come in contact
with...."
                —Paul Glassman, Society of American Travel Writers

"This is the stuff memories can be duplicated from."
                —Karen Krebsbach, *Foreign Service Journal*

"Like having been there, done it, seen it. If there's one thing traditional
guidebooks lack, it's the really juicy travel information, the personal
stories about back alleys and brief encounters. The *Travelers' Tales*
series fills this gap with an approach that's all anecdotes, no directions."
                —Jim Gullo, *Diversion*

OTHER TRAVELERS' TALES BOOKS

Country and Regional Guides
America, Australia, Brazil, France, India, Italy,
Japan, Mexico, Nepal, Spain, Thailand;
Grand Canyon, Hawaii, Hong Kong,
Paris, and San Francisco

Women's Travel
A Woman's Passion for Travel, A Woman's World,
Women in the Wild, A Mother's World, Safety
and Security for Women Who Travel,
Gutsy Women, Gutsy Mamas

Body & Soul
The Adventure of Food, The Road Within,
Love & Romance, Food,
The Fearless Diner, The Gift of Travel

Special Interest
Testosterone Planet, There's No Toilet Paper
on the Road Less Traveled, The Penny Pincher's
Passport to Luxury Travel, Family Travel,
A Dog's World

Footsteps
Kite Strings of the Southern Cross,
The Sword of Heaven

THE
FEARLESS
SHOPPER

HOW TO
GET THE BEST DEALS
ON THE PLANET

*Enjoy fearless
Shopping!*

TRAVELERS' TALES

THE
FEARLESS
SHOPPER

HOW TO
GET THE BEST DEALS
ON THE PLANET

BY KATHY BORRUS

TRAVELERS' TALES
SAN FRANCISCO

The Fearless Shopper: How To Get the Best Deals on the Planet
By Kathy Borrus.

Cover design: Kathryn Heflin, Susan Bailey, and Judy Anderson
Interior design: Art direction by Kathryn Heflin, design by Susan Bailey
Cover Illustration: Michael Surles, watercolor painting
Page layout: Patty Holden, using the fonts Berkeley, Copperplate, and Savoye

Library of Congress Cataloguing-in-Publication Data
The fearless shopper: how to get the best deals on the planet / by Kathy
Borrus — 1st ed.
        p.   cm.
    Includes bibliographical references and index.
        ISBN 1-885211-39-2
    1. Shopping Guidebooks. I. Title.
TX335.B635 1999
380.1'45—dc21   99-34442
                                                         CIP

First Edition
Printed in the United States
10 9 8 7 6 5 4 3 2 1

For my parents

TABLE OF CONTENTS

PART TWO

Fearless Shopper's Regional Shopping Guide

INTRODUCTION

Life is the greatest bargain:
we get it for nothing.

—*Yiddish proverb*

———

Sheets of rain pounded against the car's window. The intermittent fog and the glare from the headlights of oncoming trucks obscured my view. On the two-lane highway the dividing lines disappeared from my sight. I gripped the steering wheel and strained to see the road ahead of me. "How can they drive so fast over this potholed road?" I wondered. "In the dark, no less. What was I doing on this Mexican highway anyway?"

This was not my idea of fun. I had taken the wheel so Luis, our buying agent, could catch a quick nap. I couldn't wait to return the driving to Luis, a former racecar test driver. Fortunately, after an hour he woke up and took over the wheel. Every muscle in my body ached, but I was relieved to be going home safely after our business trip through Mexico. We came in search of crafts to stock the Smithsonian Museum Shops, and now our trunk was packed with samples from this buying trip.

Heading back to Mexico City from San Miguel Allende, I remembered the time I tried to leave the Nurenberg Toy Fair in Germany during a blizzard. From business treks in inclement weather to the hotel rooms with unidentifiable insects, I wondered how we not only survived, but also managed to come home with the goods trip after trip.

Whether you're buying professionally, picking up something at your local market, window-shopping in Paris, or scouring a flea market in Morocco, everyone shops. The choices can be overwhelming, but they can also be entertaining. Where do we shop? Markets, stores, catalogs, TV, the Internet, in the streets. Why do we do it? Necessity or desire? Boredom or compulsion? Diversion or depression? To pamper or reward?

The reasons are as varied as the venues. As a Fearless Shopper, you may be a determined haggler or a casual window-shopper. Whatever your role, you'll enjoy browsing these pages for hints on shopping at home or in exotic cultures. Armed with these tips, you, the Fearless Shopper, will revisit your favorite haunts as well as venture into new territory with confidence.

I still love finding back roads, cruising crowded markets, sleuthing around corners, wandering up crooked streets and down mysterious alleys. I'm a Fearless Shopper with a degree in street anthropology. Some may be born to shop, but I was born to wander. So, wander with me in these pages through alternative routes to fearless shopping—which may mean just looking—into sidewalk stalls, Third World bazaars, flea markets, open-air auctions, that new world market—the Internet, and more.

This is not a guide to outlet malls, couture houses, or department stores. Fearless Shoppers will discover hints to shop smart, bargain like a native, consume less, absorb culture, leave civilizations intact, and sustain fair trade.

For me shopping has never been about acquiring things. It's about exploring culture and preserving memory—the sights, sounds, smells, tastes, tempo, and touch of a place. And whether you actually buy anything or not, shopping is about having fun.

Someone recently asked me for my best shopping tip. "That's easy," I thought. "Travel." Most unique finds are an accident of place and time. Things are for sale everywhere—even those not for sale. You need only be open to the possibility. The buys that bring the most joy are often those things we stumble across, never looked for, and never even knew we wanted.

Wherever I've traveled, one thing is clear: the world is a marketplace. We are all traders—natural-born buyers and sellers. It's primordial. Beyond the basic needs of food, clothing, and shelter, people have always bartered and traded for things of beauty, things that delight and nourish the spirit. Whether we love it or hate it, we all shop.

For many in Western cultures, shopping is almost an addiction. Historians date the rise in consumerism to the seventeenth century, but mass production in the early twentieth century created a culture of spending that continues to grow. In fact, for the past five decades our collective buying spree has known no boundaries save an occasional pause for economic slowdowns. In the last twenty years, Americans' personal spending rose about 30 percent. We own more cars, clothing, kitchen gadgets, and electronic devices than ever before. Who would have thought, as a recent article in *The Washington Post* suggests, that America would have more shopping malls than high schools?

And so, we owe it to ourselves and our planet to try to consume less. It may mean paying greater attention to the places we shop and the reasons we purchase the things that catch our eyes. But we cannot deny human nature—it is unlikely that we will give up souvenir hunting. For, just as the earliest wanderer encountering a different civilization brought back something foreign, we also seek remembrances of our journeys. I look at my accumulated stuff and I am transported. It's less about consumption than it is about memory.

My Dutch wooden cookie mold with its film of flour hangs on my kitchen wall and reminds me of my student days in Amsterdam. My ceramic Coimbra olive dish with the floral motif and prancing deer brings me to a street market in Cascais, Portugal. My pierced-leather stick puppets remind me that everything in Indonesia is shadow play. Looking at my sculpted clay figure, I see the chalky, mud-crusted fingers of a Romanian folk artist in his workshop.

The batik wall hangings and Mogul silk paintings, the masks and carvings, the jewelry and clothes and silk scarves that I've amassed evoke images of people and places along my own silk route. One day I'm picnicking on the ruins of an old Mogul fort in India as the sun sets; the next day I'm watching a wedding procession in Bali; and another day I'm wondering if the sun will ever set in Juneau, Alaska, while I await the Eskimo artists who have even less of a sense of time than I do. And, so, I am surrounded—not by things but history and culture and memory.

When I think about shopping, the world divides into East and West. The latter shouts conspicuous consumption, while the former conjures romantic images of bazaars and *souks*, camels and caravans, spices and colors, and legendary roads like Amber, Incense, and Silk. Visions of nomads of the Eurasian steppe and Turegs kicking up dust across the Sahara fill my mind. For me, shopping links the past and present, just as the Silk Road linked cultures, religions, crafts, and trade over 8,700 miles (14,000 kilometers).

Beyond the bazaars and *souks* are other markets of the

world where the tradition of buyer and seller provides continuity of civilization. In the faces and the buzz of human activity and exchange, there is woven the fabric of daily life, and shopping is merely another access—a window through which culture beckons.

Along your own shopping route, you'll want to prepare yourself. Arm yourself with hints for shopping smarter with every purchase, every dollar spent—even for mundane things. Learn to negotiate for anything, anytime, anywhere. In the process, think about using less stuff, preserving the earth's resources, and paying fair prices. Make shopping an adventure, even at home. Above all, have fun.

PART ONE

BE A
FEARLESS SHOPPER

Chapter One

DETOURS & DIVERSIONS

Most of us would like to end our lives feeling both
that we had a good time and that we left the
world a little better than we found it.

— Philip Slater

*F*earless Shoppers in search of entertainment need no excuse to cruise the hottest retail spot or hunt for great bargains at the nearest garage sale. Stressed from work and responsibility, we need shopping adventures to break the routine in our lives.

But for many of us, shopping turns into a real diversion only when we travel and encounter other cutltures. My desire to shop increases exponentially as soon as I get in my car, board a plane, or hop a train out of town. It's then that I leave behind routine and just go looking. I find the best stuff when I'm traveling—some-

> I buy quickly when I fall in love with something, and only then. Buying for investment in art or craft is always a mistake. I collect experiences rather than objects—memories that accumulate patina rather than dust.
>
> ◆
>
> *Hans Guggenheim, artist*

thing unexpected—usually because I've made a detour. And if I find nothing, well, I'm just as happy for the diversion.

Commerce can lead us into culture. An unexpected connection with a textile artist halfway around the world can lighten your heart—as well as your pocketbook. You'll come home with a rug, a story to tell, and a wonderful memory.

Once while browsing a street market in Zimbabwe, I stopped for lunch along the dirt road, where a group of barefoot kids aged five to twelve were playing a make-shift game of soccer. I joined the game, thinking I could easily outmaneuver them.

In shopping out of town there is the pleasure in remembering the trip.

♦

Dene Garbow,
buyer and manager

Instead, they had great fun keeping the ball away from me—a cultural exchange not soon forgotten. And I thought I was just shopping.

Whether your idea of shopping is deliberate diversion or part of a grand trip, my best advice is to set forth with courage into the wide world. You may not find what you're looking for, but you may find something infinitely more valuable.

When I'm out of town, I have more time and really see shopping as a form of escape.

♦

Lauren Freedman,
e-commerce consultant

Traveling with children increases your chances of mixing cultural experiences with commerce. Given a budget for souvenirs, children have an opportunity to interact with children from different cultures, to practice their language and bargaining skills, and to learn responsibility with money.

When I was in a Mexican market with my then-seven-year-old son, he found a young girl about his age selling woven bookmarks. Running back and forth in the market, he asked me how to say various numbers in Spanish, then he bargained with the girl. He had a blast and proudly displayed the gifts he had bought for his friends.

Whether you play soccer, encourage your children's adventures, or sip tea in the back room of a rug dealer's emporium, find those detours and diversions that make life more rewarding than routine. The hidden joy in shopping is exploring other cultures— bringing back memories and leaving behind goodwill from your encounters. Remember, a Fearless Shopper doesn't have to buy anything. Sometimes just looking is enough.

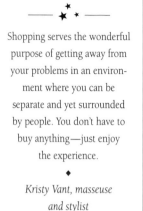

Shopping serves the wonderful purpose of getting away from your problems in an environment where you can be separate and yet surrounded by people. You don't have to buy anything—just enjoy the experience.

♦

Kristy Vant, masseuse and stylist

Tips

➣ Bring photographs and postcards from your hometown to show new acquaintances.

➣ When traveling in a foreign country, bring small items made in your country, such as pens or t-shirts, for giving away to friends you meet along the way.

➣ Increase your opportunities for personal encounters in the markets. When you are bargaining for that turquoise necklace, ask the artist what she most enjoys about her work. Or strike up a conversation about her family.

➣ When shopping in a foreign market, take time to find out

what local customs or stories accompany the object you are purchasing. Designs painted on bowls or woven into fabric may carry symbolic meaning for the people who created them. Listen to the traditions behind their work.

➤ Take photos of people you chat with—after asking their permission, of course. In some places a small gratuity is appropriate for the privilege of taking a photo.

➤ Ask a bystander to snap a photo of you with new friends. When you get home, make the photo into a postcard, and mail it back to your new acquaintances.

➤ When giving children a budget for souvenirs, review vocabulary of numbers so they can bargain in the foreign language.

➤ If traveling with children, shop in places that would appeal to them: markets where other children are present, shops with child-sized objects or objects that stimulate the imagination.

➤ Encourage children to choose objects made by hand rather than factory-made items, so they can learn the stories behind the goods and appreciate the craft skills needed to create them.

➤ Give children an inexpensive camera and at least one roll of film and encourage them to record their own impressions of the trip.

When my friends learned I was going to Antarctica, many said,
"Why? There aren't any stores there."

◆

Ramona Solberg, artist

Chapter Two

FEARLESS PREPARATIONS

A journey of a thousand miles must
begin with a single step.

— *Lao-tzu*

———

I stuffed my bags with giveaway t-shirts and pens, boxes of labels, bubble wrap, and masking tape. This was not my idea of traveling light. I hardly had room for my clothes. "At least," I thought, "we're more prepared this time." I wanted our second excursion into West African markets to be more hassle-free than our first. My colleagues and I, as buyers for the Smithsonian Museum Shops, dragged these tools of our trade along with malaria pills and granola bars to markets in Africa, Asia, and beyond. We were always determined to bring back the goods. And preparation was everything.

It still is. Whether you are headed downtown, to the next state, or to a country around the world, you will save yourself hassles—not to mention money, sometimes a great deal of it—if you spend a little time preparing for the hunt.

Think before you go about what you would like to buy, for whom you are buying, and how much you would like to spend. Knowing these three things ahead of time will help you focus, and you'll be less likely to get distracted by unworkable purchases. And if you fall in love with that impossibly delicate porcelain figurine? You'll have your own bubble wrap—even an extra bag for carrying it home.

Tips

➤ Shop smart locally. Save energy and call ahead to see if the product is in stock.

➤ Bring a calculator or create a cheat sheet of the currency rates, especially if you are bargaining in a foreign language.

➤ Research a product or a substantial purchase. Use Consumer Reports and the Internet. Visit a few stores or on-line sites to compare price and quality.

➤ Before you visit a foreign country, learn as much as you can about the customs, traditions, regional specialties, and indigenous arts and crafts of that place. You'll know what specialties to look for when you arrive. Review the extensive Regional Shopping Guide in Part Two of this book.

➤ Plan ahead for souvenir buying. Prepare lists with names of friends and relatives and their current sizes and color preferences as well as one with your own needs or desires.

➤ If you plan to buy an item to match an outfit or coordinate a color scheme, pack photographs or color swatches and a tape measure. Take measurements of floor or wall areas at home in case you want to purchase rugs or furniture.

I've always had a hard time buying things. Anything. I grew up in a family where I was taught that anything bought simply for pleasure, for the sheer enjoyment of life, was a waste of money. Not a sin exactly—Jews don't really believe in sins—but an unforgivable self-indulgence, worthy of crippling guilt. There was always some distant, abstract "future" when I might need that money—as if the $1.50 I spent on a James Bond souvenir program would cripple my retirement fund.

♦

Jeff Greenwald,
Shopping for Buddhas

➤ Pack a foldable suitcase to carry home additional or unplanned purchases.

➤ Wherever you travel, if you get hungry often, pack snacks that travel well, such as granola bars. They'll make you less cranky so you'll be more apt to make a wiser purchase decision.

➤ Pack small tokens from home—anything made in your own country—to barter for an item that interests you. They can also be given away to friends you meet along the way.

When packing, I put the least-valuable stuff in the bags I plan to check. Most people check their big bag; I check the small one with the things I can live without the longest.

◆

Ginny Hanger,
customer service manager

➤ If you don't want to overspend on impulse items, stick to your budget and your lists.

➤ Comparison shop even before you leave home. If you're planning to visit a country with a reputation for good prices on certain items, check out the prices on similar products before you leave home. Write down the information and bring it with you.

High school yearbook caption:
In ten years can be
found shopping.

◆

Laurence Bacon,
businessman

➤ Familiarize yourself with the customs policies of your own country, and learn as much as you can about a country's entry and exit requirements. See "Getting It Home" for more information on customs and shipping.

➤ If you live in the U.S., you can order a copy of "Know Before You Go" from the customs office in Washington, D.C. See the "Resources and References" section for the address, or read it free on-line at http://www.customs.ustreas.gov/travel/ kbygo.htm.

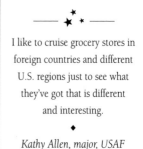

I like to cruise grocery stores in foreign countries and different U.S. regions just to see what they've got that is different and interesting.

♦

Kathy Allen, major, USAF

➤ Learn about proper documentation as well as import and export regulations on antiquities, animal products, and endangered species. See the CITES listing in the "Resources and References" section for international trade information on endangered species.

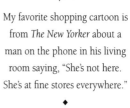

My favorite shopping cartoon is from *The New Yorker* about a man on the phone in his living room saying, "She's not here. She's at fine stores everywhere."

♦

Shelley Levin, graduate student

➤ In some countries, buying artwork and antiquities may require an export license, which could result in unexpected duty or additional fees. Know the policies of the country you will be visiting.

Dress the Part

And then there's the matter of your clothes. In the theater of commerce, as every Fearless Shopper knows, it pays to dress the part. Your costume is part of the game, giving merchants clues about who you are and how much money you are likely to spend. If you are bargaining at an open-air market, you don't want to look ritzy, so it's best to leave your good jewelry and expensive outfits at home. If you are shopping in a fancy boutique, on the other hand, you'll be treated better if you dress up. Wear suitable clothes for each shopping venue, and you're more likely to find a receptive audience.

Tips

> You'll walk more than you think, so wear comfortable shoes.

> For excursions to yard sales, dusty bazaars, or open-air markets, don't wear sandals. You never know what you might step in or on, so cover your feet with socks and a comfortable pair of shoes.

> If you are shoe or boot shopping, bring the socks or stockings you are likely to wear with each so the fit will be correct.

> If you are a woman trying on clothes, wear a body suit and tights to save time; this will also allow you to slip on garments anywhere without undressing. Dressing rooms, especially in foreign markets, are frequently unavailable.

The best shopping is when a smile of satisfaction appears in front of your mirror. The worst is standing in line to return the item purchased.

♦

Florence Lloyd, linguist

Chapter Three

SAFE SHOPPING

Put all your eggs in the one basket
and—watch that basket.

— Mark Twain

———

Once in a bookstore in New York City, three women bumped me and lifted my wallet. Those three lucky women got to split four dollars. They didn't know I had $150 in a white envelope right next to the wallet.

Fortunately for me, I had "hidden" my Smithsonian travel money. For easy accounting, I often traveled with my business money separate from my own money. But the pickpockets gained access to my wallet because I had been careless. I was so engrossed in book browsing that I had slung my bag over my shoulder and had forgotten about it. I was an easy mark. Though a kind soul later retrieved my wallet from a subway floor and returned it to me—minus the four dollars but with credit cards intact—I had already reported my credit cards stolen and requested replacements.

At home in familiar places, these occurrences are annoying and stressful but relatively easy to rectify. Abroad, the dangers and hassles multiply. Lunching one day in London, a friend reached down under the table to pay for her meal and found her bag gone. After spending the day reporting her losses and replacing her money and passport, she went to dinner at an elegant restaurant with her husband. Her bag disappeared again from under the table—an unusual coincidence. Stolen twice. She learned: keep your bag in sight.

It takes stamina, caution, and awareness to shop whether at home or abroad. On the road, especially a foreign one, pickpockets and petty thieves can cause problems, ruin your shopping sprees, and waste your time.

The best strategy against theft is to hide your cash. Do carry cash, but organize it so you don't flash a large amount of money to pay for an inexpensive item. Keep a small amount of cash in your pockets to pay for these incidentals. Also, do not keep all of your cash in one place. That way, if someone does steal your wallet, he or she will not get all of your money. This monetary organization also helps when bargaining—you can pull out your money from one pocket and say that's all you have. It may get you a better deal. You can always "find" more, if necessary.

Consumer fraud is rampant everywhere, and protection laws differ widely from country to country. You may not have the same legal protections, even with credit cards, when you step outside the borders of your own country. It pays to know the terms of the sale, including shipping arrangements, before you sign a credit card sales receipt. Foreign merchants may have a no-refund policy. Certain stores may have a "store credit only" return policy. In some countries all sales may be final with no exchange possible. In others you may be entitled to a tax refund.

If you anticipate the possibilities and plan a few necessary precautions, you'll safeguard your money and your purchases. Awareness will lessen your risk and increase your enjoyment.

$\mathcal{T}ips$

➤ Keep your passport and money in different places.

➤ Hide your cash in different pockets, wallets, or a money belt. Separate it in your bag, slip it inside checkbook covers, or seal it in plain envelopes and tuck it into the bottom of your knapsack or fanny pack.

Browsing is fun;
shopping is work.

◆

Phyllis Rasmussen,
manager and buyer

➤ If you carry a purse, swing the strap over your head so it crosses your body, instead of slinging the bag from one shoulder. It's harder to snatch that way.

➤ If you bring traveler's checks, record and store the numbers in a separate place. Check the country you are planning to visit. In some countries, such as Peru, it is difficult to cash traveler's checks.

➤ Use ATM machines for cash. Increasingly ubiquitous, money machines offer the best way to get local currency at a more favorable exchange rate than traveler's checks or dollars, and you can withdraw only what you need immediately. Always be careful when using ATM machines; try to use them in daylight, be inconspicuous about the amount you withdraw, and watch for questionable individuals.

➤ For ATM cash withdrawals, use a debit card drawn on funds from your bank account rather than a credit card. That way you'll avoid high interest rates for cash advances on credit cards.

- Bring credit cards for purchases. Cards such as American Express, Diners Club, VISA, and MasterCard are widely accepted, and the exchange rate is figured well after your purchase, often to your advantage.

- Pay attention to prices on shelves and those that are rung up at registers or added in a merchant's head. Scanners and people make mistakes, but someone working an abacus hardly ever adds wrong. Be alert anyway.

- Watch merchants in the stores and in markets wrap your purchases. Unscrupulous sellers may try to switch merchandise on you. You may pay for one thing and get something of lesser value. Check your package before leaving the shop or market.

- Never leave unattended bags in airports, restaurants, or hotels. When registering at hotels or checking in at airports, do not leave your bag

To fear the worst oft
cures the worse.

♦

William Shakespeare

Before leaving for the airport in New Delhi, India, I bargained with two Rajasthani women selling traditional textiles. After long negotiations they agreed to my price. At the airport, I realized that the women had put two different textile pieces of much lesser quality in my bag. I ran to get an auto-rickshaw to take me back to the market. I found the women and asked them to give me the textiles I had purchased. Somehow, they admitted to their trick and gave me the ones I wanted. I guess they were worried about their karma! And I made my flight just in time.

♦

Nina Smith,
nonprofit executive director

or briefcase on the floor. If you need to free your hands, put your bag on the counter.

➢ Leave valuables at home. If you must bring them, leave them in a hotel safe.

➢ Lock your hotel room windows and doors, especially those with balconies.

➢ Walk against the flow of pedestrian traffic. That makes it more difficult for pickpockets to work.

➢ When you are walking or browsing, especially in crowded areas, keep your shoulder bag in front of you. Keep your hands on it at all times, even when you go to pay for a purchase.

➢ Refuse unsolicited help, and be aware of your environment. Avoid dark alleys and poorly lit areas.

I was walking on a narrow little street in Florence, and I heard a motorcycle coming up behind me. I looked around to assess the situation and saw a nice-looking Tuscan man who smiled at me. I let my guard down, and next thing I knew, he was ripping my bag off my shoulder. I hadn't been careful—slinging the bag over one shoulder instead of wearing the strap across my body. Fortunately, my passport and tickets were in the money belt around my waist.

◆

Ginny Hanger, customer service manager

Chapter Four

FINDING THE PERFECT GIFT

Why is it no one ever sent me yet
One perfect limousine, do you suppose?
Ah no, it's always just my luck to get
One perfect rose.

— *Dorothy Parker*

———

I have a closet full of tchotchkes—all potential gifts. Most of this stuff comes from my travels. Once shopping in Japan, a colleague and I were negotiating for lacquer trays, and after we got the price for one, we asked about a discount for two. The price was so reasonable that my friend casually asked, "What about a dozen?"

The price was even more reasonable, so she turned to me and asked if I knew a dozen people who would like the trays as a gift or souvenir. I thought a minute then said, "Well, I could use about six, maybe two more."

"I'll buy what you don't use," she said, and we handed over money for two dozen. That was fifteen years ago, and I have one tray left. The other eleven made great gifts. I never actually purchased a dozen of the same thing again, but I have since bought other moderately priced gifts in multiples, taking advantage of time and place to accumulate presents for birthdays, special occasions, teachers, holidays, and housewarmings. Having these items readily available has saved me time, energy, and money over the years—especially when I've needed that last-minute gift.

It's time for a true confession: On occasion, I recycle gifts. We all receive presents we don't need, cannot use, or do not want. Perhaps, we actually hate them. We smile, say thank you, and think, "It's just not me. What were they thinking?"

What do you do with well-intended gifts that don't suit your taste? Returning a gift is one solution, though finding the time and the store can be tricky. Giving useless presents away to a charity or a school auction is another idea. But recycling a gift to someone who will appreciate it is a double pleasure: a friend gets something perfect for her or him, and you have less unused stuff cluttering your home.

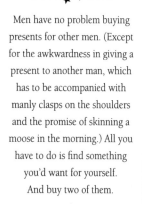

Men have no problem buying presents for other men. (Except for the awkwardness in giving a present to another man, which has to be accompanied with manly clasps on the shoulders and the promise of skinning a moose in the morning.) All you have to do is find something you'd want for yourself. And buy two of them.

♦

Tony Kornheiser,
The Washington Post

Gift giving is highly personal, and finding the right gift is an art. Even those who know each other especially well make mistakes. The more unusual someone's taste, the more difficult it may be to satisfy it. Holidays and special occasions present shopping dilemmas for anyone, particularly if the recipient has everything he or she could possibly want. If you agonize over gift purchases for someone you love or barely know, try a few of these tips. Instead of indecision and anxiety, enjoy the search and the pleasure that comes from a recipient's smile.

$\mathcal{T}$*ips*

➢ Buy gifts all year long. If you happen upon that perfect gift for someone, buy it. You'll probably never see it again. Even if you won't give it for months, you'll have it ready without worrying about shopping for it later.

> I have myself convinced that I "deserve" a gift when I am away from home. I plan ahead financially because I know that I am so deserving while away. Where this attitude developed, I have no idea, but I know myself and it will never go away!
>
> ◆
>
> *Gloria Delauney,*
> *importer and wholesaler*

➢ Avoid shopping for gifts at the last minute or in the crunch of a holiday season. You will suffer from the crowds, the traffic, harried and temporary sales staff, picked-over merchandise, and you will pay more for everything.

➢ Create your own gift store—a shelf or closet. Put all your cards, gift wrap, and miscellaneous presents there. When you need a gift or card, you'll know where to look.

➢ Make a current list of friends and relatives. Write down their sizes, color preferences, house decor, birthdays, anniversaries, etc., along with possible gift ideas. Keep it with your gift items.

> I don't like to buy things because you're supposed to give a gift for a certain holiday. I am much happier giving gifts to friends for no occasion.
>
> ◆
>
> *Alida Latham,*
> *arts patron and collector*

➢ Listen to what friends say they like, want, or need. Make mental notes when you are shopping with them. Write it down later for future reference.

➤ If you are stuck for an idea for a child's gift, ask other children the same age what they would like.

➤ If you recycle gifts, be alert to giving a gift to the same friend who gave it to you. If you think your memory might be faulty on this, keep a list.

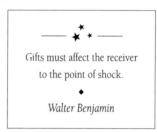

Gifts must affect the receiver to the point of shock.

Walter Benjamin

➤ Buy multiple, unisex presents such as picture frames, travel mugs, or candles. These are useful gifts for anyone but especially good for those you do not know very well.

➤ Give your time: volunteer to organize a party, read to a sick friend, chauffeur someone who doesn't drive, or babysit a friend's child.

➤ Make a gift—perhaps a basket of fruit, desserts, wine, coffee, jams. Mix any products that the recipient will love.

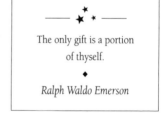

The only gift is a portion of thyself.

Ralph Waldo Emerson

➤ If you have an artistic bent or a hobby, give away something that a friend admired—a photograph, an art object, jewelry, any craft or food you create or cook yourself.

➤ Give gifts that help worthy causes. Donate money to a friend's favorite charity or plant a tree in his or her honor.

➤ Send a card and enclose funny articles. Laughter is a great gift.

➢ Share your special talents: give someone lessons—music, sports, dance, or art.

➢ Give an experience that will linger in memory. Take a friend out on the town, or wrap up theater or concert tickets.

➢ Shop from your favorite nonprofit gift catalogs. Organizations like Alternative Gifts International, American Friends Service Committee, and museum stores will help you give presents that empower people in crisis, protect our environment, or increase education. See the "Resources and References" section for suggested print and on-line catalogs.

Gift Shopping in Catalogs

Catalogs are the perfect way to go if you don't want to brave the crowds, or if wrapping and delivering are not in your Fearless Shopper repertoire. You can browse pages instead of stores, and fingertips are the only extremities likely to tire.

On-line catalogs will give you a broad selection of gift ideas in one place. See "On-line Shopping" for more about dropping dollars in cyberspace.

Tips

➢ Make it clear that your purchase is a gift. Request a gift card and wrapping.

➢ Ask the order department to block out the price of the gift if it is listed on the product.

➢ If you buy a gift and also other items for yourself, and then request shipping to different addresses, be very clear. Mix-ups often occur. Ask the operator to read back your instructions. Better yet, order the items separately. It may save you time later when you have to untangle the mistakes.

➤ If you order an item at the last minute, and you are desperate to get the gift mailed out the same day, it helps to be friendly and ask politely. Plead if necessary.

➤ Ask when the gift is likely to arrive. Get an order number so you can track the gift if there is a delay or problem with delivery.

➤ Keep records of your purchases.

When people grow gradually rich, their requirements and standard of living expand in proportion, while their present-giving instincts often remain in the undeveloped condition of their earlier days. Something showy and not-too-expensive in a shop is their only conception of the ideal gift.

♦

Saki, Beasts and Superbeasts

Chapter Five

SCORING A FIND

Good merchandise, even when hidden,
soon finds buyers.

— *Plautus*

———

*E*very time I wear my cowhide and fabric boots, I am reminded of Marrakech and the leather merchant who patiently waited for me to try every boot on his mat for just the right fit. A conversation piece, they are warm, comfortable, and durable—all for twelve dollars. I consider these boots my best bargain ever.

To paraphrase Gertrude Stein, a find is a find is a find. It doesn't matter where. Whether you comb antique shows or haunt flea markets, the fun is in the search and the accidental find. An item may fit the moment, satisfy a whim, or be a perfect decorating solution. Once in a while a find might actually be a rare treasure. If you know enough when you stumble upon that special piece, don't let it get away. If you suspect you have something of value, get it appraised. If you're wrong, don't dwell on the disappointment. You bought it because you wanted it, needed it, or loved it, and saved a bit of money. Don't worry about all the treasures you might have missed.

Kathleen Lane, a graduate student in historic preservation, says, "The thrill of scavenging is finding something that no one else recognizes as valuable." She once found an Eero Saarinen chair in a trash bin—only to discover later that it sells for $1,500 in vintage furniture shops.

Keep in mind while you scour antique fairs and dealer shows that the seller's profit margin will vary according to their cost. And depending upon the city, art and antique booths may cost anywhere from $3,000 to $50,000. The price of a booth influences the objects brought to a show, dealer prices, and flexibility for bargaining. So take stock of the venue and set your expectations accordingly.

Don't be afraid to pick up something you might hate. Sometimes I'll go for an unbelievable bargain, but it's borderline tacky. I'll buy it anyway because it challenges my taste. It's easy to keep buying things that fit a certain style, but then everything ends up looking sort of homogenous. Something different stretches my style and my perspective.

◆

Kathleen Lane, art program assistant and graduate student

Bargain hunting is entertainment. Go out and enjoy the hunt. To help you dodge the fakes and score the real finds, try these tips while rummaging around flea markets and antique shows.

Tips

➤ Bring cash. Paying in cash will often give you better bargaining leverage. As in gambling, take only as much cash as you're willing to part with.

➤ Pretend you're a seasoned

Distrust bargains. Take your time and find out as much as possible about the object and what the market value is back home. Sleep on it overnight, if you can.

◆

Hans Guggenheim, artist

buyer. Ask the price first. Neophytes tend to ask about the item first.

➤ Learn the antique show lingo. Try asking these questions: "What's your dealer price?" "Is this reserved?" "Is this piece really as old as it seems?"

➤ Be informed: carry an antiques price guide and know the trends. Be wary of fads. Sellers love them because prices escalate quickly. Scoring a treasure that you can turn over quickly is best left to the pros.

➤ Unless you can tell the difference between a fake and something that is authentic, don't buy. For the collectibles that really interest you, consider attending classes, doing research, and studying price guides.

> Antique shopping is a slippery slope: innocuous on the outside, but insidious at the core, the socially acceptable act-ing-out of one of the seven deadly sins—covetousness....
Before this last outing, I at least had devised a system for dealing with the deadly-sin angle of antiquing, that impoverishing urge to possess assorted stuff. I'd set my sights on the near-impossible to find, or better yet, the nonexistent, and the old checkbook could remain in balance.

◆

M. J. McAteer,
The Washington Post

➤ Get to know specific dealers whom you can trust.

➤ In the antique market, condition determines value, so examine an object carefully. A defect or breakage matters in some pieces but not in others and may indicate an older piece. A broken collectible or a set with missing pieces loses value. A tear in fabric or a painting can be mended, but broken clocks may mean costly repairs.

➤ Look for merchandise with "red dot" sold labels and dealers with crowded booths. Sold pieces may indicate competitive pricing and a dealer who has done enough business to negotiate with you.

➤ Bargain politely. Express a willingness to buy at the right price, and keep the negotiations friendly. Many dealers are sensitive, and aggressive tactics do not work as well as sincere questions and gracious haggling. Ask questions like, "Is this your best price?" "Can you do better?" or "I don't usually pay that much for this type of item." If you find a flaw in the antique, point that out in a friendly manner and use it as a bargaining point.

➤ Time your arrival. Early, you'll get the best selection; late, the best deal.

Buy only what you love; don't buy something because it seems like a bargain, if there's no other reason. You may have to live with your "bargain" for a long time. Take credit for good choices, because you've no one to blame but yourself for the bad ones.

♦

Jerome Spiller, antique dealer

Chapter Six

SECONDHAND VALUES

The propensity to truck, barter, and exchange one
thing for another…is common to all men, and
to be found in no other race of animals.

—*Adam Smith*

———

*I*t's just past 4:30 A.M. I'm up but not awake. What am I
doing? I'm not a morning person, so this is definitely
fearless. Last night I had a long talk with my body and
brain and convinced myself that I would venture forth
before dawn to trail behind two inveterate antique dealers.

They are making their weekly pilgrimage to Crumpton,
Maryland, an hour and a half away from Washington, D.C.,
to Dixon's outdoor furniture auction. Trucks begin unload-
ing, and buyers come early to scout the grounds before the
bidding starts at 9:00 A.M. I'm fascinated and a little bleary
eyed. This is a whole culture of secondhand shopping I
know nothing about: rows and rows of old junk piled onto
acres of farmland, separated into twenty-dollar and five-dollar bidding fields. Just a sliver of a line separates junk from
treasure, and beauty truly is in the eye of the beholder. Who
knew what I was missing all those mornings I slept in?

We pace the field, taking in whole rows at a single
glance, past brick molds, bedroom sets, cast-iron pots, cra-
dles, dining ware, metal advertising signs, rocking horses,
wheelbarrows, weather vanes, birdbaths, footstools, and
exotic things I cannot identify. My friends have keen eyes

and scan the field alert for any special pieces they can add to their antique business. After viewing the possibilities, it's inside the barnlike café for a homemade breakfast cooked up by the Mennonites (who come to sell at the indoor market). Ah, breakfast and coffee. This I can handle at any time.

Fortified, I now have energy for the bidding wars. Starting at the twenty-dollar field, I think with fearless determination, "Maybe I'll even bid on something." Of course, it would help if I knew what language the auctioneers are speaking. I can't understand a word of the bidding—not even a single price—uttered in rapid-fire syllables by the husband-and-wife team who drive a stretch golf cart up and down the field, recording the winning bids. I am amazed by the speed with which heaps of this stuff disappear—whole lots, all of it to the swift and lucky treasure hunters. The field shrinks as winners claim their spoils and runners help load up trucks that inch inward, replacing the space where the last row was.

We move to the five-dollar field—much less intimidating for a first-timer. Already in progress, the auction here is a feeding frenzy of bidders cruising aisles of hubcaps, light fixtures, glass bottles, washboards, old games, shovels, rusted wrenches, bent tin watering cans, and more. For

I believe the population of the thirteen colonies was less than four million souls, and every one of them must have been frantically turning out tables, chairs, china, glass, candle molds, and oddly shaped bits of iron, copper, and brass for future sale to twentieth-century tourists. There are enough antiques for sale along the roads of New England alone to furnish the houses of a population of fifty million.

♦

John Steinbeck,
Travels with Charley

the ultimate in recycled shopping, Crumpton is the last stop before the landfill. Amid the truly junky stuff, I spot an odd-shaped table of sorts—one side has a hollowed keg barrel with iron rails and spiral legs.

"What's that?" I ask aloud to no one in particular.

"One of those things you only see here," answers a man in passing.

Auctions provide another dimension—a game and the mystery of competition. You have a chance to get some unexpected prize or a good price.

♦

Ronald E. Becker,
museum administrator

"Wait 'til you see the pickers," my friend Andrea says.

"The pickers?"

"They pick over the leftovers no one buys."

Of course. It takes a truly Fearless Shopper to comb through the rubble left in the fields. I'm not that fearless, so I'll sleep in tomorrow dreaming about the avid fans of early-morning auctions, flea markets, thrift shops, yard sales, and swap meets.

In all of these venues, socializing is as much a part of the fun as unearthing a treasure. Each secondhand market has its unique culture where both a camaraderie and a healthy dose of competition

I check out the same thrift stores regularly because they rotate their stock. But you can keep seeing the same thing again and again and never consider buying it. Then, three weeks later, it fits the bill for what you need. You decide that you want to organize your cookbooks, you need something to prop them up, and there, tucked in the corner of the basement in the store, is exactly the thing you need.

♦

Curt Millay, exhibition assistant

thrive. Friendships form, and sellers often buy from one another. The people who attend and those who sell are attracted by the community aspects. With a little persistence, you can find one that suits your personality.

Up a notch from auctions and thrift shops are consignment shops and resale boutiques. They offer lightly worn clothing and accessories from couture to casual. My friend Ann, who is director of marketing at the Harvard Club of New York City, recommends that at resale boutiques you can try bargaining if you're buying three or more items. Resale boutiques and consignment stores are also great places for recycling clothes and accessories you no longer want. Most offer consignment policies where you receive 30 to 50 percent on the sale of your items.

In my hometown lives an antique dealer well known for pulling stunts at yard sales. At our sale she offered me fifty cents for a bookend priced at three dollars. "One bookend," she said, "is worthless." I replied that if I had both, I'd be charging twenty. About a month later, I went to her antique shop. I saw the bookend, marked ten dollars. I asked her if she'd take fifty cents for it. She said it was very valuable.

◆

Michael Gagne,
professional magician

Although each secondhand venue has its own culture and devotees, some common elements and tips apply to each. Beyond the thrill of a bargain, there's the adventure of a treasure hunt. So be observant, go prepared, and have fun. After all, picking through other people's castoffs is a fearless way to shop, and a good deal for the environment.

Tips

➢ Get an early start.

➢ Have a good breakfast.

➢ Check local papers for yard and garage sales. Use a detailed map of the local

I never pass up a dumpster.

♦

Curt Millay, exhibition assistant

areas and plan your route. Why expend unnecessary fuel or waste time getting lost when you could be searching for treasures?

➢ If you are into dumpster diving, find out when curbside pickup is in your more affluent neighborhoods (where garage sales may not be the rage).

➢ Bring change and small bills to yard sales. Often the seller cannot make change for large bills.

➢ Take a wish list with measurements of everything—rooms, pictures, plants, wall space, windows—along with swatches of fabric, color, and paint.

➢ Bring a tape measure with you.

I think it's in very bad taste to haggle a price down from a dollar to fifty cents, only to whip out a twenty-dollar bill to pay for it. Believe me, it happens. If I think the price of an item is fair, I don't bother haggling. Also, I would not drive up in a Lexus expecting to haggle. Drive the junker instead.

♦

Christina Heiska, web site and newsletter owner

➢ It gets dusty and dirty out there in the fields or trash heaps. Bring moist towelettes with you for your hands and for cleaning up what you find.

➤ Watch out for other bargain hunters. If you put down your treasures to look at something else, someone may "discover" your finds.

➤ Ask the seller to name his or her price first. Then, bargain.

➤ If you cannot come to an agreement after bargaining, leave your phone number. A seller may contact you if no one bought the item by the end of the day.

➤ Avoid unlabeled electrical devices. It may be illegal to install them without UL markings and safety labels.

➤ Look for warranties on defective appliances. You may be able to return them to the manufacturer for a refund or replacement.

➤ Examine everything you want to buy carefully for potential problems. If salt shakers and pepper mills are on your wish list, make sure they actually grind or have holes in the top. Many old ones are just decorative, but the things you want to function should.

> Once, I shadowed a very formidable man, who had picked up a beautiful tapestry before I could reach it, because I had a feeling he would change his mind and put it down. He did!
>
> ♦
>
> *Norma Ryan, book buyer*

> One early Saturday, I began garage sale hopping. I had rented an apartment and needed everything—kitchen items, linens. We stopped at a house where some plain white modern dinnerware was for sale. I was about to bargain but started laughing instead. My friend wanted to know what was so funny. I said, "I can't bargain because she's nursing her baby." If you can't bargain with a nursing mother, pay her price.
>
> ♦
>
> *Lenore Brindis,*
> *retired homemaker*

➤ Ask sellers to hold large purchases for you so you do not have to lug them around while you look at other things.

➤ Come prepared to cart away any large pieces you buy. Sellers usually do not deliver.

➤ Bring your own tote bag or cardboard boxes and newspapers to pack your purchases and protect them on the ride home.

My sister and her husband went driving around recently looking for yard sales. They spotted a man in his driveway getting ready to set up. They parked the car on the side of the road and started searching through all his boxes. After digging around for ten minutes, my sister found something and took it over to the man and asked, "How much do you want for this?" He said, "It's not for sale." She said, "Well, it's a yard sale, isn't it?" He said, "No, I'm just cleaning out my garage."

♦

Carolyn Lind, mother

Chapter Seven

CONSUMING LESS

Never doubt that a small group of thoughtful,
committed citizens can change the world;
indeed, it's the only thing that ever has.

—*Margaret Mead*

*B*uying something is often touted as the answer to just about every ill. You can purchase things to help you look better, feel better, smell better, eat better, or communicate better. You will be happier, advertisers say, if you purchase our product. We get lured into believing we will get more love or more self-esteem along with the product.

But Fearless Shoppers don't shop out of fear or fall for the bait. Fearless Shoppers know how to stop themselves from buying for the wrong reasons.

And just how much stuff do we need, anyway? I often wonder about the abundance of products available in U.S. stores. I happened to be in the former Soviet Union six months before Communism fell—one of the worst times for empty shelves. In Moscow, lines snaked around the block for a Big Mac or a bottle of vodka. In a local grocery in Kiev,

> I am guilty as hell of over-consuming! It's this sick need for collection. At my age, I still collect and have collected more than anyone I know of. My children dread my death, for they will have to sort through all of my "treasures!"
>
> ♦
>
> *Gloria Delauney,*
> *importer and wholesaler*

34

crowds leaned into the meat counter for a chance to buy stacks of packaged crackers. Would they have been overwhelmed to visit a supermarket in the States—the land of conspicuous consumption? Juliet Schor says in *The Overworked American,* "We used to recoil at stories of how the Russians spent so much time in lines shopping. However, when the Russians came to this country, shopping took them just as long because there are so many choices to make!"

Many Americans believe it's our unalienable right to spend and accumulate stuff faster than any society in history. Two-thirds of our nation's economic activity derives from consumer purchases. In a National Public Radio special, the commentator noted that we shop on average about six hours a week but spend only forty minutes playing with our children. Public television aired a program called "Affluenza" that contended we are drowning in excess consumption, overloaded with debt and waste, and we are wrecking the environment. A United Nations human development report indicates, "The richest fifth of the world's people consume 86 percent of all goods and services while the poorest fifth consumes just 1.3 percent."

Shopping itself, as we all know, can be a very liberating experience. It is a measure of our self-esteem that we allow ourselves to shop; a measure of even greater self-esteem if we shop for something expensive. In Western civilization, of course, this is taken even a step further, and the truly respected people are the ones who can spend money hand over fist on the utterly useless, or the wildly extravagant. My father was fond of saying that ours is the only society where people actually go out and spend three or four dollars a week for plastic bags to throw out their garbage in.

◆

Jeff Greenwald,
Shopping for Buddhas

We are masters of planned obsolescence. I had an art professor once who told me he had to stop designing cars in Detroit because his ideas were too durable. They told him he should design cars to fall apart after a few years.

Landfills overflow with abandoned, useless stuff. The link between consumerism, consumption, and the fate of the Earth is often addressed by advocates of recycling. Our throwaway society has learned to recycle. It's no longer a radical idea, and it feels good.

I don't like to shop! I think people waste a lot of money on stuff.

♦

Lars Messler, businessman

Recycling purchases certainly helps, but there's a movement afoot to use less stuff. In their book *Use Less Stuff,* the authors, Robert Lilienfeld and William Rathje, suggest a strategy of source reduction. They argue that "recycling by itself cannot solve our environmental degradation/resource conservation/solid-waste dilemma. It is a means to an end, not an end itself. The real end result is the conservation of resources and the minimization of waste." They say that recycling can achieve positive

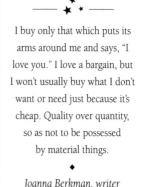

I buy only that which puts its arms around me and says, "I love you." I love a bargain, but I won't usually buy what I don't want or need just because it's cheap. Quality over quantity, so as not to be possessed by material things.

♦

Joanna Berkman, writer

results, but in the long term it merely delays the impact of consumption. Consuming less solves the problem at its root; we don't have to think later about what to do with all the stuff we don't want anymore.

When we were children, my brothers and I used to watch Saturday morning cartoons. Once, after a particularly enticing commercial, I remember begging my mother for a toy called Haunted House. After trying to persuade us it was trash advertising, she relented and bought it as a holiday gift for us. Upon unwrapping it, we discovered a few junky pieces of printed cardboard. Talk about disappointment. We learned our lesson about consuming early: we didn't need everything we wanted.

Fearless Shoppers find ways to buy smarter, to recycle, and to take care of planet Earth in the process.

Tips

➤ Shop with a list so you do less impulse buying.

➤ Ask yourself: Do I absolutely need this purchase?

➤ Save time, energy, and gasoline by consolidating shopping trips.

➤ Buy recycled items. Shop consignment stores, thrift shops, yard sales, and at antique shops.

➤ Resist shopping for products that you'll only use once or

Don't buy something unless you love it. Even following this rule, you will end up wondering why you have half the stuff you do.

♦

Kelly Smith,
technical writer

twice. Rent dishes and glassware for special occasions. Wash and reuse plasticware instead of throwing it away.

➤ For black-tie parties, consider renting formal clothes. For Halloween or theme parties, put together your own outfit.

➤ Buy longer rolls of film. You save about four dollars, or 40 percent, by purchasing rolls of thirty-six exposures instead of twelve, and you reduce waste by 67 percent.

➤ Wrap your presents in usable fabrics or comics, or have children color and decorate brown bags. They can decorate their schoolbook covers the same way.

Thrift and flea market shopping is an outing, an adventure, an exploration. I come home, spread everything out, and admire it. It's serendipity—give chance a chance. Things need patina. With age and history, things look better, feel better, have better vibes! Besides, recycling is also a bonus.

◆

Norma Ryan, book buyer

➤ Reuse supplies: packaging, padded envelopes, wrapping paper, gift bags, and ribbon.

➤ Cancel any catalogs you don't order from.

➤ Give old magazines to hospitals and nursing homes, or bring them to work to share with colleagues.

➤ Donate unwanted items to charities, or recycle them to secondhand stores.

➤ When asked "Paper or plastic?" say "Neither." Take along your own bags when you shop.

When I was little, my family's only shopping choice was the Sears catalog. I soon realized that products were never as good as they looked in the pictures.

◆

Sharon Nelson, judge

➤ Use Co-op America's Green Pages to find more than 10,000 consumer products and services that are Earth-friendly. Research environmentally responsible businesses at www.greenpages.org. using word searches like clothing or toys. Or search by store, state, catalog, or product type (art supplies, sporting goods, etc.).

➤ Shop for "organic" fabrics grown from chemical-free crops. "Natural" fabrics may only mean that the fabric contains no dyes.

Buy less, but of higher quality. Make things last longer.

♦

John Wilson, importer and wholesaler

New Uses for Old Things

Figuring out new uses for old items is one form of creativity. Says Cecile Andrews in *The Circle of Simplicity*, "It's challenging to find ways to 'make do' instead of just going out and buying something. It is called ingenuity." Yankee ingenuity made it possible for many rural and frontier families to get by with next to nothing, but in the age of shopping malls, this kind of creativity has evaporated.

Fearless Shoppers can learn to be creative with second-hand finds. Try transforming old junk into something beautiful or useful. An old ice bucket makes an attractive planter; a large candlestick works for a lamp base; a

No one in our building actually throws anything out. They just put it in the hallway, and someone grabs it. A friend and I once found a kitchen table with an interesting base and leaves in the hall. We cleaned it, took it apart, and used it for three different things. When our neighbor saw what we had done with it, she was sorry that she hadn't been more creative.

♦

Curt Millay, exhibition assistant

framed but cracked mirror could be a perfect fit for an old photograph; and that antique iron might make a fine book-end. Fallen in love with that gorgeous, etched-silver cigarette case, but you don't smoke? You can use it for business cards, stamps, or tissues. Shop smarter and discover satisfaction creating new uses for old things.

Tips

➤ Use old clothes for rags and wash them instead of using paper towels.

➤ Don't throw away paper printed on one side. Use it for scratch paper or print first drafts on it.

➤ Use old containers such as jars or film containers for paints, spices, change holders, etc. Be creative.

➤ Try sturdy shoe boxes for storage or to file cooking recipes, slides, odds and ends, etc. Boxes from sports shoes work the best, and index cards and dividers fit easily inside.

I have a use-it-up, wear-it-out philosophy regarding both durable and perishable goods and am not a slave to fashion— comfort is key over style.

◆

Kathy Allen, major, USAF

➤ Salvage or purchase wood from old barns or buildings, and use it for remodeling rooms or for art projects. An artist friend bought a stash of exotic wood from an estate sale and used it to build wood-sculpted desks and tables.

➤ If you're tired of your old finds, have a swap party and

exchange things. Send invitations to about ten friends. Ask them to bring over what they no longer want—CDs, books, art objects, toys—in boxes or bags. When everyone is present, put all the packages in the one place. Make sure no one peeks. Then, the fun begins as everyone grabs whatever they want. Donate the leftovers.

—— ✦ ✶ ——

Call them hand-me-downs and no one wants them. But label old children's clothes vintage, and you can sell them instead of giving them away.

♦

Amy Synnott, The New York Times

Chapter Eight

ON-LINE SHOPPING

I generally avoid temptation
unless I can't resist it.

— *Mae West*

———

y first foray into the wide world of Web shopping began with a search for a new car. Though not inept at technology, I'm far from a tech wizard. Well, O.K., if you really must know, my idea of a great technological advance is "cut and paste" in a Word document. But the idea of shopping for a new car intimidated me far more than using the Internet to find the best deal in town. In fact, it was remarkably simple. After reading an article on where to look, I logged onto edmunds.com and autobytel.com. The rest was a matter of filling in the boxes and clicking. Once I got past the basic question of what model car I wanted, the site did all the work.

Armed with *Consumer Reports*, dealer costs, leasing versus buying options, and dealer holdback information, I shopped for my new car at the site-sanctioned dealer who was obligated to honor the on-line price. Even though car sites say that the price they quote is the final price and that there is no bargaining at their recommended dealer, I still was able to shave a few hundred dollars off by standing firm and buying at the end of the model year. I also got them to throw in a cover for the car when they forgot one of the extras I wanted.

Though I wasn't fearless enough to buy it on-line, the experience made the dreaded task of car shopping easier, and I was hooked. My next foray was relatively safe: Amazon.com. Although I'm an inveterate bookstore browser and purchaser, time often leaves no other choice. Days before I would have had the car keys in the ignition, books arrived on my doorstep. I have shopped for books many times on-line since that first order and, though it was a bit disconcerting—eerie even—to log on the second time and find a personalized greeting welcoming me back, I have enjoyed speedy communication and delivery.

Internet shopping lets you bid or browse twenty-four hours a day in privacy. On-line shopping can give you nearly

There's something very gratifying about being able to shop naked.

◆

Anonymous

instant product information and price comparisons. But beware. The Internet is not necessarily a time saver. Even with fast connections, you'll be amazed at how quickly two hours pass—or three or four. But it connects you to places you've never been and may never get to. Enter this global shopping world fearlessly for some of the best deals on the planet.

On-line Shopping
DOS & DON'TS

DO

Read the site's privacy policy before buying.

Check out the merchant with the Better Business Bureau or Consumer Affairs.

Answer only the minimum questions necessary to make a purchase.

Buy from secure sites.

Stay away from sites that want a registration fee.

Understand the delivery terms before buying.

DON'T

Give out your social security number.

Buy from a company with a negative report from one of the consumer bureaus.

Agree to put your name on a mailing list unless you want e-mail from that merchant regularly.

Accept substitutes.

Answer unsolicited sales pitches or offers that insist on instant action.

Believe everything you read.

ℐips

➤ Shop with companies you know and trust.

➤ Use a secure browser (the software you have to navigate the Internet). Most computers come with this software already installed. It should use industry standards to scramble or encrypt your purchase information to guarantee a secure transaction and minimize your risk.

➤ Do not submit your order until you have checked that the merchant's site is secure.

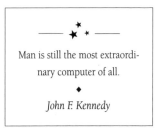

Man is still the most extraordinary computer of all.

John F. Kennedy

A URL address that starts with "https://" indicates a secure server. Another indication of a secure site is an image of an unbroken lock or key in the lower left corner of your screen.

➤ Never buy from a site without a mailing address, phone number, and contact listed.

➤ To avoid incorrect orders, double-check all information you have entered before submitting your on-line order.

➤ Before you buy, read all customer service agreements, return/exchange policies, merchandise information, and special offers or trial periods. Sometimes products such as computer software and recorded music are not returnable.

➤ Think about your shipping options. Normal delivery and consolidated shipments are most cost effective. If some products are back ordered and others aren't, consider waiting for one complete package to avoid additional freight charges.

➤ Pay by credit card. If you are in the U.S., under the Fair Credit Billing Act you have the right to dispute charges and withhold payment while a case is under investigation. With most credit card companies, you have a fifty-dollar liability limit, so you are also protected against unauthorized charges on your card.

➤ Keep records. Print a copy of the order with all the details, including a confirmation number.

➤ By law, a company must ship within thirty days (unless you also are applying for credit) or notify you. You have the option of approving the delay or canceling the order.

➤ Bookmark the shopping sites you like, especially if you click on many related links. It's easy to forget the internet address of your favorite sites.

➤ Find practical consumer advice and product information at sites such as www.consumerreports.org and www.con-sumerworld.org.

Privacy Tips

➤ Protect your password and your privacy. Create an unusual password, and avoid ones such as birthdays, anniversaries, and pet names.

➤ Look for a company's encryption capabilities on their home page: 40-bit is standard and 128-bit is better. If you are unsure about the security of a site, don't buy. If a site has several secure transaction screens, you can feel comfortable giving out your credit card information in cyberspace.

➤ Read the privacy policy posted on a web site to understand how personal information will be used. Be cautious about shopping at sites that request this data but do not post privacy policies.

➤ Do not give out social security numbers, phone numbers, or other personal information unless you are sure it is appropriate for the transaction.

➤ Be careful giving out personal information. Most shopping sites want to capture personal data for their mailing lists, and many sell these lists. If a site will not let you continue without personal information, go to a different one.

➤ Teach your children to check with you before giving out any personal information on-line.

➤ Never hang up and redial into the site at the request of the merchant.

To err is human, but to really
foul things up requires
a computer.

♦

Anonymous

➤ A Better Business Bureau seal of approval (BBBOnLine Reliability Seal) indicates a willingness by a company to stand behind its goods and services, and maintain privacy commitments.

Tips for Complaints & Returns

➤ Be alert to scams on the Web. Avoid limited time offers, any requests for your password (no matter how official they sound), miracle cures, anything free, work-at-home schemes, bulk e-mail address lists, investment possibilities, vacation promotions, bad credit clearances, outrageous promises of money, and other "opportunities." As the saying goes, if it sounds too good to be true, it probably is.

➤ Contact the Better Business Bureau at www.bbb.org for consumer alerts and information on scams. Use their on-line form to file a business complaint.

➤ You can also file complaints about bad business practices with the Federal Trade Commission (FTC) Bureau of Consumer Protection using the on-line complaint form at www.ftc.gov/ftc/complaint.htm, or call the Consumer Response Center: 202-FTC-HELP (382-4357).

➤ To file complaints by mail, write to: Consumer Response Center, Federal Trade Commission, 600 Pennsylvania Ave., N.W., Washington, DC 20580.

➤ The FTC cannot resolve individual consumer problems, but it can take action against companies with a pattern of possible legal violations.

➤ Consumer World's Company Connection will also link you to business complaint pages. Go to www.consumerworld.org/pages/company.htm. You'll find product reviews, shopping advice, price comparisons, and many other articles.

———— ★ ★ ————

The future is made of the same stuff as the present.

◆

Simone Weil

➤ Keep all your receipts, product literature, boxes, and packaging material until you are sure you will keep your purchase.

➤ If your order arrives damaged or is incorrect, call the company immediately. It will usually pick up the order at its expense and send you a replacement.

➤ Be careful of person-to-person trading on-line. It is much harder to track down and take legal action against an individual on-line than it is against an Internet business.

On-line Auctions

While my on-line shopping habits have been relatively tame, my friend Rebecca, an art historian, has joined the bidding wars at on-line auctions. The eBay site, only a few years old, holds thirty-four million auctions each year, selling everything from 1970s Mork and Mindy lunch boxes to farm equipment. Recently, after an important meeting with a university vice president about a rare, lucrative job possibility, Rebecca began to question her own priorities.

"What was I thinking while he was talking?" she asked me. "About an eBay auction ending in minutes! Before leaving for the meeting, I had placed the

Going, Going, Gone on Line.

♦

—*Headline,*
The New York Times

high bid by a comfortable margin on a beautiful Depression-era print by Claire Leighton. I had to have it!"

Rebecca explained what on-line auction shoppers know: items frequently go to the last-minute bidder who bids for the first time just as the auction closes.

"I was helpless—I could find no decorous way to rush to the computer in the VP's office to check on the status of my bid. It was awful."

"Well," I asked, "did you get it?"

"Someone had snatched the print from my hands. But, at least, I got the job and a pointed lesson in how to schedule meetings. Around eBay auctions, of course!"

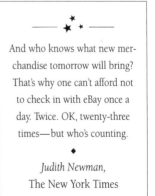

And who knows what new merchandise tomorrow will bring? That's why one can't afford not to check in with eBay once a day. Twice. OK, twenty-three times—but who's counting.

♦

Judith Newman,
The New York Times

Old, established auction houses are also developing Internet businesses. Sotheby's hopes to attract "new clients who weren't comfortable crossing the threshold of our august establishments in the past," according to its executive vice president, David Redden.

"You'll be able to wander the halls of the most exalted galleries in the world and attend the most notable auctions in your pajamas," he says.

Bidding on an item at an auction site can be as intimidating as the first time you participate in a live auction. On-line, you can bid anytime, twenty-four hours a day, at whatever sites you choose. You have instant access to an astounding array of categories. The components for auctions on-line are similar to live auctions: registration, bidding, selling, closing the transaction. But think before you hit that "Submit Bid" button. Do you really want the item? If you have the high bid, you are entering into a legal agreement to buy.

Some on-line auction sites, such as eBay, offer chat rooms for sharing interests with other buyers, as well as the opportunity to bid on items for sale. At eBay it is also possible to record impressions of business transactions, so you can review other buyers' experiences with a seller. As Rebecca says, "When was the last time you experienced this in a major department store?"

Tips

➤ Many on-line auction sites offer tips for amateur bidders. Read them.

➤ Find hundreds of auction sites through www.yahoo.com or other search engines. Search for "on-line auctions."

➤ Learn what is sold on the site before registering.

➤ Before you bid on an item, check comments and ratings from other users. You can get a good idea about who you want to do business with from these on-line comments.

➤ Read all the user agreements and legal notices before you register at the site. Print out the pages for your records and put them in a folder and label it with the auction site name.

➤ Take notes when you bid. Write down the details; it will ease the final transactions.

➤ Avoid a frenzied bidding war during the auction time period (usually a week). If you really must have that item, wait and place your maximum bid in the last hour of the auction.

➤ E-mail the seller immediately when winning an auction. Give the details of the auction in the e-mail. Clarify all payment and shipping issues. If you cannot confirm the arrangements by e-mail, ask the seller to send along his or her phone number so you can discuss the specifics.

➤ If you buy an item, be prepared to pay shipping and insurance as well as the site's finder fees. You also may want to pay extra for an escrow account that holds the money until the exchange of goods.

> ——— ✦ ✦ ✦ ———
>
> Avoid a frenzy of bidding on any individual item, as fast and furious bidding can drive up the price. Instead, bid modestly at first, or not at all. Only as the auction nears its end should you bid more aggressively. But, remember to decide on what your maximum bid is in advance and to stop when you reach it.
>
> ◆
>
> *Rebecca Phillips Abbott, art historian and photographer*

Chapter Nine

BAZAARS, SOUKS & THIRD WORLD MARKETS

In the souk no one less than God
himself sets the prices.

—Attributed to Muhammad the Prophet

———

*T*he markets of the world pulse with a rhythm
unique to their culture and time. Some swagger and
shout; others buzz and hum. In certain places, a frenetic energy ignites market activity. In others, merchants settle
in for a long, languid day while
incense wafts through the air.

In this gathering of buyers
and sellers, discover the heart
and soul of any city—its traditions and complexities. It's
here that people work, social-

> Travel is the sherbet between
> courses of reality.
>
> ♦
>
> *Cartoon in* The New Yorker

ize, display their wares, demonstrate their skills, and bargain. It's here that the Fearless Shopper can soak up the culture, taste the flavors, and hear the music of this microcosm.

To shop in a bazaar, a souk, or a Third World market is
to feel the link with the first traders who bartered and sold
along the Tigris and Euphrates, supplying the basics of the
day—weapons, food, beads, and cloth. Camel convoys
moved goods from Africa, Asia, and Europe along trade
routes that intersected in the Middle East. Traders brought
silk from China, spices and perfumes from India, amber

from the north, and ivory from Africa. These ancient markets spread via the Islamic tradition of the caravansaries (the resting places on the early caravan routes) and were the precursors of modern city markets. Today, from Marrakech to Istanbul, Cairo to Samarkand, these bazaars are a shopper's paradise and the places to bargain till you drop.

I used to travel with a buyer who was masterful in these markets. She whirled from vendor to vendor in her long, flowing skirt and negotiated prices with dramatic gestures. She was especially effective in West Africa using her mangled French. When a merchant would mention a price, she would place her hand to her brow in a manner reminiscent of Scarlet O'Hara, feign fainting, gasp with horror, and proclaim, *"Oh, non, mon Dieu, c'est très cher."* Then, she would name a rock bottom price as absurd as the merchant's opening bid, and the fun would begin. The game went on until both sides were satisfied or a deal just wasn't possible. Sometimes I'd intervene, play the bad guy, or we would switch roles. If the negotiations lasted too long and only a few dollars or cents were at stake, it was time to move on. But the point is bargaining was fun and expected in all markets. So, browse among the shopkeepers and craftspeople and, in the process, you'll discover treasures that are more than you bargained for and valuable beyond the things you set out to find.

Tips

➢ Get the feel of the marketplace. Look around before you buy.

➢ In a foreign market, shop with a native, if possible. You'll get better deals.

➤ Always bargain, and do it in a spirit of fun and friendliness. See the "Fearless Bargaining" chapter for a course in negotiating with the best of them.

➤ It's easy to get dehydrated in a hot, dusty marketplace. Carry bottled water, and drink before you get thirsty. Make sure the top is sealed. If you have reason to be suspicious of the bottled water, buy the local cola or beer instead.

In Turkey, while being shown rugs in a bazaar, I noticed the rug the vendor was sitting on. I said, "I'd like to buy that one," but he said it wasn't for sale as if it had been in the family for a long time. I left, but casually dropped by the next two days. On the last visit, he offered to sell.

◆

*Constance Bond,
writer and editor*

➤ Bring cash. Though some merchants may accept credit cards, you are in a better bargaining position if you have local currency. U.S. dollars also help.

➤ If you want to buy more than one item, ask the price of one unit. Then bargain for quantity.

➤ The small tokens you brought from home, such as pens, key chains, caps, or t-shirts, can be used to

Respect local customs, haggle hard, and look carefully at the merchandise.

◆

Karen Peterson, photojournalist

barter for an item that interests you, especially if the merchant has expressed an interest in them.

➤ Learn as many phrases and numbers as possible in the

native language of the marketplace. Learn to say "too much" in any language. This will help you bargain with confidence.

➤ Ask permission to take photos of a stall or shopkeeper. If your purchase is a gift, you can use the photograph as a gift card.

➤ Be adventurous. If you are serious about buying and the merchant looks trustworthy, accept an invitation to see more goods behind the scenes, or ask to see other, more exclusive items that may be not be out.

➤ If you want a particular item from a country, bring photographs with you from home and ask your hotel concierge or a market vendor where you can get a similar item or have a copy made.

➤ Buy traditional crafts. Before you go, learn what crafts a market is famous for, and research the craft technique.

In Beijing, a man started to talk with us in rather good English about the area and its history. We ended up following him through an alley and into an art studio. A teacher at the university, he showed my son and me his students' paintings. My son was struck by a piece that turned out to be the teacher's, so he purchased it. What at first felt uncomfortable—following a stranger down an alley—resulted in a rewarding experience.

♦

David Begelfer,
executive director

➤ Go on educational craft-shopping vacations. There are groups that offer trips to visit artisans and craft markets in different countries. They will customize your trip, educate you about traditional crafts, and arrange meetings with indigenous groups from which you can purchase directly. See the "Resources and References" section for organizations.

➢ When shopping in dubious areas, you are vulnerable to hustlers and petty thieves. Instead of taking a map or guidebook with you, carry a local newspaper or magazine. You can clip photocopies of guidebook pages or your map to the inside of the journals, to appear less like a tourist.

Only through the yoga of true pushiness, only by being relentlessly pushy in the most charming possible way, would I ever find the prize that I was seeking: a Buddha that really said something; or, a Buddha that really said nothing—and said it loudly enough for me to hear.

♦

Jeff Greenwald, Shopping for Buddhas

Chapter Ten

FEARLESS BARGAINING

Necessity never made a good bargain.

—*Benjamin Franklin*

———

$\mathcal{I}$ wandered into a jewelry store in Hong Kong, peered into the narrow counter, and asked to see a Seiko watch. I knew the suggested retail price in the States was about $200. I didn't really want to spend more than $100, so when the merchant said $150, I was tempted. I tried it on, admired it, and handed it back.

"Too much," I said. "I only wanted to spend $100."

"You from America?" he asked. He wanted to know where, and what had brought me to Hong Kong. He chatted about everyday things and tried to interest me in other watches.

"I really only like that one, but it's too much." I shrugged, thanked him, and walked out the door. Perhaps I even looked disappointed.

He chased me down the street. A smile broadened his already wide face. "You my first customer of the day. First customer, last customer rule. Unlucky if I don't make a sale. I sell it for $100."

First customer, last customer—I didn't even know I was bargaining. I bought it and realized that I got what I wanted because I was ready to walk away.

Another time, after dinner in Bali, the grounds of my hotel transformed into a temporary market with blankets lining the paths and traders hawking their handicrafts. I spotted batik cloth paintings and stopped to admire them. I chose two and asked the price of one.

A slender young man with a broken tooth started to sell the merits of both. "Fifty dollars each," he said.

I must have looked like a rich tourist to him. They weren't worth more than twenty-five to me.

"Too much." I countered with an offer of twenty-five.

"Thirty," he said.

"Too much." I shrugged and walked away.

As I wandered away looking at other things and thinking about sleep, I felt a tap on

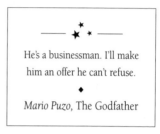

He's a businessman. I'll make him an offer he can't refuse.

Mario Puzo, The Godfather

my shoulder. He had followed me, the two batiks in his hands.

"You are my last customer of the day," he said. "I sell both for twenty-five dollars total."

First customer, last customer—sometimes you get more than you bargained for. Two for the price of one—how could I resist?

"I'll take them," I said, even though I knew the frames I'd put them in at home would cost far more.

My dumb luck worked on these occasions, but often negotiating is more complicated. It's a skill and one that the merchants have long perfected. But whether you are buying one souvenir or multiple items, it's also fun. For the Smithsonian, we often dickered for hundreds. Because of our volume buying, we had an occasional behind-the-store-front tour to select more goods. The quantity of our purchases gave us leeway to haggle with the merchants.

Whatever the answer to our questions "*Cuanto cuesta?*" or "*Cambien?*" we inevitably said, "Too much."

After negotiations, depending on the country, we carted away any variety of goods—wood carvings, jewelry, textiles, one-of-a-kind crafts (all to be boxed and mailed later). Of course, we always thought that we got great bargains, but the truth is that merchants and shopkeepers have been at this game far longer. They know just where their margins are and what they can afford. I'm always reminded of the film *Casablanca,* where the merchant professes to give Ilsa a good price. He quickly drops his price, however, for "special friends of Rick's," leading one to ponder the intricacies of market negotiation and whom you know. We always tried to negotiate for the best deal even when prices were already good. It was part of the game.

So enjoy it, but remember merchants are savvy bargainers in any language—even the young children. And they're quick to size up tourists. Once in the Arab quarter of Jerusalem, I watched a young boy, no more than ten, try to interest a tourist in buying souvenirs. He addressed different customers, switching within seconds from Arabic to Hebrew, English, German, French, Spanish, and rattled off his prices. Merchants may not converse fluently in another language, but numbers are universal.

Bargaining 101

Haggling does not mean harassing. Being pushy, rude, or belittling merchandise will not win you points with merchants in any part of the world. "This behavior does absolutely nothing for cultural understanding and global goodwill," writes fearless bargainer Katie Cooney, author of

Window on the World: Straightforward Advice for Today's Woman Traveler. "Be casual and polite when asking for prices and information," she advises. "The more polite and respectful you behave, the chances are the same respect and kindness will be reciprocated."

Once you and a vendor have agreed on a price, it's usually impolite to back out. You've taken the merchant's time, and reneging now is considered rude. Wait to bargain until you are ready to buy. If you feel pressured, you can always step outside the shop to think the deal over.

In many countries, some items are negotiable and others are fixed. Such things as train and plane tickets, museum entrance fees, and safari tickets are usually considered set prices. But taxi rides, crafts, artwork, jewelry, clothes, rugs, and textiles are often negotiable. If in doubt, watch other travelers or ask them what's appropriate.

> Don't let negotiations get in the way of purchasing.
>
> ◆
>
> *Jim Greene, consultant and fly fisherman*

It pays to get the feel of a market before you start to bargain; check out the quality and pricing at other vendor stalls. Knowing the relative value of an item will help you decide how to counter a merchant's offer.

Bargaining is a game around the world—a game of wit and skill and words. Bring your best poker face, and prepare for fearless entertainment.

Tips

➤ Before you bargain for anything, decide "What is this worth to me?" Ask yourself, "What is the most I am willing to pay?" Then ask the price. That way you'll know how much bargaining room you have.

➤ See what the locals are buying and paying.

➤ Try to avoid shopping during peak holiday or tourist seasons when demand often leaves little negotiating power.

➤ Learn numbers in other languages.

It never hurts to make an offer, even in a place you think would never discount. Always carry cash—it's the international negotiator—and don't be afraid to walk away.

◆

Lissa Spiller, real estate agent

➤ If a merchant asks an absurd price, offer an equally ridiculously low price. You'll probably meet somewhere in the middle. But if you start in the middle, you'll have less room to maneuver and you'll pay more than you should.

➤ Carry a calculator.

➤ Always ask. All anyone can ever do is say no. Often I've asked for a discount for buying so much. Sometimes the clerk will laugh. And I always respond, "You're laughing, and I'm serious." Sometimes that's enough to get an extra ten percent off.

Buy what you like at a price you think is fair.

◆

Jonathan Kaufelt, lawyer

➤ Be willing to walk away. In bargaining, as in life, you can get what you want if you're not attached to it.

➤ Time your purchases for that lucky first or last spot of the day.

➤ Maintain a sense of humor.

Advanced Bargaining

Many people think of bargaining as something to try in Morocco or Hong Kong, never in Western countries. But even in the U.S., negotiating can work, including in stores that have "fixed" prices. This is especially true if you are spending a considerable amount.

In a pleasant manner, always ask for a discount. If you are friendly and polite, you'd be surprised how many stores, even upscale boutiques, department stores, and chains, will extend one. Salespeople often have leeway for small price breaks—ten percent—to handle on-the-spot markdowns, but if a clerk cannot make a large purchase discount decision, ask to speak to a manager or the owner. Rather than lose the sale, a merchant will often extend a courtesy discount or mention a "special" for the month.

In Europe, bargaining is more common than you'd expect and fairly routine in small owner-operated stores, open-air markets, art galleries, and antique shops. In countries such as Portugal and Spain, and in Greece, Turkey, and various islands, paying the asking price is only for the uninitiated. Bargaining is accepted and, indeed, expected.

And then there's the matter of the "American price." In

My husband and I spent two days schmoozing with an old merchant and negotiating for jewelry in the New York City diamond district. In the end my husband had the diamond merchant in tears with old family stories—and he got the best price.

◆

Judith Katz Nath, public relations and marketing consultant many parts of the world, prices of souvenirs are set higher for American tourists, since all Americans are considered wealthy. If you are American, and a vendor asks where you're from, he or she may not just be making small talk. If you are aware of this practice, you can bargain accordingly.

Tips

➤ Always bargain up from your price, never down from the merchant's.

➤ Learn to be an actor. If something in a market is too expensive, act horrified. Do not be enthusiastic for or show much interest in the item you really want. Pretend you don't care.

There have been times when I have been asked where I was from when the bargaining began, England? Germany? France? America? Canada? I wondered, What was the price if I was to say Germany or Canada? I would ask in a humorous way, "What country will get me the best price?" Their reaction was a combination of perplexity and embarrassment. We both ended up laughing at the situation.

◆

Katie Cooney,
Window on the World

➤ Try bargaining first for something else that doesn't interest you as much. Wander around, then start negotiating for what you really want.

➤ Let the vendor make the first offer, take your time before suggesting a counteroffer, or try silence. The offer may drop even before you respond.

➤ Do not budge from your highest price. But if you really want it, ask the merchant for his or her best price.

➤ In small luxury shops, polite bargaining works best. Instead of aggressive tactics, ask any of these gentler questions: "Is there a cash discount?" "When will this item be on sale?" "Do you give professional discounts?" "Do you give discounts for traveler's checks?"

➤ Do not be intimidated with aggressive bargaining, especially in many Third World countries. Counter bold tactics with equal vigor. Remember, you can always walk away.

➤ When you are shopping abroad anywhere, ask, "Do you have a discount for foreigners?"

➤ If an item might go on sale soon, ask a clerk to hold it for you or ask if you can get the sale price immediately.

➤ Ask for a discount at any store or market in the following circumstances:

You would be surprised how little vendors will accept if they are hungry to make a sale.

♦

Vera Hyatt, exhibit curator

With just a few hours left in New Delhi, I broke one of my cardinal rules: never buy anything at a hotel boutique. I saw a finely embroidered jacket in the shop window, just my size and in flattering colors. It was $400, the product of Kashmiri men who ply their needles during long, snowy winters. I offered $100 in cash dollars for it, was turned down, and left the store. I was walking away when the shopkeeper changed his mind and chased me down to accept my offer. Better a low sale than no sale that day for him. What did I learn? No place is above bargaining.

♦

Ann McClellan,
marketing director

- for the last item on the shelf
- for buying an older model
- for a slight flaw that really doesn't bother you (but pretend that it does)
- for paying in cash, checks, or traveler's checks
- for various professions or memberships in certain organizations
- for buying more than one of the same thing
- for taking the floor or display sample off their hands (Often you can get about twenty percent off, and many items still have a valid warranty.)

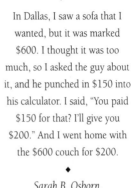

In Dallas, I saw a sofa that I wanted, but it was marked $600. I thought it was too much, so I asked the guy about it, and he punched in $150 into his calculator. I said, "You paid $150 for that? I'll give you $200." And I went home with the $600 couch for $200.

◆

Sarah B. Osborn, documentary filmmaker

➤ If you think you are paying too much but really want the merchandise, ask the merchant to throw another item into the bargain.

➤ Remind the merchant that you are helping them get rid of their inventory—especially at the end of a season. To a small business owner that translates into immediate cash flow to buy new goods or pay bills.

Give the lady what she wants!

◆

Marshall Field to a manager in his Chicago department store

➤ If something is too expensive, but you really want it, be indecisive. Pick it up, put it down, look at other things, ask lots of questions. Be persistent, but not demanding.

The more a shopkeeper has invested in time and the longer you can string out the negotiations, the more likely you will arrive at a good compromise. The merchant will want to convert that time to money in order to get on to the next customer.

➤ Bring duty-free lists and catalogs from home as a way to compare prices and know if you are really getting a bargain. Tell the shopkeeper what price you'd pay for similar goods at home, if that will help with your negotiating.

> When negotiating, keep it fun and happy. Don't get so fixated on getting a better price that it becomes an adversarial or unpleasant experience.
>
> ◆
>
> *Alida Latham,*
> *arts patron and collector*

➤ The sight of real money is a powerful inducement for the vendor to close the sale. Pull out just what you are willing to part with.

➤ In foreign countries, often pulling out dollars in a lesser amount will be acceptable. But in any currency, pull out less cash than asked for and try saying, "This is all I have on me. Will you take it?"

➤ Enter into the bargaining only if you really want the item, and don't leave behind something you really must have.

Many years ago, two brothers had a family clothing store on the Lower East Side of New York. The brother who waited on the customers wore a large hearing aid, while the other brother at the rear of the store was in charge of the books. After finding out a family wanted a blue suit for the son for the holidays, the brother in front would hold up the suit and shout to the brother at the rear, "Sam, how much is this blue suit?" From the back, the reply, "Thirty-five dollars." The first brother promptly turned to the family and said, "The price of the suit is twenty-five dollars." Quickly the suit was wrapped and paid for, and the family left very satisfied. It is remarkable how many fifteen-dollar suits were sold in this way.

♦

Marsha Shaines, lawyer

Chapter Eleven

FAIR TRADE

Everyone lives by selling something,
whatever be his right to it.

— *Robert Louis Stevenson*

———

lies hung in the air and swarmed the alley. Like beads in a curtain, they momentarily blocked my way to a craft workshop. My Indian agents, who had brought me to this part of New Delhi, seemed oblivious. They walked straight through the passageway. I covered my mouth and nose with one hand, brushed aside the thick veil of flies with the other, and followed them.

The alley opened into an airy courtyard where a dozen Indian women, clad in multi-colored saris, squatted over a wide, rectangular blanket on the stone ground. Babies huddled to their bodies or sat beside them. Pieces of fabric and accessories lay in heaps in

I like to patronize shops with
another aim besides profit.

♦

Florence Lloyd, linguist

front of the women. They hunched over the blanket and formed a makeshift assembly line to cut, paste, and sew. One cut, another stitched, others glued felt pieces to fabric. I came here to buy patch-cloth dolls and learn about traditional handicrafts. I watched as the women pasted eyes to cloth doll heads for a dollar a day.

The women seemed happy, and the government agency with whom we worked claimed the women received a good wage for their work, but I felt uncomfortable when I had to negotiate lower costs. The price the government wanted from us bore no relation to the wage these woman earned. If I got the agency to lower their wholesale price to us, would the women earn even less than one dollar? I kept thinking that the Indian government was taking advantage of our situation. With only two weeks to cram in all our buying, we didn't have time to find other resources or learn about working conditions. In our limited time, we had to trust that the agency was paying fair wages, but it was never clear even when we asked. And what was a fair share?

Judging worker salaries in Third World countries by Western standards was unrealistic. What would be a pittance in the West would feed many families in other parts of the world. We felt compelled to pay an equitable price based on the country's own economic standards. Wherever possible, we bought from craftspeople rather than an intermediary so that they would benefit directly. We tried to be alert to exploitative conditions where artisans were treated poorly, had no ventilation, or appeared overworked. Seeing that would have prevented us from buying the products no matter how much money we might have saved.

> It's impossible to wear something and feel good about it when I know it was made in sweatshops. I discourage my students from doing so since I've become aware of the choices.
>
> ♦
>
> *Kristy Vant,*
> *masseuse and stylist*

The problem, of course, is actually seeing the factories. Government-run stores say they represent the interests of the artist, but some Third World countries are notoriously corrupt and irresponsible about worker conditions and wages. Importers and manufacturers may, in fact, pay their producers more than they would get from a local company, but unless you tour the workplaces and factories, you'll never know for sure. So, the closer you get to the source, the more likely you will be to promote fair trade and equitable standards. When traveling and shopping, take advantage of any opportunity that brings you into indigenous artisan homes and marketplaces. You'll find unique buys and help sustain communities.

My friend Gloria, an importer, believes in shopping as close to the source as possible. She was purchasing clothing in Nogales, Mexico, when she spotted a young woman behind the counter wearing a blouse that was more typical than anything found on the rack. She asked the young woman for a blouse exactly like that but was told the blouse came from the village and was not for retail sale. Gloria offered to pay the young woman for the blouse—double. Spotting an offer she couldn't refuse, the young woman agreed to the sale. But what would she wear the rest of the day? No problem. Gloria slipped out of her plain white Anne Klein blouse, and the young woman slipped it on. Says Gloria, "She loved it, and I loved my new blouse. It's called fair trade."

> ─── ★ ───
>
> I love to buy directly from artists. In Costa Rica, I found rain forest products—journals and paper goods made from coffee, banana, and tobacco by-products created to support sustainable development.
>
> ♦
>
> *Bette Ann Libby,*
> *artist and ceramist*

Tips

➤ When buying directly from artisans, bargain if it is part of the culture, but don't quibble over nickels and dimes. Save the aggressive negotiating for middlemen and merchants or for expensive merchandise.

➤ Buy from companies that pay fair wages and maintain decent working conditions. For a list of stores and information on companies, contact the Fair Trade Federation. See the "Resources and References" section in this book for the address or check their web site for consumer news at www.fairtradefederation.com.

> When you buy a product, you're endorsing a way of doing business.
>
> ◆
>
> *Nina Smith,*
> *nonprofit executive director*

➤ Write protest letters and boycott businesses known to treat workers unfairly.

➤ In stores, read labels on clothing and crafts to find out how they were made and who made them. Those made by special artisan groups usually have an interesting story on the hang tag.

➤ Join nonprofit groups that contribute to artisan development. See the "Resources and References" section for appropriate organizations.

➤ Take an arts and crafts vacation. Groups like Aid to Artisans sponsor specialized craft trips, and eco-travel companies can customize a trip for you. See the "Resources and References" section of this book for contacts.

Questions for Researching Companies & Products

➢ How is an item made?

➢ What are the materials used?

➢ What is the country of origin? What laws does it have regarding worker hours, wages, safety regulations, the use of pesticides, and ventilation?

➢ Does the company have a good or bad record regarding workers' rights?

When buying anything handmade from its maker, ask about the process and materials and understand pertinent traditions. I seek value and try to match social and environmental responsibility to price and value.

♦

Lloyd Herman,
art exhibit consultant

➢ How much energy is consumed in the manufacture or packaging of the product?

➢ How does the company dispose of waste? Does the company recycle scraps and postproduction material?

➢ Will the product itself be energy efficient? Will disposing of it cause harm to the environment or your own health?

➢ What effect do chemicals used have on the workers or the environment?

I wish to reinforce consumer opinions against exploitative labor and abuse of environment. Ask lots of questions about how things are made, by whom, under what conditions, and what percent of the price goes to the maker.

♦

Caroline Ramsay Merriam,
crafts specialist

➢ Does the company use timber from rain forests?

➢ Have animals been used in testing? If the item is a by-product of animals, are they well treated?

➢ How much fuel is used in transportation and distribution?

➢ Can you recycle the product or its packaging?

Business in our society has lost the notion—if it ever had it—that it should do more than create wealth and move goods back and forth, that it should be of service to greater society. We learn from the farmers about life's basic priorities, about getting by with less, about living in harmony with the earth. They learn from us about international business, the marketplace, promotion, and finance. Our customers hold the web together. As more take part, the web grows stronger, and we all gain hope from our exchanges. That's alternative trade.

◆

Jonathan Rosenthal, executive director

Chapter Twelve

GETTING IT HOME

As the Spanish proverb says, "He who would bring home
the wealth of the Indies, must carry the wealth of the
Indies with him." So it is in traveling; a man must
carry knowledge with him, if he would
bring home knowledge.

— Samuel Johnson

———

While combing through dusty back rooms of an antique shop in New Delhi, India, I found a small wood-and-brass chest with hidden drawers. I thought I could use it as a table between two chairs in my living room. Perfect. It needed no repairs and had an added bonus—those neat, hidden compartments. I had no clue what I'd put there, but what fun to think I could hide a treasure. Not being an antique maven, I also had no idea about the real worth of the chest, but I was with Francis, a savvy French businessman who had lived in India for the past twenty-five years. He knew the reputation of the dealer, and so I bargained a bit and got the chest for about $300. (I still don't know what it was actually worth, but the price seemed fair to me.)

My unexpected find thrilled me. On a previous trip to India, I had purchased my requisite souvenirs, now I could hunt for old Indian treasures. My first mistake? I hadn't completely inspected the chest. Later at home when I was cleaning it up, I found a small brass plate that read, "Made in Germany." So much for Indian treasures. I still love the piece; it still reminds me of rummaging through that old shop, but I thought I was purchasing native goods.

However, buying a piece made outside the country was a minor mistake compared with my freight mishap. Because Francis exported merchandise all the time, I left the shipping arrangements to him, and because I wasn't in a hurry, I assumed he would send it the cheapest way. Wrong. He sent it air freight. Not only did I have to drive two hours round-trip to the airport at home, I also had to shell out more than $300 to retrieve my bargain.

When I asked him why not a slow boat, he said it might have gotten mildewed and warped. But if I had thought to ask how much the air freight was, I might never have purchased it in the first place. Obviously, we didn't communicate even though we were both speaking English. Just imagine how tricky it can get to negotiate about shipping in another language.

Taking It with You

The best advice I can offer when sending things back home is, Don't. You're better off carrying your purchases home than spending unknown quantities to get them shipped. Try these tips for hassle-free transport of your treasures.

Tips

➤ Give away old clothes you've been traveling with. The recipient is happy, and you have more room in your suitcase for your purchases.

➤ Be prepared in advance with a copy of "Know Before You

Go," free from the U.S. Customs Service or on their Web site (www.customs.ustreas.gov/travel/kbygo.htm).

➤ Know the duty-free limits of your own country. For Americans, you can bring $400 worth of goods duty-free into the country; above that, up to $1,000, you pay 10 percent duty.

➤ Save your receipts to prove retail value. If you've bought a real bargain somewhere, leave the price tag on so a custom agent does not place a higher value on it and charge more duty.

> Rather than get carried away with the moment, consider how you are going to get the object home and what kind of shape it will be in.
>
> ◆
>
> *Phyllis Rasmussen, manager and buyer*

➤ If an agent needs to inspect your purchases, you'll save time if you pack your bags so that the items are readily available. Or consider packing your purchases separately.

➤ When you calculate the exchange rate, write it down directly on all your receipts (whether cash or credit). This will help when you fill out customs forms and also when you reconcile your credit card bills later.

> I love shopping for ceramics, and the best way to carry them back is to pack my laptop computer bag, which is a small padded backpack, in my suitcase. Then I carry it on the plane on the way back.
>
> ◆
>
> *Ginny Hanger, customer service manager*

➤ Answer all customs questions clearly, and keep it simple. Never volunteer information about purchases. You may inadvertently say something that causes suspicion and delays your arrival.

➤ Customs officials know the basic retail value of most things, and they're hip to all the tricks. You usually won't win trying to slip something past them. If an agent catches you with something you haven't declared, avoid arguing and admit that you simply overlooked it.

➤ Declare purchases from duty-free shops abroad on your customs declarations. They count toward your personal exemption amount. The term duty-free means free from taxes or duty only leaving the country.

➤ Certain items such as textiles may be subject to quotas. Textiles bought for gifts or personal use are usually not subject to restrictions, but large quantities and unaccompanied textiles and

When living in Spain, I went to Morocco to buy carpets. When we returned, I presented my receipts to the Spanish Guardia Civil. I didn't realize that there was a tremendous duty on carpets (something like 70 percent), although as a military person I was exempt from such tariffs. Apparently, most people get falsified receipts for carpets. The Guardia, worried about the size of my bill and believing that nobody could be so dumb as to present a true receipt, thought I was up to something. They called in their sergeant, a large and humorless fellow, and the situation became quite serious. I pulled out my military identification. Instantly, the atmosphere changed from stern questioning to solicitation. I declined their offer to carry the two heavy carpets to my car, scurried to the parking lot, and zoomed off.

◆

Gregory Gallardo,
commander, U.S. Navy

apparent item, textiles apparel might have quotas. You may need a "visa," "export license," or exempt certificate from the country of origin.

➤ Be aware that many countries restrict or prohibit the import or export of merchandise such as elephant ivory, fireworks, fur, leather, fruits, vegetables, pirated music cassettes or computer software, and certain types or amounts of liquor.

➤ Avoid purchasing restricted products. If customs confiscates an item you purchased by credit card, your credit card company has no obligation to give you a refund and will not get one for you from the merchant.

➤ If an item is too heavy or unique, consider shipping no matter what the cost.

Shipping

If you really can't carry home the four-foot-tall smiling Buddha, it is possible to ship it. Try these tips for getting it home with the least possible expense. Remember, however, that when it comes to discussing shipping arrangements in a foreign language, little things get lost in translation. But even if you're speaking the same language, mix-ups can occur.

Tips

➤ When you ask questions about shipping, be as specific as possible. Communicate your preferences clearly. Repeat them if necessary, or write them down.

➤ Factor in the cost of shipping when you think you are getting a bargain. A bargain is only a bargain if the price you pay to get it back home is less than you would have paid to buy it at home.

➤ If you ship goods back home, you cannot prepay duty or include them in your customs exemption. In the United States, they are subject to duty when they arrive. (Separate procedures apply for merchandise brought in from the U.S. Virgin Islands, American Samoa, Guam, or Caribbean Basin countries.) Customs must clear all incoming shipments, and they collect duty based on a tariff schedule. They may also collect state user fees or IRS taxes.

➤ Any freight forwarder, broker, or an agent can clear shipments for you, but they will pass on their fees based on the amount of work they do, not on the value of the goods. These charges are separate from customs duties, and they can be expensive—especially in relation to the value of your purchases.

➤ Mailing shipments back via UPS International, FedEx, DHL, or such can be cost efficient if the parcels are small or lightweight and meet the mailing requirements of the exporting country in terms of weight, size, and measurement. These express companies will arrange customs clearance and charge a fee for this service.

I sold four European watercolors to my client in Texas. None of them measured more than about 6" x 8" unframed. Despite the tiny size, the customer did not want to carry them with her and arranged shipping back to Texas. A couple of weeks later an oversized truck pulls up to the curb, and four wrestler-type guys walked in to pick up the Texas client's package. I handed them a small bundle in an equally small shopping bag.
Puzzled, they asked,
"What's this?"
"My client's four watercolors."
"We came to pick up four water coolers."

◆

Anonymous antique dealer

➤ Sending items via parcel post to the U.S. is easy but slower than express mail. Customs inspects foreign mail shipments, and, if no duty is required, the Postal Service delivers the package to you without additional charges for postage or handling. If duty is owed, expect to pay the duty plus a $5 processing fee and a U.S. Postal Service handling fee when your parcel is delivered.

➤ If you are having clothes made abroad, get recommendations for reliable tailors with export experience. Expect additional fees, and ask about store shipping policies. Some may charge a flat fee; others add insurance and actual shipping on top.

➤ If you ship items, get complete details in writing from the store merchant, including a shipping date, method of shipping, and insurance details, including who will be responsible if the item arrives damaged or is lost, and instructions on what to do if that happens. If your purchase is forwarded by boat, it may take up to three months to receive.

> ★ ★ ★
>
> I had a leather coat made in Thailand based on my own cloth raincoat. I didn't really want to do it, but the salesperson pushed—saying I'd only have to pay if I liked it—and friends convinced me the shop was reliable. On my last night in Thailand, the salesperson showed me a picture of my proposed coat. It looked more like a tent. Everyone convinced me that I should trust the seller to tailor it as I wanted and that it would be shipped to me. Somehow I did this, paid for it, and, yes, never got it.
>
> ◆
>
> *Sharon Nelson, judge*

➤ If you pay to have something sent, charge it on a credit card so you might have recourse if your package doesn't arrive.

➤ Ask when you will receive your shipment. If the length of time is unacceptable, take it with you.

The Value-added Tax (VAT)

Value-added tax is a tax assessed to purchases above a certain amount, and it is a tax that is refunded at the end of your travels. Getting the refund, however, can be a hassle if you don't have your receipts in order and you have to wait in line at customs. Because of these difficulties, it is wise to make sure the return will be large enough to invest your time and effort in the process. So learn about the process before you go. For additional information and tips on VAT, see the Western Europe section of Part Two.

Tips

➤ For more information, call Global Refund (800-566-9828) or check its Web site: www.taxfree.se.

Many years ago in Pakistan, I bought a large Bukhara-style rug. It was draped over a shed roof to dry, having just been finished and washed. The knots were tight and the background color a lovely, natural camel hair. It had not yet been sheared. They tie all those knots and then roll up the whole carpet and shear it. When we finally received the carpet and unrolled it, we found deep furrows and lumps where the shearing had been extremely badly done. I called the rug dealer in Lahore, an adventure in itself, and he blithely said that I should put the rug out in the road and let cars run over it for a while—that would flatten it out!

♦

*Clare Brett Smith,
nonprofit president*

➤ Refund policies and percentages change frequently, so contact the tourist board of the country you intend to visit for current VAT information.

➤ Stores participating in VAT refund programs will refund your percentage after they receive the forms you complete at customs. If you're paying by credit card, ask them to credit your account so that you don't have to pay possible fees cashing a foreign check.

PART TWO

FEARLESS REGIONAL SHOPPING GUIDE

Throughout this section, unless otherwise specified, country shopping tips refer to capitals, main cities, or areas that most travelers are likely to visit. Where possible, I've listed shop names. But be aware that situations change quickly in politically unstable regions, and a particular shop may be in a new location or simply no longer exist.

AFRICA &
THE MIDDLE EAST

For time is the longest distance between two places.

—Tennessee Williams

———

To shop in Africa, you need time: time to move across this vast continent, time to understand its tribal nature and years of colonial rule, time to appreciate its different cultures. Folklore, geopolitics, religion, and language—often within a country as well as the entire continent—make African and the Middle Eastern complexities almost impossible to categorize. So, I'll narrow our shopping explorations to three areas: North Africa and the Middle East; Sub-Saharan and West Africa; and East, Central, and Southern Africa.

In each of these regions you'll discover exotic markets with their own traditions and treasures. Before you go, always check State Department travel warnings. Political instability and other potential hazards can be a risk anytime.

Choose your route with care, then leave your inhibitions at home and bring along

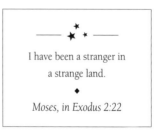

I have been a stranger in
a strange land.

♦

Moses, in Exodus 2:22

your sense of adventure. Drop your notion of time, put on your bargaining hat, and don't forget your camera. Wonders await you.

NORTH AFRICA & THE MIDDLE EAST

When I first arrived in Morocco, I was anxious to see the market in Casablanca. My romantic visions of a grand souk from the movie *Casablanca* faded rapidly. A crooked street with a few local merchants hardly enticed me. My one purchase? A can of olives. But by the time we got to Marrakech, the northern connection for the ancient Saharan caravan routes, I knew I had found real magic, not Hollywood legend.

Surrounded by orange trees, olive groves, and gardens, Marrakech enchanted us in daylight and at sunset. In this place where Africa and Arabia meet, my buyers and I discovered anything is negotiable—even a horse- and buggy-ride. And everything is for sale in Djemaa el Fna—an open market square suspended in time. As we made our way through this twelve-acre bazaar, vendors pushed stacks of oranges and nuts on their carts while monkeys squawked and begged a photograph. Veiled young women hawked

In the Arab Quarter of Jerusalem I learned never to bargain unless you intend to buy. I spotted a long Bedouin dress in bright orange and purple. The shopkeeper saw the need in my eyes and began to bargain. I asked to try it on. With great irritation, he ushered me into a makeshift closet. I emerged, thanked him, but said I couldn't buy the dress as it was too small. He lowered the price again, and again, until I finally explained that no matter how reasonable, I could not take the dress as it did not fit. He became furious, hurling at me what I imagined to be a string of the choicest Arab epithets. As I turned to leave, he spat on my back, right between the thin straps of my tank top. My next stop was the Wailing Wall.

◆

Janet Borrus,
actor and writer

silver bracelets ("here, *petit cadeau,* little gift") and costumed water sellers in tassel-brimmed hats jangled metal cups in front of us. Clowns and acrobats, dancers and drummers, fortunetellers and faith healers, snake charmers and storytellers swarmed around us in continuous motion, vying for our dollars. At night, veiled old ladies sat cross-legged on mats, shuffled tarot cards, and sought to read our fortunes. Merchants and beggars competed for our attention.

We bought necklaces and camel toys from the sidewalk vendors, then maneuvered beyond the open space into a maze of streets and merchant stalls. We crisscrossed streets, browsed down alleys, up others, and around corners. Somehow we never really got lost, and our search for crafts was easy. Everything imaginable was crammed into every available space. It was a soft sell, and negotiations were laid back.

"Come here, lady, just one look," merchants routinely beckoned in French. "Come in, hello." Some treated us to tea in their back rooms; others showed us how their inlaid furniture was made.

We soaked up the culture and bought rugs, leather, jewelry, boots, fabric, wood, pottery, brass, pillows, and small home furnishings. We found treasures everywhere, especially those not for sale. You will, too.

General Tips

➤ Many countries have state-run cooperatives where prices are reasonable. So, if bargaining makes you uncomfortable, you can select indigenous gifts without the pressures of the markets.

- Dress conservatively. Leave your tight jeans, short shorts, and halter tops at home.

- Don't worry about getting lost in the markets. Shop every nook; you'll find a pattern to the souks.

- Often you'll find clusters of similar merchants, making price comparisons easy.

- Both beggars and merchants will vie for eye contact. Be firm in your refusals.

- Respect tradition. Bargaining in bazaars is an expected ritual with its own customs and gestures. There is an unwritten sense of trust between the seller and prospective customer. You may be treated or spoken to like a member of a family— offered tea and told a family story—in order to create a friendly atmosphere. After a time the seller will mention his price. Always reject the first offer. Do not be surprised if he shows you a book filled with notes or

If you want shopkeepers to bother you in the souks, just carry previous purchases openly.

◆

Miriam H. Labbok,
physician

We were shopping for a rug in the walled cities of Morocco finding our way through the narrow and confusing walkways, the language, and cultural differences. Everything was negotiable. We were dependent on the ethics of our driver— who it turns out was very honest and helpful (probably my child in tow influencing him)—and his knowledge of the local businessmen. When we were served hot minted tea in tiny glasses, I was charmed. Unfortunately, we left without buying the $500 rug. He wouldn't go lower. This was 1970. I've always regretted that, but have very fond memories of the whole experience.

◆

Claudia Minnicozzi, artist

postcards from foreign customers who were satisfied buying similar items to those that interest you. It's all part of the negotiating process.

➤ If you are offered tea or coffee and an invitation to go upstairs or to the back room, accept it. You're under no obligation to buy. It's an opportunity to watch a craftsman at work, view a local interior, and absorb a bit of culture.

➤ If you mention that the shop has been recommended by a friend, you indicate that you may become a regular customer.

➤ Bargain in the early afternoon when the heat is the strongest and the seller may be weary.

➤ For the best deal, try negotiating just before evening prayer, when convention dictates that the last customer is entitled to a discount.

Country Specialties & Tips

Algeria
Specialties: rugs, carpets, and Tuareg crafts.
- Visit SNAT, the official arts and crafts organization with locations on Rue Didouche Mourad for crafts overview. Use this visit for price comparisons before you shop the market in Algiers.
- If a family invites you to their home as a guest, buy flowers or food as a gift.

Bahrain
Specialties: gold, perfume, fabric, brass, dates, pottery, embroidery, and raffia.
- Shop at the Crafts Center, the museum shop, and the souk at Bab

al Bahrain in Manama.

- Gold—usually 18 or 22 carat—is priced daily by the gram at the gold souk on Shaikh Abdulla Avenue. Graded sieves used to assess the value of pearls in the old days may still be for sale in Bahrain antique shops.

- To the west of the gold souk, visit the fabric shops to purchase silk, cotton, worsted and brightly colored material. The perfume merchants are nearby.

- On Wednesday at Ladies' Market, Bahraini women sell their goods, including typical masks.

- Find pottery made today using traditional methods in the village of A'ali.

- Buy traditional weaving in west coast villages: watch basket weavers in Karbabad near the Portuguese Fort and fabric weavers in Bani Jamra.

When haggling over anything, stick hard to your prices. Don't be intimidated. A tradesman may act as if you insulted his entire clan when you offer your low price. He will want to drop the whole deal. Let him. It's just a bluff! When you stick to your guns, he may pretend you have invoked the wrath of some godly force and give you images of men sweeping across the desert, machetes raised to take your head. Another bluff. Play hardball, walk away. You can probably find it somewhere else.

◆

Brandon Zatt, student

Egypt
Specialties: cotton clothing and towels, leatherwork, gold, silver, jewelry, ancient reproductions, rugs, spices, henna, perfumes, brass, copper, and camel saddles.

- When in Cairo, visit el-Qahirah and shop at the Khan El-Khalili bazaar for souvenirs and antique treasures, but not on Sunday when many stalls are closed.

- For gold and silver, try Suq

Cairo has the most richly atmospheric market in the world, great buys.

◆

Karen Peterson, photojournalist

el-Sagha. Simple gold pieces are usually 22 carat and more ornate pieces are generally 18 carat.

- Browse around Suq el-Nahassin for copper and Suq el-Muski for clothing and leather. Carefully inspect the findings—buckles and clasps—for quality.

- Be alert for forgeries. Fake bronze castings, coins, and old drawings may be factory-made today.

- If you have the time, ask a jeweler to create a cartouche with your name in hieroglyphs.

- Visit Wakalat el-Ghouri, the arts and crafts center in Cairo, and the glassblowing shops at el-Daour.

- Find the perfume dealers in the souks and ask them to mix your favorite fragrances as a souvenir. If the scent is too strong when you get home, dilute it with alcohol.

- If you're in the market for a tent, watch traditional sewing in Suq Khiyamiya.

- Northwest of Cairo, visit the Camel Market on Friday mornings.

- Buy pottery and batiks near Cairo in Harraniyah village. While you're there, visit the Wissa Wassef School for woven carpets and rugs.

- In Alexandria, don't miss the

Cairo is a shopper's paradise—everything from ultramodern plastic arts to prehistoric relics and everything in between. One excellent source of traditional copper and brass pieces is Atalier Ahmed. Just ask other copper merchants for him. In addition to the genuine old items, he makes excellent reproductions as well.

◆

Odis Kendrick, businessman

I had seen a necklace in the main market that I wanted to get for my wife. I left my wife and mother-in-law in the middle of the Arab bazaar in Cairo and found my way through a maze of passages, steps, and alleyways to the manufacturer. I was gone so long before I returned with the fabulous necklace, they thought I had been killed.

◆

Rich McNally, businessman

opportunity to forage around the antique stores off Attarine Street. In the late nineteenth century, wealthy Europeans, attracted to this port city, helped it flourish as a cultural and intellectual Mecca. But during Nasser's rule, they fled the city and left behind home furnishings that formed the basis of today's antique business. For reputable, family-run establishments try Au Petite Musée, Omar Antiques, Habashi, Mohammed Moussa Antiques, Gallery Odeon, Nahas Antiques, Magdy Moussa Antiques, Mustafa Moussa Antiques, and Gamel Antiques. Many of these stores are generations old.

- If the antiques you find on Attarine Street are too costly, look for antique reproductions on St. Youssef Maghariah and Sheikh Aly El-Leithy streets. Merchants who specialize in antique replicas include PATCHO Reproductions and Antiques and Shouman Reproductions Gallery.

- For low-quality flea market finds that need work, shop on Ibn Khaldoun Street.

- Egyptian law prohibits the export of antiques more than 100 years old.

Iran

Specialties: carpets, kilims, prayer rugs, gold, silver and mother-of-pearl jewelry, camel hair toys, and Persian slippers.

- If you are a woman, buy a *rupoush* or long, loose coat to wear over your clothes to comply with local dress codes.

- In Tehran visit the Grand Bazaar for local crafts. Start at 15th Khordad Street to find gold and carpets and try Manucheri Street for antiques and leather.

- You might still find miniature paintings and a carpet of excellent quality in souks in Esfahan, Iran. Most carpets in the bazaars there, however, are bought by wholesalers and sent to London, Hamburg, and Zurich.

Israel

Specialties: silver filigree, gold and silver, jewelry, Roman glass, antique pottery, olive wood crafts, old coins, gold necklaces with your name in Hebrew, contemporary art, brass oil lamps and other Judaica items, diamonds, and Dead Sea toiletries.

- Shops are closed from midday Friday until sundown Saturday for the Sabbath.

- In Tel Aviv, shop at the open-air Carmel Market, the Diamond Exchange, and Bezalel Market. On Tuesday and Friday buy crafts at Carmel Market.

- For superb reproductions—from Roman coins and ancient glass to jewelry and religious replicas—visit the museum shop at the Israel Museum in Jerusalem.

In Israel, stop by the kibbutz where they make Naot shoes. They are great, good quality shoes. The kibbutz has an outlet store on the premises with a huge selection and good prices. They are a fraction of what they cost in the U.S.

◆

Dana Lansky, law student

- Bargain without mercy in the old Arab quarter of Jerusalem.

- Buy handblown, painted glass in the Neker craft workshop in the Mea Shearim quarter of Jerusalem.

- In Jaffa, check out the flea market and the artist workshops.

- Visit the artist's cooperative at Ein Hod between Tel Aviv and Haifa to buy contemporary work.

- Plan visits to kibbutzim where they make and sell merchandise. Prices are usually quite reasonable.

- Kibbutz Megiddo sells traditional filigree jewelry.

- Locals say you can actually find bargains at the duty-free airport shops.

Jordan

Specialties: Bedouin rugs and jewelry, Dead Sea products, local crafts such as ceramics, embroidered items, and Bedouin dolls.

- In the gold souk in Amman look for contemporary gold and silver jewelry.

- Visit the Noor Foundation workshops for local crafts.

- Check out the used clothes bazaar on Nixon Street. Although it specializes in Salvation Army donations, you can find a surprising array of designer jeans and other fashions.

Kuwait

Specialties: museum shop reproductions, handicrafts, and Bedouin weavings.

- The Kuwait Museum of Islamic Art in the Salmayah area has a museum shop with an extensive assortment of museum reproductions and adaptations. Take home superb reproductions of Islamic art and related souvenirs to remember your visit.

- In Salmayah near McDonald's, stop in at the Sedu Gallery for a selection of Arabian handicrafts, cards, graphics, and prints.

- Look for the new shopping arcades next to the souks and older shops where you can find both Western goods and traditional crafts.

- Be careful of pirated videos and cassettes as it may be illegal to import them into Western countries.

Lebanon

Specialties: blue glass, jewelry, copper, silverware, inlaid jewelry boxes and game boards, pipes, and fruit tobacco.

- Once the Paris of the Middle East, Beirut is trying to raise its standards again; so, look for upscale fashion and jewelry in the area of Jounieh.

- Purchase traditional crafts at the Artisanat du Liban.

The Ladies Cooperative (Bedu Society) is an interesting group devoted to the art of Bedouin hand weaving of the Arabian Peninsula. The craft and training center is housed in a restored 19th-century, Arabian Gulf-style house in the center of Kuwait City. Various items are for sale, including rugs, runners, bags, and cushions. They also demonstrate weaving on certain days.

◆

Odis Kendrick, businessman

Morocco

Specialties: hand-tooled leather goods, tiles, rugs, leather-and-fabric boots, pottery, beaded jewelry, inlaid furniture, copper, brass, silver, and local music cassettes.

- In Casablanca, shop at the New Medina (Habbous) and at the Coopartim and Ensemble Artisanal cooperatives for traditional crafts.

- Try Aït Manos on Boulevard de la Résistance in Casablanca for handmade, decorative tiles.

- Bargain in the souks in Marrakech or Fez for the best deals on everything.

- Learn about the craft traditions of Morocco by visiting the Handicrafts Center and Dar si-Said, the folk art museum, both in the old city of Marrakech.

- During the summer, the heat in Marrakech can reach 120°F (50°C), so visit the souk at Djemaa el Fna right before sunset when the heat dies down.

- Don't pick the oranges from the trees in Marrakech. They are bitter and are used as essence for toilet water. To quench your thirst while shopping, buy the freshly squeezed orange juice from the vendors in the square. They use imported oranges.

I knew about ten words to bargain in the souks in Morocco. I was doing so well that the salesman said, "Come speak to my father. He will be so impressed by your Arabic that he will give you a big discount." Although I demurred, he dragged in his father. Of course, when the hajji spoke to me, I didn't understand a word, embarrassing myself and the son, who then upped the price on everything.

♦

Miriam H. Labbok, physician

- In Marrakech, discover good buys for rugs, textiles, shoes, spices, brass, and pottery.

- Find market jewelry at both ends of the price scale, but little in between. The inexpensive, beaded earrings there make great, lightweight gifts. Or select an expensive, crafted jewelry piece.

- Save your leather purchases for Fez and find pottery everywhere in Safi, a seaside town just northwest of Marrakech.

Shopping in Marrakech you need energy and perseverance and protective armor.

♦

John Wilson,
importer and wholesaler

- Expect to find bazaars filled with men as merchants. But in northern Morocco in the Er Rif mountains, look for the Berber women's markets where you can purchase clothes and pottery.

Oman

Specialties: gold, silver, and crafts.

- The Oman Heritage Center in the Shati Al-Qurum Center sells ethnic crafts such as textiles, weavings, copper, and pottery.

Saudi Arabia

Specialties: gold and silver jewelry, pearls, Asian carpets, rugs, Bedouin jewelry, pipes, coffee pots, antiques, perfumes, pottery, wall hangings, baskets, and camel stools.

- Wear conservative clothing in Jeddah as it is a strict Islamic city.

- In the Balad area in Jeddah, gold and silver jewelry is sold by weight. Bring cash.

- Shop for spices and silk in the Bab Makkah Souk.

- Find good bargains around New Year.

- Dictated by prayer times, store openings vary several minutes each week. Shopkeepers close their stores at prayer call. Do not linger in the shop to finish bargaining as the owner may be fined. Businesses reopen later after the conclusion of prayer.

- In the town of Hofuf, between Riyadh and Dhahran, you'll find palm-frond baskets, ideal for shopping or decoration. In the Thursday morning market,

If you go to Zagora in southeastern Morocco, stay out of the cheesy tourist shops on the main strip. Ask to be taken to the Casbah—the old city, no streets, only sand. You get there through a wonderful series of trails and irrigated, mud-built housing communities. It's gorgeous and invigorating. I found a wonderful home that ran our camel trips and had high-quality carpets and great silver jewelry.

♦

Brandon Zatt, student

The Arabian port city of Dubai is noted for its selection of electronic goods (multivoltage) and 24-carat gold jewelry from India in traditional and modern styles. Many of the old souks are air-conditioned and expect traditional haggling over prices. Be aware that most shopkeepers have up-to-the-minute computer reports on the international prices of gold. Most of the price negotiation is based on the value of the work only.

♦

Odis Kendrick, businessman

discover Bedouin goods such
as infant carriers, woven mats,
shepherd crooks, old and
modern copper teapots, and
camel bells and bags.

- Buy woven Khamis and Najran
  baskets with lids decorated
  with camel leather in the
  Asir province.

- For delicate, white pottery visit
  the sandstone cliffs area of Whiff.

- Stop in at local Saudi bakeries
  for piping hot pita bread, a
  delicious buy.

Syria

*Specialties: Damascus silk brocades,
damascene crafts, rugs, carpets,
brass, gold, copper, embroidered
table linens, and inlaid boxes and
furniture.*

- Don't miss the ancient Souk al Hamadiyeh in Damascus.
  Bargain hard.

- Visit the glassblowing factory
  near Bab Sharqi in Damascus.

- Watch perfume dealers mix
  musk, amber, and essences of
  flowers such as violets and
  roses. Ask them to mix a special
  fragrance for you.

Tunisia

*Specialties: felt caps, olive oil, kilims,
copper pots, olive wood bowls,
spices, and perfumes.*

- In Tunis, prices are better in the
  medina, the Souk et-Trouk,
  than at the Rue Djema Zitouna
  next to the Great Mosque.

Most stores are closed in
Damascus on Friday except for
some shops near Bab Sharqi
and the shops in the gold souk.
When shopping in the old city
souk, try these stores: Ahmad
and Hassan for assorted handicrafts, Dabdoub's for handicraft
and antiques, Garo for gold,
Laham and Nazeer for carpets,
and Tony Stephan for
handicrafts and brocade.

♦

*Kari L. Carey, embassy
community liaison offficer*

Most of the other areas in the
Emirates have traditional
Market Days where indigenous
people sell, trade, and barter
goods. Check with the hotels
in Dubai and other capitals
for dates and locations. To
reach some of them, you can
actually rent a camel to
arrive in grand style.

♦

Odis Kendrick, businessman

- Vendors in the souk will blend floral scents for your own perfume souvenir.

- Do not buy coral as it may conflict with import regulations in Western countries.

United Arab Emirates

Specialties: gold, watches, electronic equipment, cameras, rugs, antiques, and jewelry.

- In Dubai, shop duty-free for Hong Kong-type bargains.

- Dubai is the best place to buy Persian rugs outside of Iran.

- Visit the gold souk in Dubai near Sikkat Al-Khail Street.

- Discover the antique shops behind the Arab Monetary Fund Building on Al Nasr Street.

- In Abu Dhabi souks, buy inexpensive cotton caftans to use at the beach.

Yemen

Specialties: traditional jewelry, spices.

- Visit the Suq al Fidda, the silver souk in San'a.

I was shopping in the souk in Yemen when a spice merchant, whom I had passed a couple of times and had photographed, called me over and offered me some Yemeni saffron. I said, no thanks, and, though I hadn't bought anything from him, he said, "Please, take it, it is a gift."

◆

Alida Latham,
arts patron and collector

SUB-SAHARAN & WEST AFRICA

Some markets are tame; others teem with life. Some are quiet; others push. The souks in Marrakech are calm compared with Marché Kermel and Marché Sandaga in Dakar, Senegal. Dakar markets are not for the weary or jet-lagged. Bleary-eyed, my colleagues and I struggled to focus on market crafts in Dakar, our first stop on a three-week buying trip in Africa. Merchants tossed wares in front of our eyes, shouting out prices and vying for our attention. Whenever we wanted quantities, word spread through the market, and the merchant's friends and relatives continuously shoved crafts in our way. We learned to ignore it all and bargain on our own terms—in French, of course.

Our next stop was the more civilized Grand Marché in Bamako, Mali. This market and other West African trading centers are slower and move not in a frenetic pace but on "African time." In the streets everyone walks slowly, in business people write slowly, at restaurants waiters pour drinks slowly, bring the check slowly. If you ever saw the Bertolucci film, *The Sheltering Sky*, you understand African time.

In Bamako, we found treasures along its dusty, red-clay streets. I was heartbroken to learn recently that the Grand Marché—a medieval, covered market where my Smithsonian colleagues and I had purchased so many crafts—had burnt down in the mid-nineties. While the market undergoes renovation, the vendors have spread out their wares along the street where you can shop for handicrafts, observe the scene, and soak up the culture. Women carrying bundles—textiles, assorted fruit—on their heads saunter down these streets in multicolored print dresses. They walk with sensuous deliberation and a model's posture. (Back at the hotel I had practiced walking down the halls with books on my head to emulate their carriage, but to no avail.)

The pace and path of life here is loose and meandering like the men in regal, billowing robes and dashikis who glide down unpaved streets and greet each other with warm words and smiles. Some of them and children trade goods while others carry home live chickens and guinea hens upside down by holding onto their bound feet. Women sit or squat selling pineapples, bananas, or bolts of fabric on the sidewalk. Bicycles, motorbikes, cars, wagons, and pedestrians stream by as if in a slow dance.

Savor the atmosphere as you negotiate for gifts and souvenirs.

General Tips

➤ As always, buy what you love; but, the symbols and patterns of many West African crafts have special meaning and function. So, to appreciate your purchases beyond their basic design, learn about each country's craft traditions, religious symbols, and tribal usage before you visit. Masks, textiles, body accessories, gold weights, Dogon doors, musical instruments, kitchen tools, fertility dolls, and headrests all have functional or ceremonial purpose in daily life and are available in the markets.

➤ Wander lively markets in Bamako (Mali), Dakar (Senegal), Abidjan (Côte d'Ivoire), Lomé (Togo), Kano (Nigeria), Ouagadougou (Burkina Faso), and Niamey (Niger) for the widest selection of indigenous crafts.

➤ If time permits, visit individual villages away from the main cities where you can often buy directly from the artisans. Prices will be lower usually and the quality of the crafts probably better.

> Visiting a craft village in Ghana, I was surprised by the quality of the items. Having to fly back to the U.S. was the only limiting factor in purchasing.
>
> ◆
>
> *Vera Hyatt, exhibit curator*

➤ Brush up on your high school French, the common language in most of the West African markets, though English is regularly used in Ghana and The Gambia. In all these countries, if you can use a few words in the local tongue, you may delight the vendors.

➢ The merchants in these markets are often middlemen, not the original craft artists. Ask if they made the goods. If not, bargain hard.

➢ Be prepared for aggressive hustling and hassling in the markets. Sellers will pull and push you to see their goods. Watch the locals and emulate their air of nonchalance.

➢ Petty thieves also roam the markets, so hide your money. I know a craft importer who used to shop the markets with thousands in cash tucked into his boots.

➢ Carry a fan or pick up a handwoven one in the markets as the heat and humidity can be overwhelming.

➢ Take precautions against the sun. Bring sunscreen and wear a hat or bandanna. Shop the markets in the morning when it is cooler.

➢ For a light lunch, buy inexpensive fruits on the street—anything you can peel—bananas, oranges, etc., but not watermelon—too porous. The pineapples are particularly delicious. Lunch will be considerably less expensive than in a restaurant. Save your money for dinner and souvenirs.

➢ Prices in the markets are about half of the prices in the local stores around hotels, especially for gold and silver.

➢ Gold and silver are often sold by weight in the markets so bargaining may be more difficult. But measures and weights are not always standardized. Be aware that the gold and silver jewelry you buy in the markets may not be stamped

14k or 925 silver. Nonetheless, these are usually good buys.

➤ Look for bargains in malachite jewelry. Brass, cowrie shell, and leather bracelets are plentiful and make fun accessories and inexpensive souvenirs.

➤ Traditional textiles, such as mud cloth, *kente*, *adinkra*, tie-dye, make wonderful gifts and decorative art. Bargain hard for these in the markets.

➤ Printed African cloth is sold by the yard or meter in local stores. The designs are both contemporary and tradition-al. The cheaper cloth is of African origin. The more expensive and better quality printed cloths are imported from Holland, which local women buy also. The cloth makes a great souvenir if you sew clothes or home acces-sories, but the prices on the imports are pretty firm. A shopkeeper may extend a small discount of 10 percent when you bargain, but don't expect much. Even if you don't sew, it's fun to wander into the shop just to see the bolts of cloth crammed into every shelf and stacked to the ceiling.

I had bought a carved giraffe when I was in Namibia, carried it with me through customs there, went on to South Africa, Côte d'Ivoire, then to Guinea. Up until then, I had had no problem at any of the airports, but when I tried to leave Guinea, a customs official stopped me and asked me for a receipt. "I bought it in Namibia," I said. "I don't have a receipt." "You don't have a receipt," he kept repeating. It wasn't even from Guinea, but he wouldn't let me go on. It was obvious he wanted a little *bak-sheesh*, in full view of all the other inspectors. Finally, I hand-ed him the local equivalent of about seventy-five cents. He was satisfied and I was on my way.

♦

Richard Solloway,
international consultant

➤ Bring home a bit of the local culture. Purchase native music on cassettes in many local stores.

➤ All the old, valuable crafts or museum-quality pieces are long gone. Be aware of sellers trying to pass off new crafts as old. It is common practice to carve a mask or other wooden object, then bury it in the ground so that it is caked in dirt to appear old.

➤ If you do stumble across a valuable artifact, you may have trouble getting it out of the country because authentic art may not be exported. In Ghana or Nigeria, you may need museum permission to remove an art object that looks old. Have the seller give you a written money-back guarantee if the export of your purchase is rejected.

➤ Rarely will you get a receipt in the markets, but you may need to show proof of your purchase to a customs official when you leave the country. Write up your own receipt in a notebook, and ask the vendor to sign his name or stamp it.

➤ Bribery is common in many West African countries. You may even be subject to a body search. Be firm in your refusal; but, if you are trying to get your purchases through customs to another West African country and encounter too much difficulty, offer a small gift to the official—local currency or a single dollar. Sad but true.

➤ Always carry a book or two. Trying to get out of any land-locked West African country is like being pregnant and overdue. You know it will happen eventually, you just don't know when. Flights leave erratically and only on certain days. There are few shops at the airports, and you are not likely to find much to do. You spend time just waiting— perfect for reading.

➤ Carved wooden objects may be infested with insects. Usually a trail of white powder around an object or bore holes are a good clue. Even if you don't see these telltale signs, as a precaution, try these solutions at home: put the items in a plastic bag with mothballs or freeze the items for three to four weeks, nuke the pieces in the microwave, or pour lighter fluid over them.

Country Specialties & Tips

Benin
Specialties: appliqué tapestries, wood carvings, bronze sculptures, leather goods, batiks, stone jewelry, and voodoo dolls and accessories.

- In Cotonou, you'll find artisan crafts at *Artisans du Soleil* and *Centre de Promotion de l'Artisanal* on Boulevard St-Michel.

- *Coronné d'Or* on Avenue Steinmetz sells crafts, stone jewelry, and bronze. Ask the staff there to design a piece of jewelry for you. They will also restore your jewelry or art.

- For a large selection of Beninese music, listen for the music blasting just behind the Marché Ganhi, and you'll find cassette vendors selling both contemporary Beninese artists and traditional recordings.

- The Marché de Dantokpa, near Boulevard St-Michel and the lagoon, is the place to shop for everything from pottery and baskets to bat wings and love fetishes.

- For the best pottery in Benin, travel south of Cotonou to the town of Porto-Novo and about six miles east on a back road to the Grand Marché d' Adjara. Every four days, the market there also sells tie-dyed blue and white cloth, baskets, and musical instruments.

- In Abomey, north of Cotonou, watch craftsmen carving wood and making appliqué cloth and bronze sculptures at the Centre des Artisans. The quality here is higher than in Cotonou, but the prices are generally higher also. Don't forget to bargain. For better prices on appliqués, ask for the Yemandje family workshop nearby.

- For all your voodoo paraphernalia visit the market in Abomey. Dead insects and animal parts will fascinate the strong of heart.

Burkina Faso
Specialties: leather goods, baskets, bronze, masks, pottery, calabashes, musical instruments, wood carvings, blankets, beads, and batiks.

- Shop at one of West Africa's best markets, The Grand Marché in Ouagadougou. In this open-air maze of vendor stalls, you can forage for food and find almost everything you want from fabrics and baskets to small souvenirs. If you do not have correct change after you've settled on a price, a merchant may disappear to find you the correct amount. Don't worry, he will come back with your change. You can hire local boys to carry your purchases. Be alert, however, for professional pickpockets in this market.

- Every other year in October, there is a handicrafts festival at *Maison du Peuple* with merchants from all over Africa. Contact the embassy for dates.

- Look for a small market around the Rand Hotel where you'll discover artisan woodwork such as carved animal stools, birdcages, and musical instruments.

- For other African wood carvings, try Sortileges on Avenue Mandela and Boutique d'Artisanat at the Wasa Club.

- If you want to buy a large quantity of baskets, musical instruments, and other crafts, ask for the family of Nacoulma Boukary. They are reliable and will ship your purchases. As always, negotiate for the best prices.

- Purchase cassettes and recordings of local music at Top Music on Avenue Yennenga.

- Le Centre de Tannage is a tannery on the road to Niamey where you can find leather gifts such as wallets, boxes, and bags.

- For embroidered tableware, visit the women's cooperative, Le Centre de Formations Feminine Artisanale in Gounghin, west of the city on the road to Bobo-Dioulasso.

- In the Grand Marché in Bobo-Dioulasso, tailors will make African cotton print shirts and dresses for you while you shop for bronze and gold.

- In northeast Burkina Faso visit the market in Gorom-Gorom for a variety of crafts and desert foods. Trade goods and gossip with the Tuareg, the Bella, and other ethnic groups.

- In the market for a donkey or camel? Or maybe just a goat? Check out the animal market on the outskirts of Gorom-Gorom.

Côte d'Ivoire (Ivory Coast)

Specialties: Korhogo cloth, Sénoufo weavings, bronze, beads, West African music, and masks.

- Abidjan, the capital, is one of the more sophisticated French cities in West Africa; so if you crave a taste of France while in Africa, you can buy a variety of imported French food in the supermarkets there.

- The Marché de Treichville in Abidjan has the widest selection of crafts. Bargain there for traditional African textiles and wood carvings, bronze, malachite, jewelry, beads, and cotton prints.

- Marché d'Adjamé has a smaller selection and lower prices. Other markets to visit are Marché Sénégalais, Marché du Plateau (both on or near Boulevard de la République), and Marché de Cocody (near Hôtel Ivoire).

- Watch out for pickpockets in the markets.

> In the Korhogo area of Ivory Coast, the best quality and best selection of pitch/cotton cloth paintings, known as "Korhogo cloth," is in the village that makes the genuine article, located some 20 kilometeres outside the town of Korhogo. Tour companies and hotels in the area can make arrangements to visit at the appropriate time, as can the local craft co-op. Beware of inferior imitations available at the tourist bazaars in places such as Abidjan.
> *shop buyer*
>
> ◆
>
> *Ernesto Pazmany, buyer*

- Be aware that many of the cotton printed bolts of cloth are imports from Holland. The local cloths are generally less expensive.

- Vendors sell "hot" designer watches for a few dollars on the streets in Abidjan.

- Hôtel Ivoire shops sell West African music on cassette, 18-carat gold, silver, and high-quality crafts. Prices are more expensive than in the markets.

- Not far from Abidjan on the east coast, look for textiles and contemporary wood carvings at the Artisanat cooperative in Grand Bassam. Purchase pottery next door at the Centre Céramique and watch potters at work. In old Bassam meander around the artisan shops until you find Karim Coumara's shop near a Vietnamese restaurant. He will help you distinguish between old and new crafts.

- For the best buys in batiks go north to the city of Bouaké in the center of the country. Ask for Mamadou Diarra who will customize pieces for you.

- Farther north to the city of Korhogo the best cloth and Sénoufo weavings are available at La Co-operative Artisanal.

The Gambia

Specialties: hanging batik prints, tie-dyed gambishirts, straw hats, leather goods, and silver filigree jewelry.

- A sliver of a country on the west coast, The Gambia is like a tropical island. In Banjul, the capital of The Gambia, the Albert Market—a food and craft market on Wellington Street—welcomes the Fearless Shopper to open-air stalls and balmy breezes from the ocean. Bargain in English.

- Swap the paperbacks you've been traveling with at the book exchanges in the beach hotels.

- For antique Venetian beads visit the markets in Serekunda.

Ghana

Specialties: adinkra and kente cloth, trade beads, fertility dolls, Ashanti stools and sandals, leather,

At a Ghana marketplace my eyes went immediately to a black stone necklace. The vendor gave an outrageously high price so I walked away. One of my male friends spotted the same necklace and the vendor gave him a significantly lower price than he gave me. I told my friend what had happened. Disgusted, we both walked away. But my mind was still on that necklace. I asked him if he would go back and buy it for me at the lower price. He agreed but he returned with no necklace. He told me when he had tried to buy it, the vendor agreed to sell it to him but only on the condition that he not give me the necklace later. I stood shocked. He didn't want to do business with a girl.

♦

Nicole Maisel, student

brass, wooden masks, wood coffins in any shape, magic fetishes, and herbal medicine.

- Visit National Museum on Barnes Road in Accra, the capital of Ghana. With this introduction to Ghanaian crafts you'll appreciate the rich artisan heritage in this prolific West African country.

- Look for artisan goods and lively entertainment from Thursday to Sunday at the Arts Center. Listen to African music here. Nearby galleries sell local contemporary art.

- To practice a little magic, purchase fetish paraphernalia at Timber Market on Hansen Road. Dead or alive, all the jujus you need are here: lizards, reptiles, animal skulls, teeth, skin, porcupine quills, and assorted charms.

- While in Accra, visit Kaneshie and Makola markets for textiles.

- Buy glass beads in Koforidua (north of Accra) at the bead market.

- In collaboration with the Smithsonian, the Museum Development Project renovated and developed museums and tourist facilities in Ghana's Central Region. Look for fully stocked museum shops at Cape Coast, Elmira Castle, and the Kakum Visitor's Center. The museum stores, especially at the Castle, highlight the best local handicrafts with stories about the makers.

Once in Ghana, I spotted a woman with baskets on her head. She was on her way to the market to sell them, but I asked if I could buy a few. The price was so reasonable that I asked to buy all her baskets. We negotiated and agreed on the price. I figured she was happy she didn't have to sit in the market all day. But, at the last minute, she backed out of the sale. I later learned that in their culture the men stay in the village while the women go to market. She would lose face if she went back home without going to the market.

♦

*Richard Solloway,
international consultant*

- Don't miss the Ashanti crafts in and around the city of Kumasi. The market in Kumasi center has thousands of traders. Have an outfit made the same day by a local tailor. Buy *kente* cloth and other crafts here and in the nearby villages. All along the village roads look for artisans weaving *kente* strips, printing *adinkra* cloth, making pottery, goldsmithing, and carving stools. Everything is for sale.

- Prized family possessions and symbols of status, Ashanti stools are the souvenir to take home with you. Carrying one around may prove a bit burdensome though.

- In the north in Tamale, buy woven clothes made by the local Gonja and Dagomba.

- If you buy wood carvings that look old, you'll need a certificate from the Arts Center or the National Museum in Accra to get them out of the country.

Guinea
Specialties: traditional Malinke music on cassettes, koras *(harplike musical instrument), African printed cloth, gold, and silver.*

- Craft prices are lower than in other West African countries, but the quality may not be as high.

- Try the Marché du Niger in Conakry for printed cloth and music. Look for the jewelry shops nearby for gold and silver.

- Women's cooperatives, Les Centres de Promotions du Pouvoir Féminin, in Conakry sell table linens and tie-dye fabric.

Liberia
Specialties: fanti *shirts and dresses, masks, tie-dye and batik prints, beads, baskets, and soapstone and wood carvings.*

- Shop the Waterside Market in Monrovia for beads, batiks, carvings, clothes, and other crafts.

- Be aware that the traditional shirts and dresses are not colorfast.

Mali
Specialties: leather crafts, mud cloth, musical instruments, tie-dye cloth, saddles, trade beads, brass figures, gold, silver, wood carvings, Mopti blankets, Fulani wedding rugs and blankets, Ségou blankets, Bambara pottery, Dogon doors and masks, and Tuareg knives and swords with inlaid handles.

- The markets, the supply, and the prices are among the best in West Africa.

- The Grand Marché in Bamako burnt down, but while it undergoes renovation, shop the vendor stalls on the streets around it. Mahamane Cisse is a reliable merchant there.

- Buy gold and silver in the Maison des Artisans.

- Find traditional mud cloth and tie-dye at La Paysanne, a women's cooperative. Fabrics and ready-made clothes tailored to appeal to Westerners are available here as well.

- For an honest guide in the markets and assistance shipping goods home, ask for Issa Sacko around the taxi stand at the Grand Hotel. He speaks French only.

- Dress down. Bamako is a dusty town.

- The Grand Marché in the town of Ségou is the place for Ségou blankets and cloth as well as Bambara pottery.

- Thursday is market day at the Grand Marché in Mopti, if you want dried fish and rock salt. Otherwise, purchase Mopti blankets and the more ornate Fulani wedding blankets at the Marché des Souvenirs, near the waterfront. Bargain hard.

- In the town of Djénné, between Bamako and Mopti, don't miss the lively Grand Marché on Monday where mud cloth is a good buy. Ask for the workshop of artist Pama Sinatoa for the best designs.

- If you manage to reach Timbuktu, be prepared for lots of desert sand everywhere. Try the city's whole-wheat bread, buy a camel ride to the Tuareg camps, and search for handicrafts at the Petit Marché.

- Buy goods directly from the Tuareg artisans at the Fédération des Artisans Tuareg on the main street in Timbuktu.

- Try to get to Dogon country. Hardly any old doors or masks remain so don't be fooled by promises of antique ones for sale. But those made new are still unique, decorative souvenirs of good quality. The Dogon will try to sell anything from masks to old tools, but avoid purchasing older carvings, fetishes, and doors off houses that might destroy their culture. Look for newer crafts.

Mauritania
Specialties: silver, wooden chests with silver inlay, camel and goat hair rugs, hand-inked leatherwork, hand-painted Kiffa beads, batik cloth, saddles, cushions, daggers, and jewelry.

- A combination of Arab and Berber culture in Mauritania gave the Moors a craft tradition that will tempt you.

- In Nouakchott, shop at the Marché Capital for silver inlay boxes, silver jewelry, and traditional teapots.

- Though hard to find these days, old silver jewelry has a fine patina and no sharp edges.

- On a small street in the market, look for old men selling ancient beads. Local goldsmiths will turn your bead purchases into jewelry for reasonable prices.

- Try the French bread at the local bakeries.

- Artists from the town of Kaédi sell colorful batiks.

- If you are looking for a quick pick-me-up, try a few glasses of green tea—sweet, but strong.

Niger

Specialties: Tuareg silver filigree crosses and leatherwork, gold, bronze artwork, soapstone carvings, tie-dyed cloth, batiks, rugs, and camels.

- In Niamey, choose from five main markets for your shopping excursions: The Grand Marché on the Rue de la Liberté sells household goods, African cloth, food, bicycle parts, and miscellaneous things. The Petit Marché offers food. The Rue du Combat tourist stalls are considered Rip-Off Row where veteran bargainers push African art at tourist prices. Wadata, a market in the Poudrière area specializes in household items, food, and clothing. Boukoki vendors hawk recycled things

Outside Niamey, each group of villages has its own designated market day. Certain areas of Niger are notable for different artisan crafts. The major markets in Niger and their specialties: Ayorou (Sunday) for terracotta beads, wooden bowls, and Tuareg woven leather; Baleyara (Sunday) for blankets; Boubon (Wednesday) for pottery; Maradi (Monday & Friday) for woven blankets and leatherwork; Tahoua (Sunday) for silver rings and pounded indigo cloth from Nigeria; Tillabéri (Sunday—large & Wednesday—small) for blankets; and Zinder (Thursday) for leather work and *chuku,* a local cheese. Don't forget to bring a market basket, a hat to guard against the sun, and a gourd of water.

◆

Catherine Ostick, embassy community liaison officer

made from steel drums and automobile parts.

- The Wadata Artisanal village, not to be confused with the market, is a craft cooperative built with funds from the Luxembourg government. Buy items at set prices on the showroom floor. But wander to the back, watch the artisans at work, and bargain a bit with them.

- Find Tuareg artisans who specialize in silver at Château Un. Ask them what they have in gold.

- In Agadez in the north, buy Tuareg crosses, which the men use for buying cattle, at the Artisana des Handicapés and Centre Artisanal. Don't miss the action at The Grand Marché near the mosque where Tuaregs dressed in native garb sell traditional crafts.

- Trade for anything at the Tuareg Market just outside of Agadez.

- Visit the camel market early morning on the northwest outskirts of Agadez. Buy a camel ride for a few days.

Nigeria

Specialties: bronzes, batiks, calabashes, wood carvings, textiles, traditional indigo and tie-dye cloth, trade beads, printed cloth by-the-yard, jewelry, pottery, fetishes, baskets, and old coins.

- Although there is a wealth of traditional crafts for sale, Nigeria is

---

If you are looking for African art try Rip-Off Row at a stall owned by a man named Ibrahim or at Château Un (also known as Château d'eau) across from Presse where the owner, Issaka Yacouba, has a large selection of wood art, rugs, bronze work and masks. He is very fair and honest. For baskets, the easiest place in Niamey is right on the parking lot side of SCORE, about four stalls from the corner or try Château Un. The best quality and selection is at the Catholic Mission, but they are only open now on Thursday afternoons. Another good shop is Jane, a clothing and arts place around the corner from Buropa. If you are going to be headed to Ouagadougou, consider waiting to purchase there as prices and selection are far better.

◆

Catherine Ostick, embassy community liaison officer

notoriously corrupt and dangerous. It's best to shop elsewhere.

- In Lagos, buy native goods at Jankara market, Bar Beach on Victoria Island, and the nonprofit craft center at the National Museum.

Senegal

Specialties: Jewelry, cotton trousers, bronze, wood carvings, masks, music, leatherwork, and other traditional African crafts.

- In Dakar, find aggressive vendors, but lively markets at Marché Sandaga and Marché Kermel. Bargain hard and be firm in your refusals. Often there is one price for the Senegalese and another higher price for *toubabs* (foreigners).

- Prices in the markets may vary from day to day depending on the customer's attitude, the vendor's mood, or an approaching holiday.

- Vendors may become offended if you bargain for an item you have no intention of buying.

- The crafts at these markets come from all over Africa and tend to be more expensive.

- Pick your own cotton fabric and have baggy trousers made for you within twenty-four hours at Marché Sandaga.

The vendors in Senegal are among the most aggressive in the world. Also, there are more beggars here than I have seen anywhere and they can be aggressive as well. No is not an answer to any of them. Bargaining is a must, and a shopper should probably pay no more than half of the quoted price (usually a lot less than that—one-third). I start at one-tenth of what's quoted and work up. Shop Marché Kermel for veggies, meats, seafood, and craft stores all around it (though it is also considered one of the most expensive because so many tourists visit it).

◆

Trudy Bagley,
embassy personnel officer

- Buy gold or silver at La Cour des Mours north of Marché Sandaga at 69 Ave Blaise Diagne. Even though it is sold by weight, try bargaining.

- Take the ferry to Île de Gorée just east of Dakar to discover a calmer tourist market for souvenirs, behind the row of restaurants near the ferry ramp.

Sierra Leone

Specialties: woven cotton country cloth blankets and clothing, tie-dyed or batik-printed gara *fabric, and* shukublai *baskets.*

- In Freetown, Victoria Park Market has a wide selection of fabric.

- Shops along Howe Street sell West African crafts.

- Up north in the town of Makeni, buy *gara* cloth and *shukublais*—coiled grass baskets made by Temne women. Find these crafts in the town market at less expensive prices than in Freetown.

- The grass baskets are also sold at the Mamunta-Mayoso Wildlife Sanctuary south of Makeni.

Togo

Specialties: Brass, wood carvings, tie-dye cloth, handicrafts, leather sandals, and voodoo accessories.

- At the Grand Marché in Lomé, imported cloth from Holland is sold in two-meter lengths (about six and a half feet) called *pagna*. African women buy it in a package of three *pagnas* to make an outfit. It may be difficult to bargain for less, and the prices on the cloth are pretty

Avoid shopping around any of the major Muslim/Christian holidays, Ramadan (Tabaski), Christmas, Korite, etc.— because you will probably have your pocket picked or purse snatched. During these times, everyone is expected to buy a sheep or goat for the feasting and have money for new clothes. If the person is short on cash, then the tourist or foreigner is fair game.

◆

Trudy Bagley,
embassy personnel officer

In Lomé at Grand Marché and Marché du Bé, you can find voodoo things such as dog's teeth, snake's skeletons, crocodile heads, furs, calabashes, ritual irons, mummified monkey skulls, dried owls, decayed gray parrots, chameleons—living ones—and also rats. Go with a strong stomach.

◆

Richard Solloway,
international consultant

firm. Ask the vendor for a small discount. The prices here are better than in other West African countries.

- Bargain for souvenir-quality wood carvings and brass on the Rue des Aretisans.

- The BricàBrac shop near Hôtel de la Plage sells high-quality African art.

- Find a good supply of Ghanaian *kente* cloth in Lomé and other city markets in Togo.

- In the Akodessewa area of Lomé, wander the largest fetish market in West Africa. Amid the skulls and bones, you may find a few charms or gri-gris to buy as souvenirs. To ward off evil spirits, wear them around your neck.

EAST, CENTRAL, & SOUTH AFRICA

As we wandered though the city market in Nairobi, we stopped to purchase beaded key chains from a young child. They were inexpensive and would make great impulse items to sell in our African Art Museum Shop. So after we settled on the price for one, I asked about quantity.

Sweat trickled down the boy's face. He looked no more than ten.

"How many?" he asked incredulously.

"Four hundred," I said.

He squatted in front of his mat and started to count.

"There's, there's only 200 here," he stammered. "I don't know if I can get more. Can you, can you come back later?"

We could see he was trying to think fast. He didn't want to blow it. His father had left him in charge momentarily, and this was his big chance. We said we'd return. When we came back later, he had rounded up another batch. We had our 400 key rings. The rest of the market community had chipped in and helped conclude the deal.

Though the vendors were all different, it seemed that their attitude was similar: if they helped each other make a sale, they all benefited. We had witnessed this communal sense even in West Africa, where merchants were more aggressively competitive.

In general, this part of Africa does not have the rich craft variety of West Africa. While some of these countries have their own distinct craft traditions, others have established trading cooperatives and workshops that promote handicrafts. With the help of outside organizations, they have managed to organize an infrastructure which helps communities become self-sustaining.

Kenya, for example, has a thriving art and craft scene. Once on a trip with one of my buyers to Kenya, we found variety in the local markets, craft shops, cooperatives, and the store at the National Museum in Nairobi. But the best find was a handmade clay bead factory, Kazuri, established by a Danish woman to give work to the local women. The women roll, paint, bake, and string colorful necklaces. They have a wonderful retail store attached to the premises, and they are adept at shipping. I found necklaces to match every outfit and gifts for everyone back home—inexpensive, easy to carry, and a depth of selection not usually found in sub-Saharan African markets.

General Tips

➤ Shopping is more Westernized in East and South Africa than in West or North Africa. You encounter more city and suburban-type malls especially in larger Southern African cities. But the Fearless Shopper can still find unique arts and crafts by searching in smaller curio shops, the city markets, and makeshift street stalls.

➢ Often these craft cottage industries are just outside the main cities on unmarked roads. Some just have P.O. Box numbers. The best way to locate them is to ask locals where to find a particular craft. Or contact the community officers at your embassies for additional help.

➢ The shopping atmosphere is generally laid back and easy to understand. While there are local dialects in use everywhere, English is widely used.

➢ Bargaining and bartering in the markets and with street traders and artists is expected.

➢ Gemstones and carvings are good buys, but do not buy ivory. It is illegal to import it into the United States and many other countries.

➢ Look for handwoven baskets in Botswana and wall hangings throughout Southern Africa. Both can be quite intricate and make great decorative art back home.

➢ If you send purchases back home, the shipping is generally

Time in East Africa is not the same as in the rest of the world and African people have a very relaxed attitude to it. If you ask when something will arrive the answer invariably is, "It will come." I often found myself waiting endlessly with locals under a tree for a bus to arrive. The real problem is the Swahili clock, which is different because they start counting from the 6 where we would start from the 12. A posted time (such as a bus timetable) could be from a Swahili or a non-Swahili clock—there is no way of knowing—and so the posted time could be plus or minus six hours from what any clock says. Remember this, and you will get along fine in Africa.

♦

Anthony Cameron, surfer, ski instructor, and sailor

reliable in Nairobi and in Johannesburg. I have used Kuehne & Nagel to ship large purchases, and they have offices worldwide.

Country Specialties & Tips

Several countries do not have a tradition of indigenous arts and crafts or may have frequent travel warnings, so I have listed only those with best buys.

Botswana
Specialties: baskets, pottery, and ostrich egg jewelry.

- In Gaborone, unless it's just after the rainy season, you can generally find a broad selection of the famous grass-woven Botswana baskets at Botswana-craft in the mall near the President Hotel.

- For more baskets and other crafts, try the Ditso Curio Shop and the Bushman Craft Shop, both in Broadhurst.

- Mokolodi, established by an expatriate to give work to local woman, sells great contemporary African clay jewelry.

- A visit to the Oodi weavers is just a short distance from the center of Gaborone and well worth the drive for the atmosphere. Dyed yarn strands in multicolors hang on clotheslines all around this weaving coop. Contact the Lentswe-la-Oodi Producers Cooperative.

No matter where you shop in Africa, you never know what to expect. One time we planned a trip to Botswana where we tried to purchase from the craft cooperative, Botswanacraft. Finding a basket supplier who could actually ship things back to the States was a major coup. Unfortunately, the rainy season had just wiped out the entire crop of grass needed to make the baskets. We arrived at a huge showroom filled only with samples. The most we could hope to get was about twelve baskets when we came for several dozen.

KB

- Take another drive about twelve miles outside Gaborone to Pelegano Crafts and Pottery Shop in the village of Gabane. You'll find handmade traditional African terra-cotta pots, masks, candle-holders, and bowls as well as grass mats, baskets, and corn-husk dolls. After shopping, wander the surrounding hills where you might stumble on remnants of an ancient settlement that dates to 800 A.D. Contact the Pelegano Village Industries.

Cameroon

Specialties: masks, wood carvings, gemstones, jewelry, bronze, hand-tooled leather goods, and baskets.

- English and French are spoken, but it's useful to know some French for shopping.

- Look for the Artisan Center in the Central Market for local crafts.

- Purchase old and new tribal passports made of clay. Hand-painted and multicolored, they are configured as faces and make decorative masks.

Ethiopia

Specialties: jewelry (especially Ethiopian Coptic crosses), gold and silver, rugs, embroidery, leather goods.

- In Addis Ababa shop at the Mercato, one of the largest markets in Africa.

Kenya

Specialties: Kisii stone tableware and sculpture, traditional Masai jewelry, stools and spears, walking sticks, clothing, kangas (beach wraps), colorful clay-bead necklaces, safari gear and clothing, polished agates, mineral specimens and gemstones, Makonde statues, tea, and coffee.

- Find local crafts at the shop in the National Museum.

One of my prized shopping coups in Nairobi was beautiful trading beads, hundreds of years old, that had been used to trade slaves. The beads were thrown in a dish in a case jammed with beads at the African Heritage Center (the big one on Airport Road). Some were whole, many were nicked or slightly broken, but I thought that just added to the charm. And at about fifty cents apiece they were much cheaper than the $200 necklaces with one or two beads.

♦

Mari Radford, embassy community liaison officer

- The Spinner's Web on Kijabe Street, around the corner from the Norfolk Hotel, is a consignment shop that offers handmade crafts from workshops and self-help groups throughout Kenya. Look for wall hangings, clothing, baskets, and other home furnishings.

- Buy clay-beaded necklaces to match any color in your wardrobe at Kazuri.

- Kenya Weaver Bird sells handwoven Kenyan cotton and soft hand-spun wool made on traditional looms by Kenyan weavers.

- Find contemporary wearable art including hand-stenciled fashions, designer jewelry, and accessories at Kichaka on Kijabe Street.

- African Heritage on Kenyatta Avenue in Nairobi sells handicrafts, unusual tribal jewelry and fashions, and decorative Kisii stone tableware. They will ship.

- The Rockhound on Ring Road off Riverside Drive sells indigenous mineral specimens and polished stone gifts.

- For crafts produced by women's groups in the Kitui District, try Ormolu on Haile Selassie Avenue opposite the Kenya National Library. The designs on baskets, cloth, and ornaments are a mixture of traditional motifs and natural dyes.

- Other craft co-ops or cottage industries in Nairobi include Maridadi Fabrics, Kenya Crafts Cooperative Union, and Jisaidie Cottage Industries.

I bought a pair of white (probably fake) Reebok sneakers in Pusan, Korea, for $5. I didn't wear them much until six or so months later on a photo-safari in Kenya. Though not exactly "cruel shoes," they just didn't feel good on my feet, and I was completely sick of them after three days in the bush. While walking down a street in Mombasa, Kenya, a man at a wood carving stand offered to buy my shoes from me. I'm sure that it was just a come-on line because he was surprised when I enthusiastically agreed. He was quite happy with those awful shoes, and I thought that the wooden zebra that he traded for them was the better part of the bargain.

◆

Gregory Gallardo,
commander, U.S. Navy

- The city market at Muindi Mbingu Street in Nairobi is the place to bargain. Sellers will often ask double and triple an item's worth. Examine merchandise carefully.

- Many stores sell gifts made from Kisii stone, which is a form of soapstone. The carvings and tabletop items are decorative and functional.

- Violent crime and mugging are common in Nairobi. Dress down and do not wear jewelry while shopping the central market.

- In Mombasa, buy copper and jewelry from Bambolulu Gardens, a rehabilitation workshop. For wood-carved products, try East African Curios.

Lesotho

Specialties: Zulu crafts, baskets, and wall hangings.

- Many items for sale here are imports from South Africa.

- Mohair wall hangings are woven free-form on hand looms.

Madagascar

Specialties: polished stones, wood, leather, raffia, and shell and horn crafts.

- Many goods are imports from France and South Africa.

Malawi

Specialties: baskets, pottery, woolen handicrafts, furniture, spices, and Indian food.

- Go to Blantyre for a range of goods and lively shopping.

When we lived in Lesotho, I became very interested in Zulu baskets. I asked at several markets where I could buy good baskets and was given a map for the "Zulu Basket Store." My husband complained as the map led us through cornfields and around rocks and into the wilderness. Just when we thought we were hopelessly lost, we ran across a farmer. Since we couldn't speak his language, I showed him a picture of the baskets. He directed us over two streams and through another cornfield where we found a tiny hut that was the "Zulu Basket Store." We were at least an hour from the main road and could have ended up lost forever. We were so grateful that it was a real store, and that it sold the most exquisite baskets.

♦

Carole Soden,
international consultant

- Shop the Old Town Market in Lilongwe for a range of products including clothes, clay pots, and baskets. Locals refer to the clothing area as the bend-over boutique. Buy Indian foods and spices at Jogees.

- Find traditional wooden crafts in the small market just outside the Old Town.

- On Blantyre Road, the Macoha Tie and Dye Center sells fabric and clothes.

- In New Lilongwe, also referred to as Capital City, look for art objects and crafts at Gallerie Africaine, Cat's Whiskers, and other shops in Centre Arcade House.

Mozambique

Specialties: baskets, Makonde carvings, batiks, ceramics, and walking sticks.

- Bargain in the open-air craft market on Saturday in Maputo at Praca de 25 Junho Street.

- On other days try the Central Market on Avenida 25 Septembro for just about anything including handicrafts.

- Avoid the ivory. You won't be able to get it through customs in many countries.

- Be alert for petty theives in the markets.

Namibia

Specialties: leather and wool jackets, ostrich-skin products, gold jewelry, and gemstones.

- In Windhoek, purchase goods at the Post Street Mall and the Bushman Art and Namibian Crafts Center.

- Merchants in exclusive boutiques will customize jackets and shirts in about three to five days. Design your own jacket or bring photos they can copy. Most will ship it to you. The Karukol wool they use has a swirl pattern that will make your design unique.

- Goldsmiths will also design your own jewelry using tourmaline and other precious gemstones.

South Africa

Specialties: diamonds, traditional crafts that include beadwork, basketry, weavings, wall hangings, dolls, and pottery with Ndebele- and

Zulu-design influences, ostrich skin items, wood carvings, and rugs.

- Just about everything available in the West is also available in Johannesburg shopping malls. If shopping malls don't make you dizzy, try Rosebank Mall, Carlton Centre, Eastgate Centre, Hyde Park, Sandown Centre, and Killarney Mall.

- Look for the tribal crafts at the Rooftop Market in the Rosebank Mall and Serendipity Gallery at Killarney Mall.

- Find an array of Zulu crafts in Durban at the Saturday-morning market on Essenwood Road.

- Look for other handmade goods in Durban at the African Art Centre on Gardiner Street and the BAT Centre in the Inkonkoni Building on Victoria Embankment.

- On weekends hunt for treasures at the flea market in the North Beach area of Durban.

- Pretoria also has a variety of flea markets and ethnic craft shops to satisfy your buying impulse. On Saturday hunt around the State Theatre flea market at Prinsloo and Church streets, and on Sunday try Sunnypark.

- Find more crafts at street or park markets while you're in Pretoria. Outside the Pretoria Zoo any day of the week, buy from the street vendors. Or try Art in the Sun on Saturday mornings at Barclay Square, Craft in the Park on the first Saturday of the month, and Art in the Park on the last Saturday at Magnolia Dell.

- The Pretoria's National Parks Board Shop on Leyds Street also sells crafts.

- In Cape Town, shop the open market on the Parade or the Waterfront area.

- The burgeoning crafts movement in South Africa is responsible for innovative design in furniture and decorative accessories. Look for artists who combine traditional African motifs or mix old pieces with contemporary design.

Swaziland
Specialties: Sisal baskets, ceremonial swords and shields, and fabric wall hangings, handmade glass animal figures.

- Create your own wall hanging or modify an existing design to suit your taste at Phumulanga, a women's weaving cooperative. Also, try Lentsela Dodi weavers near the Swaziland/South Africa border.

- Sisal woven baskets and other items are for sale at Mantenga Crafts, a Belgium government-sponsored craft project to help local artisans in Mbabane.

- Shop for more crafts at Hoagey's Handicrafts on Sheffield Road and the Mbabane central market.

- At Ngwenya Glass, Swazi men and women handcraft glass animals and birds using recycled glass. These make great, portable souvenirs and gifts, and a percent of your purchase helps preserve the African rhino and elephant from extinction.

Tanzania

Specialties: Tinga Tinga paintings, Makonde carvings, Zanzibar carved furniture, gold, silver, and precious stones, spices, teas, and coffee.

- Browse Dar es Salaam's many curio shops as well as the Kinondoni Market.

- In Zanzibar, look for the teas and spices in funky packaging.

- When a merchant names his first price, cut it in half and start bargaining from there. If you use a few numbers in Swahili, he may think you understand and might be willing to give you a better price.

- Learn language basics in Swahili to help you bargain: Use *Asante* (Thank you) after being greeted by the shopkeeper. To refuse an offer, say

In Tanzania, I traded my own tempered steel chisels for wonderful Makonde carvings with the sculptor. It wasn't exactly technology transfer, but it certainly was an enabling barter experience for both sides.

♦

Peter Howard, exhibit designer

You can buy the most beautiful shells down at the Dar es Salaam city fish market. Many of these shells are poisonous when occupied so it's better to buy them already cleaned. Sometimes the Tanzanian officers will ask for an export "license" (bribe) to take shells out of the country.

♦

Mari Radford, embassy community liaison officer

Hapana (No), and if the price or pressure is too high, try *Unaniua* (You're killing me).

Zaire
Specialties: malachite and masks.

- Browse Boulevard du 30 Juin in Kinshasa.

- Bargain at the Grande Marché. Carefully examine the merchandise you are buying.

- Adapt an air of indifference when bargaining and start at one-third to one-half the first quoted price.

- Rather than lower their prices, the vendors may give you a gift.

Zambia
Specialties: silver jewelry, gemstones, and wood carvings.

- Price stones at home so you know competitive pricing.

- Never buy gems on the street; they will probably be glass.

Zimbabwe
Specialties: Shona stone sculpture, baskets, and local folk paintings.

- The museum shop at the National Gallery of Zimbabwe in Harare sells colorful folk art paintings of village life on wood as well as Shona stone carvings.

- Visit the outdoor Shona stone sculpture garden and gallery in Chapungu Village. Small Shona animal sculptures make great gifts from Zimbabwe, but shipping large pieces back home can get very expensive. Also, be aware that this stone chips easily.

- Do not plan any weekend shopping sprees in Harare. Most stores and malls there are closed Saturday afternoon and Sunday. It is a good time to join a day-long safari. Along the way outside the city, you can find street vendors selling a variety of souvenirs.

ASIA & DOWN UNDER

If we are always arriving and departing, it is also true that
we are eternally anchored. One's destination is never
a place but rather a new way of looking at things.

— *Henry Miller*

———

*A*s I was leaving India, I passed through the security
gate at the Delhi airport. The electronic system
never worked so I waited for the inevitable body
and bag search. A short, middle-aged guard pulled me aside
and ran her too-friendly hands all over my body. Next, an
imperious Indian man took charge.

"Open your bag," he commanded.

Though he was dressed in a drab-green uniform and
black boots, I imagined this security guard—shirtless with
billowing pantaloons—a bouncer outside Ali Baba's den of
thieves. Polished and buffed, his bald head shone burnt-
copper, and his bushy mustache curled up at the ends like
the handle of an umbrella. He peered at me through
sunken, midnight-black eyes.

Not wanting to upset him, I unzipped my shoulder bag.

He hunched his massive body over my bag and extracted
ordinary things: an eyeglass case, books, pens, camera, a
travel journal, lipstick, eye shadow, my Smithsonian business cards, a calculator, chocolate-chip granola bars, mois-
turizer, a contact lens case, eye-drops, a minitissue packet.
More things.

Engrossed, he examined everything one-by-one, holding

each piece up to the light, turning it this way and that, then setting it aside in a growing pile. What could he think? How did I fit all that in there? When will this end? Still his hands searched and revealed more.

Uncomfortable, I shifted my weight from leg to leg and waited for this prolonged agony to end. Exposed, I felt my personality unraveling piece by piece. Soon he would know more about me than my boyfriend. What's he going to find next? Like a camera panning with a wide-angle lens, his eyes scanned my bag for the smallest detail.

This man took his job seriously. The silence was too much. I needed contact, a little comic relief.

"Do you have any idea how embarrassing this is?" I asked.

He held my gaze. A grin widened slowly across his face.

"Don't worry," he said. "I've seen worse."

Like my shoulder bag, India is a cultural blend of so many stored things. You never know what you'll find as you dig.

From inexpensive souvenirs to esoteric art, you'll discover not only an amazing array of products, but also an exotic and ancient culture. Keep your eyes open because images rush by in a blur—fragments of a civilization with 4,000 years of history—too fast to absorb fully. Street scenes and marketplaces are hypnotic: cows, donkeys, goats, camels, chickens, elephants sharing the roads with cars, buses, trucks, motorcycles, human-powered rickshaws, and three-wheeled, motorized vehicles. Life teems and flows at a frenetic pace in India.

My eyes were always riveted in the marketplaces where the whirl of humanity swept by—in colored threads and layers of silk saris—along with products of every color and smell. Wide, inverted, cone-shaped mounds of powdered dyes and spices covered tables and blankets on the ground.

Smoke and scents rose in the air from food merchant carts. Colorful glass, bangle bracelets and silver nose and toe rings jangled from market vendors as they hawked their goods. Puppets and mechanical animals danced in the streets.

On one buying trip, we visited the home of jewelers. Two brothers draped in white cotton tunics showed us their rooftop garden (a sign of wealth), offered us tea, and brought out trays of sparkling gems: rubies, garnets, sapphires, emeralds. They delighted in showing us their expensive treasures, but since we did not have high-paying customers back home, we selected only affordable garnet necklaces.

On that same trip, we stayed on the outskirts of Jaipur at the Rambagh Palace Hotel, the former residence of the Princess, the Maharani of Jaipur. It looks like an art deco, fantasy palace with brilliant-colored bougainvillea, fountained lawns, wandering peacocks, and snake charmers. At lunch one day while feasting on grilled tandoori chicken and *nan*, a puffy flat bread, I watched as a musician called a snake out of its basket and a mongoose ran around it in circles. With his snake wrapped around my shoulders and another folk artist reading my palm, I tried to negotiate with a kite maker who demonstrated his skill maneuvering multicolored fighter kites in the sky overhead.

Steeped in a rich tradition of crafts, India offers the Fearless Shopper opportunities to purchase a bit of history, culture, and entertainment. Shopping the streets is where the fun begins in any Asian country but, particularly, in India. Bring cash and be ready to negotiate for everything from spices and glass bangles to brass gods and dancing toys.

General Tips

➤ Bargain freely in Asian street markets and with sidewalk hawkers, but this is more difficult in state-run stores.

➤ As a general rule of thumb, when you haggle in the markets, offer half the original price and work your way up. While bargaining is a normal part of life in many Asian countries, remember that a few extra nickels or dimes are more likely to help your adversary than hurt you. So, bargain with a bit of compassion if you're dealing with an artisan.

➤ In Asian countries, taxi drivers and locals who befriend you may offer to take you to reputable stores. There is nothing wrong with this if you see something you like, but you are not obligated to buy if you don't want anything. Merchants may give commissions to "friends" who bring you to specific shops. If you purchase an item, you will probably be absorbing the cost of the "friend's" commission.

➤ In more traditional stores, you may try for a discount especially if you are buying quantity. In the art department in a major department store in Tokyo, I asked for a discount when I bought two watercolors and easily got it. Always ask for a better price in stores in Korea.

➤ You can bargain in the small shops in Taiwan and Korea, but common language problems may arise. While English-speaking shopkeepers exist, hardly anyone is fluent.

➤ If you're in the market for cameras or any electronic devices, check out the comparative prices in your hometown to know if you are really getting a bargain. If you live in New

York City, for example, you can probably get cheaper Japanese electronic equipment on 42nd Street than you can in Japan or Hong Kong.

➤ In China and Japan, watch out for misleading sizes. A medium t-shirt I bought in a store in Tokyo fit like a small. An extra-large in China is often equivalent to a medium in the U.S.

➤ Check your receipts for accuracy before leaving a store. Keep them handy for customs and any possible return problems.

➤ Opportunities abound for purchasing silk throughout Asia. To test for real silk: light a match to a thread. If it melts or curls, it's fake; if it leaves a residue of fine ash, it's real.

> ───── ✶ ✶ ─────
>
> Just because everyone you see is wearing copy-cat Chanel skirts in Japan, you have to stop and think would I REALLY wear this back home? And please take into consideration that size does matter. Most Japanese women's clothes just aren't going to fit taller Western women.
>
> ◆
>
> *Maureen McCarthy, mother*

➤ Visit the open-air food markets all over Asia—Thailand, Malaysia, Philippines, Indonesia, Japan, China, Korea, and Taiwan. And bring a camera. You won't take back souvenirs, but you will bring home memories of things you never saw and never knew people ate. If it wiggles, flies, swims, or crawls, it's for sale and often slaughtered on the spot. Not for the squeamish shopper.

Country Specialties & Tips

I've separated the big three in Asia: India, China, and Japan. Then Australia and the rest of the countries are listed alphabetically. If tips do not refer to a specific city, you can assume the reference is for the capital city in a country.

India

Specialties: textiles, jewelry, brass, ceramics, silk paintings, dhurries, wood carvings, papier-mâché boxes and trays, terra-cotta, stone work, incense holders, silk scarves with Lurex strands, tie-dyed fabrics, batiks, wooden Rajasthani horses, mirrored fabric from Gujarat, Kashmiri lacquered boxes, paisley shawls, spices, gemstones—garnets, rubies, sapphires, emeralds—and one-of-a-kind art objects.

- India has a strong tradition of handicrafts, and the entire country overflows with tempting goods at affordable or cheap prices.

- For an overview of the crafts available in all of India, don't miss the state emporiums. If Delhi is your only stop, you can purchase crafts from all over the country in these stores. If it's your last stop, you can pick up something you missed or wish you had bought elsewhere.

- In the state-run emporiums (State Emporia) as well as the handicraft cooperatives that often benefit welfare groups, you'll discover good quality and selection, but often fixed prices. Central Cottage Industries (CCI), a government-sponsored outlet, has a large retail store on Janpath, New Delhi, and branches in other cities, as does State Emporia. Look for state and regional crafts at government stores on Baba Kharak Singh Marg, off Connaught Place.

- In New Delhi, experience shopping at Main Bazaar, Karol Bagh Market, Janpath, and Connaught Place. Find antiques at the Sundar Nagar Market.

- In Old Delhi, browse around Chandni Chowk Street and the back alley shops for jewelry and carpets.

- Visit the Red Fort's covered market, Chatta Bazaar, in Old Delhi. The merchandise and the prices might be a bit touristy now, but it's worth a look.

- Virender Art Emporium is a reliable source in the Red Fort for crafts and silk Pichhwai paintings. I also found fine-line paintings on paper both here and in roadside stores between cities. Most have images of romantic scenes, florals, or battles and early hunts of Mogul glory. Lines within lines form hidden pictures. An image of a horse's body, for instance, might contain two other painted stories. Many are contemporary copies of traditional Mogul miniatures; others may actually be old replicas or torn pages from old manuscripts.

- If you are not an expert, shop for rugs, *dhurries*, and carpets at official emporiums.

- Contemporary textiles, as well as antique fabrics, are treasures to own. Shop for silks, saris, *pashmina* shawls, scarves, Kashmiri carpets, and more. Whether you want brocades, appliqués, mirrorwork, embroidery, block prints, tie-dye, woven or waxed fabrics, you'll find something for every occasion and season. The vibrancy of color and pattern and the range of technique make any textile here a souvenir worth owning. Many states have special traditions, so spend time researching and looking before you make your decisions. For designs on silk visit Indu Arts in Pitam Pura, Delhi. Try Ahujasons on Ajmal Khan Road in Karol Bagh, New Delhi, for a large selection of shawls from all over India.

- *Pashmina* shawls, made from the down of high desert goats, are luxuriously soft—the Indian version of cashmere—and make wonderful gifts. But don't buy articles made from *shatoosh*—a crop that comes from hunted and killed antelope and is illegal to import into some countries. Ask if it's *pashmina* or *shatoosh*.

- Many hotel tailors offer twenty-four-hour tailoring if you'd like to create a quick outfit out of your fabric purchases.

How you look and how you dress, and whether you are shopping with an Indian all have an impact on the price you are charged. If possible, shop with an Indian friend. For hand-painted miniature copies of Rajasthan paintings, the foreigner price might be Rs.2,000 If you bargain, you might pay Rs.1,500 and be happy. But an Indian would pay Rs.500.

♦

*Apurva Sanghi,
economic consultant*

- Do not miss any opportunity to watch crafts people in action. Village potters still turn their potter's wheel with their big toe as they continue ancient forms and traditions. Look for the famous blue pottery in Jaipur, intricately painted lacquer boxes from Kashmir, damascene from Jodhpur, wood carvings in Rajasthan, and marble mosaics from Agra.

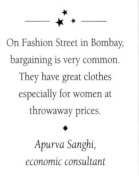

The women who sell beside the road just off Janpath Road, a few blocks from Connaught Circle in Delhi, have wonderful fabrics.

♦

Ramona Solberg, artist

- If you are traveling around Delhi, make time to visit Jaipur—the "pink city" and capital of Rajasthan, built in 1728. Though originally light gray, the city was painted pink, the traditional color of welcome, to honor the visit of Prince Albert in 1883. Surrounding Jaipur are forts of the previous capital, Amber. Buy an elephant ride up a hill to an ancient fort, accompanied by screeching monkeys, to the grounds and peddlers selling postcards and token gifts. After touring, you'll be ready for serious shopping.

- Jaipur is the place to purchase jewelry and precious gems if you know your stones. Try the shops on Haldion ka Rasta and Gopalji da Rasta alleys near the Hawa Mahal. For handcrafted gifts and textiles go to Rajasthali Emporium and Rajasthan Handloom House on MI Road, and Anokhi on Tilak Marg.

On Fashion Street in Bombay, bargaining is very common. They have great clothes especially for women at throwaway prices.

♦

Apurva Sanghi, economic consultant

- Varanasi, renowned as the Holy City for Hindus, is also famous for silk. So, find your way through the streets to shop for silk brocades and saris, but be alert for cotton and silk mixtures that look like pure silk. Try the Golghar market for silk brocade.

- In Calcutta, search for crafts on Chowringhe Yaar.

- Be alert for beggars when you pull out your money. Begging is a profession here, and it can be overwhelming especially when mothers thrust their babies in your face. We were told by local Indians that beggars deliberately maim themselves or their babies to get a few more rupees. If you give out coins to one child, swarms of children will envelop you for more.

- Indians have an ambivalent way of nodding their head yes. It's a tilted head roll between yes and no. If you inquire about the availability of an item that you want but do not see, you may get a quick "no problem" response accompanied by the rolling nod. Even though the surface gesture means yes, do not count on getting what you want. In my experience the words "no problem" often meant a polite "no."

China & Hong Kong

Specialties: jade, cinnabar, porcelain, embroidered crafts, cloisonné, silks, jewelry, calligraphy, furniture, hand-painted umbrellas, pottery, baskets, teas and teapots, Buddhas, objets d'art, reverse glass paintings, chops (seals), custom clothing, watches, cameras, electronics, and sporting goods.

- A word of warning: any tip listed here for China may change before you finish reading it. With a Starbucks already open in Shanghai, the pace of change is pumping as fast as the adrenaline rush residents may develop from the coffee. In fact, a friend

---

★ ★ ★

My sister and I were lost after no more than fifteen minutes in Varanasi. An Indian student named Ahmed offered directions. Then he began walking with us, and before we knew it, we had a tour guide for two days. We fretted over who Ahmed really was and how much he was getting on the side every time he took us to a shop where we bought something. In retrospect, Ahmed took us to sites and stores I'm certain we never would have found on our own. We later learned from a shopkeeper that the percentage he earned was far less than we had assumed. And as we comparison shopped along the rest of our trip, we realized that Ahmed had led us to some great bargains tucked away along the labyrinthine streets of Varanasi.

♦

Leah Kaplan,
development director

recently told me that when she went looking for a traditional dress for a wedding in Beijing, she couldn't find one in a local boutique for Chinese women. It was filled with Western styles so she had to go to a store that catered to tourists.

- Except in the larger fixed-price stores, shopkeepers expect polite bargaining. Ask for a discount and try to get the Chinese price not the foreigner's price.

- Along with groovy bands and great food, a Shanghai shopping spree is a West-meets-East cultural adventure. Stroll along the tree-lined boulevards of Nanjing Lu and Huaihai Lu to begin. From department stores to boutiques, you'll find arts, crafts, upscale imports, Western designer fashions, and more.

- Go antique and souvenir hunting at Yuyuan Bazaar in Shanghai. Look for porcelain teapots, cups, and other ceramics along with a variety of collectibles. Bargain hard and watch out for fakes.

- For more expensive porcelain reproductions, try the Shanghai Museum Shop.

When shopping in China, store owners want you to haggle with them. If you don't, it's almost an insult, like you don't have the time or inclination to establish some kind of interaction beyond the exchange of money. For foreigners, first offers are usually 300 to 500 percent above the price you should be paying and sometimes over 1,000 percent of what a local pays. Hard bargaining can get you local prices. If you can't speak Chinese, you can use Chinese hand signals for bargaining and communicating. It's easy to learn and lots of fun.

◆

Brandon Zatt, student

- In Beijing, if you can maneuver around the thousands of bicyclists, you can easily shop. For a good deal on Chinese and Western clothes, bargain at the outdoor Russian Market near the American Embassy. For antiques, try Liulichang Street; for silks, haggle at the Xiuxhui Silk Market on Jianguomenwai near the Friendship Store.

- After wandering Beijing's Forbidden City, mingle with the locals nearby at the Beijing Department Store on Wangfujing.

- Xidan Shipin Shangchang (Xidan Food Center) in Beijing is

packed with everything Chinese you could ever want to eat including many local and regional foods, a wide variety of teas, and a large assortment of sweets.

- Guangzhou (formally Canton) is just a short trip from Hong Kong and one of the first Chinese cities to go commercial. Shopping complexes continue to sprout up everywhere so find the smaller shopkeepers and market stalls around Cultural Park and on Shamian Sijie for more traditional souvenirs like ceramics and jade.

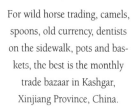

For wild horse trading, camels, spoons, old currency, dentists on the sidewalk, pots and baskets, the best is the monthly trade bazaar in Kashgar, Xinjiang Province, China.

♦

Mac McCoy,
importer and wholesaler

- For squirming, crawling, scaly, and dried things—dead and alive—have a look around Guangzhou's Qingping Market. After your eyes take in all the snakes and lizards and other creatures, you may want to purchase medicinal herbs in the market to relieve your stomach.

- Follow the ancient Silk Road to Kashgar, the oasis in the desert and China's most western city. Bargain with the traders and craftsmen for jewelry, silks, knives, rugs, housewares, and more at Sunday Market and the Bazaar.

Two of the more well-known stores in Beijing are Yan Shan and Lan Dao, which are quite modern. Chinese and Western clothing are plentiful in both, and the top floors of each contain a large traditional arts area. The prices in these stores generally are cheaper than those at the Friendship Store.

♦

Sian Seldin, librarian

- The Friendship Store, in the large cities throughout China, sell just about everything including clothing, jewelry, Chinese paintings, and calligraphy.

- Most shopping centers and tourist shops in China have currency exchange services.

- Check your money whenever you receive change because counterfeiting of the 50 and 100 notes is common. Do not accept any damaged bills; they may be difficult to unload. Vendors don't want them, but you can exchange them at the Bank of China.

- Modern copies of antiquities abound in China and are valued like museum reproductions in the U.S. Real antiques dating from 1797 to 1820 are legally offered for sale and may be cleared for export by the Cultural Relics Board. These items usually have a red seal affixed to them. It's illegal to export goods made prior to this period.

- You might find a rare old treasure in the markets and bazaars, but be aware: fakes abound.

- Chinese crafts can often be purchased cheaper in Hong Kong than on the mainland.

- Hong Kong is like no other port in the world: a true shopper's haven and the place to shop and bargain till you drop. Anything you want, you can have yesterday. A quarter of a turn in any direction will get you shops, malls, shopping centers, and specialized markets, but prices are not what they used to be.

- While you can still find bargains in Hong Kong, you must know the comparative prices back home if you want to save money shopping. Come prepared with a written list or bring catalogs from home.

Two stores in Beijing are well known to tourists: Liu Li Chang and the Friendship Store. The Friendship Store was once the principal shopping spot for foreigners, but this has changed. Now there are many other large stores and boutiques that cater to wealthy Chinese and foreigners. Service at the Friendship Store used to be somewhat slow, but as China has developed so has service, and most everyone at these stores speaks English. Liu Li Chang is famous among shoppers for paintings, calligraphy, and other Chinese arts. There are good buys here, but you have to know the particular store—fakes are prevalent—and you must bargain.

◆

Sian Seldin, librarian

- The best bargain is the ride on the Star Ferry, between Kowloon and Hong Kong, eight minutes across the incomparable harbor for about thirty cents. Hard to beat.

137

- Contact the Hong Kong Tourist Authority (HKTA) for a shopping booklet of member stores and a discount coupon card (Privilege Card)—up to twenty percent at member stores. The HKTA has an office at the Kai Tak Airport arrivals lobby open from 8:00 A.M. to 10:30 P.M.

- If you're visiting Hong Kong for the first time, plan a trip around the island to Stanley Market, a bit touristy but worth the view.

- Bargain fearlessly in Hong Kong's Jade Market (twenty to forty percent off the original asking price is possible), but watch out for fake jade—soapstone posing as jade. Bring a file or your trusty Swiss Army knife and ask the dealer if you can test the stones. You cannot scratch real jade with steel so if he says yes, you'll know it's the real thing. Quality or imperial jade is white, and good jade (called jadeite) is translucent shades of yellow, light green, lavender, pink, red, black, and orange. The deep green is usually nephrite—a cheap grade of jade.

- In case of problems with a jade purchase, note the market vendor's official license number and report it to the HKTA.

> ── ★ ★ ──
>
> I tried to buy a large, round Oriental rug and went all over China. I finally found just what I wanted in Hong Kong.
>
> ◆
>
> *Jane Jasionawsky,*
> *traveler*

- Don't miss the Night Market in Hong Kong, also known as Thieves' or Temple Street Market. Don't bring much money, hide it, and dress down. Pushing and shoving are the norm. The Fearless Shopper comes for the action: fortune-telling birds, Chinese opera singers, food vendors.

- Think shopping is for the birds? Try the alley called Bird Market. Vendors hawk birds and supplies including live grasshoppers. You might just go home with a birdcage.

- Hong Kong is still the place for internationally famous designer-name clothes, jewelry, and accessories, but prices are no longer inexpensive. Tailor-made clothing is still a worthwhile purchase, however. Bring pictures from home if you want a tailor to copy an outfit you love. If you sew your own, bolts of silk fabric are reasonably priced.

- If you need prescription eyewear in a day, don't hesitate to walk into one of the hundreds of optical shops in Hong Kong.

- Every tourist knows Tsimshatsui and Nathan Road shopping in Kowloon, but you can still find something you didn't know you needed.

- If you're looking for computer products and games, go to the Golden Arcade Shopping Centre in Sham Shui Po and the Convention Center in Wan Chai. For cameras, electronics goods, Mong Kok. Unless you're a pro in electronics and related goods, you're better off buying at home. If you do purchase equipment in Hong Kong, make sure it works the way it should before leaving the store.

- Check out *Orientations* magazine for the antique scene in Hong Kong. You'll find plenty of shops to scavenge. Trust the dealers who love to discuss their pieces, or hire an expert in Hong Kong to help you. If you are a serious buyer, ask dealers for an appointment to look in their warehouses or back room. Charlotte Horstmann Gallery is well-known in Ocean Terminal or try Honeychurch Antiques on Hollywood Road.

Buying a yak bell in the Barkor in Lhasa, Tibet, I spent a lot of time walking from stall to stall looking at a brilliant array of traditional turquoise jewelry, Buddhist ritual items, old carpets, prayer flags, postcards—it was so hard to decide what to buy. Then I saw the big old yak bell with a brown and white woven yak hair loop, and knew I had to have it. I bargained and bargained with the stubborn Tibetan woman who was selling it, and finally we agreed on a price. Part of me felt guilty about bargaining too hard, but as I walked away, I could feel a hundred laughing eyes upon me as my bell jangled off into the distance.

◆

Nina Smith,
nonprofit executive director

- For ceramics, grab a U-Haul and head out to Wah Tung China Company factory in Aberdeen. You won't be able to carry everything you buy home, but they'll ship. Try asking for a discount if you buy quantity.

- For an atmospheric selection of traditional handicrafts, don't miss one of my favorite spots, Mountain Folkcraft on Wo On Lane. Along with recognizable craft purchases, I've also discovered odd-shaped things there. These serendipitous finds had no function I could understand, but I bought them anyway for their aesthetics.

Japan

Specialties: ceramics, kokeshi *dolls with the bobbing heads, lacquerware and chopsticks, handmade* Washi *paper products, pearls, jewelry, electronics, cameras, handmade silk kimono and ceremonial items, antiques, tea sets, and fans.*

- On the surface, Japan feels Western. In particular, Tokyo (where most visitors are likely to start shopping) has it all: the big-city bustle, the neon, the fast-food chains, an efficient subway, department stores, and souvenir kiosks. Though a consumer mentality permeates the air, shopping here is a different cultural experience in both obvious Western and subtle traditional ways.

- It's easy to shop in various districts using the subway to get around, but make mental notes of where you entered. With multiple exits, more underground shopping opportunities, and few English signs, it's just as easy to get lost going back to your hotel unless you read Japanese.

- Vending machines are ubiquitous, and the Japanese have filled them with more than drinks and snacks. You might find surprising souvenirs with your change.

- From fashion and art to toys and t-shirts, the department stores in Tokyo sell everything

Akihabara is an electronic center in Tokyo where the newest equipment is sold in many little shops. When the dollar was worth more, I was able to get top-of-the-line stuff there that was not yet available in the U.S. We also bought a Japanese cello for Becky who studied here. When she left Japan, she sold it to a Japanese student who was very happy to get it since it was about half what she would have had to pay. And it was twice what we had paid, so Becky made a nice profit—enough to buy another better one when she got home.

♦

Hava Rogot, piano instructor

you want and package it with a flair. Wearing pristine uniforms, the sales staff at most department stores still know the meaning of customer service. Be prepared to shop in elegant surroundings with quality attention, but don't expect to find bargain prices.

- A few department stores to consider: Seibu, Daimaru, Matsuya, Hankyu, Tobu, Takashimaya, Mitsukoshi, Isetan, Matsuzakaya, Mariu, Parco, and Seed. Many offer a bit of culture and education along with shopping. Often, you can see an art exhibit on the top sales floors.

- Ginza still has *the* shopping cachet, but wander almost any district in Tokyo, and you'll find excellent shopping choices. Don't miss browsing around Shibuya, Harajuku, and Shinjuku where each area has a distinct tempo and culture. For a bit of old Tokyo, Asakusa has both atmosphere as well as souvenirs.

- If you're craving a new novel to read, try Kinokuniya—a department store of books—in Shinjuku. Go to the sixth floor for English titles and other languages. Go to Maruzen in Nihombashi to browse in Tokyo's oldest Western bookstore.

- Kiddyland in Harajuku is a five-story toy shop where I left my then eleven-year-old son for a few hours while I attended a business meeting. While I had slight guilt pangs, he had made friends with several of the young sales clerks. When I finally retrieved him, they wanted him to stay, and I had fun browsing.

In Tokyo, I got a kick out of the Kappabashi, or kitchen district, which was a few blocks of stores that sell nothing but kitchen and restaurant supplies. The plastic-food shops were particularly amusing, but they made me hungry, and there is a frustrating lack of restaurants on the street.

◆

Gregory Gallardo, commander, U.S. Navy

- Don't miss Tsukiji—the fish market in Tokyo. The best time to watch the action is 4:30 A.M. Ask your hotel how to get to Tsukiji (pronounced skee-jee) or have them write it out for the taxi driver. Dress down and wear shoes you don't mind getting wet. Side-stepping piles of tuna, eel, bluefin, salmon, octopus, sea urchin, among 400 other varieties scattered across the slippery concrete floor, the Fearless Shopper can wind in and out a labyrinth of food stalls and listen to the cacophonous auction that moves about five million pounds of seafood each day. Then, find a nearby shop and buy a sushi breakfast.

- For a bit of Japanese heart and soul and tradition, visit Kyoto by train. Catch a glimpse of Mount Fuji on the way, visit the temples, then head for the old Kyoto shops in the Teramachi-dori area. The shopping district around Shijo-dori and Kawara-machi-dori is worth your time also, and look for more crafts and antiques on the streets near the Kiyomizu-dera Temple.

- In Nagoya, after you've viewed the castle, look for traditional arts and crafts such as, pottery, tie-dye material, ceremonial knives, and *Washi* paper. Tour the Noritake factory and purchase your porcelain from its craft center.

- For the pearl devotee, visit the famous Mikimoto Pearl Island in Toba. I once watched the meticulous efforts of workers in a cultured pearl factory in Kobe and now understand why these strands are so expensive. To string the best pearls, this work is labor intensive and

When I asked about finding the Central Wholesale Market in Tokyo with my son, no one in my hotel could understand my English. I kept saying "fish market," and they kept saying "What?" with quizzical looks. I almost gave up, but finally, I thought to write "fish market" on a piece of paper, and someone said, "Oh, you want the fish market." Apparently, many Japanese read English, but cannot understand our accents so well.

◆

KB

They looked relieved to be going home and carry with them souvenirs from Tokyo: cookies wrapped in cellophane, flowers in paper cones, dried fruit bound with ribbon, dolls in tissue, stuffed toys in boxes. The Japanese are marvelous packagers of merchandise.

◆

Paul Theroux,
The Great Railway Bazaar

requires keen eyesight. Don't worry if you don't make it to Pearl Island. Mikimoto has jewelry stores in Tokyo and elsewhere.

- Look for cultured pearls in Kobe as well. Though Kobe is renowned for its beef, you can also buy great Chinese food here.

- If you are island hopping, visit the pottery towns of Karatsu, Imari, and Arita in Saga-ken on Kyushu Island.

- The Japanese wrap gifts as an art form. It's worth buying anything just to get the package.

Australia

Specialties: opals, Aboriginal art, wool sweaters and sheepskin clothing, boomerangs, contemporary crafts, and wine.

- Australia offers a wealth of shopping and you don't even need to be particularly fearless, except in the Outback. The major cities can accommodate all tastes and budgets, from souvenirs to fine arts and crafts, gemstones, bush-style clothing, and designer fashions. Your choice: cruise cosmopolitan shopping centers, malls, department stores, bargain factory outlets, specialty shopping arcades, and plenty of street markets.

- Export restrictions exist on protected wildlife and products made from shells, skins, feathers, and bones of protected species or anything that may disturb Australia's national heritage. Contact the Australian Customs Department for advice.

- Aboriginal artisans exhibit and sell their work throughout Australia in galleries, stores, and Aboriginal art centers.

My best shopping was on Bathurst Island, off the north coast of Australia. Although everything was drenched while I worked with the Aborigines during the monsoon season, I still managed to buy Tiwi Aboriginal folk art and crafts.

♦

Caroline Ramsay Merriam, crafts specialist

- Most markets, where bargaining is expected, are open on Saturday and Sunday throughout Australia.

- Bush clothing—the style of clothing that evolved from rural Australia (the Bush)—is available in many stores. Try Canberra

Center for cowhide boots, wide-brimmed felt hats (Akubra), moleskin trousers, loose shirts, and oiled coats (Driza-Bone).

- Australian opals from Queensland are world famous. You'll also find diamonds, sapphires, and South Sea pearls for sale.

- Don't forget to try the wines from the South Australian vineyards.

- In Sydney, visit The Rocks, a restored historic site of convict-built stone buildings, and browse in the art and craft shops lining the cobblestone streets. The Argyle Stores there sell jewelry from Australian and international designers.

- Shopping complexes in Sydney offer endless possibilities. Try a few of these: Pitt Street Mall, Sydney Central Plaza, Skygarden (after shopping, dine under its crystal dome), the Strand Arcade, Mid City Centre, Glasshouse Shopping Centre, and Centrepoint. (Don't miss the view from atop the AMP Tower.)

- Check out the food hall in David Jones store anytime and its flower display in early September.

- For designer boutiques in Sydney, roam Elizabeth, Castlereagh, and Hunter streets; and browse in the restored Queen Victoria Building, on George Street near the Town Hall.

- Visit Darling Harbour by monorail for Australian fashion, duty-free goods, and souvenirs. On Oxford Street from Darlinghurst to Paddington and Woollahra, you'll discover innovative stores and galleries.

- At the eastern end of Paddington, along Queen Street in Woollahra, look for antique shops specializing in colonial pieces, art galleries, jewelry and fashion boutiques, and designer furniture stores.

- Search Sydney's markets for unique Australian crafts, gifts, and antiques: Over 150 years old, Paddy's Markets on Hay Street, Haymarket, has more than 1,000 stalls selling anything from fresh produce to bric-a-brac on Saturday and Sunday. Paddington Village Bazaar on the corner of Newcombe and Oxford streets, offers crafts and fashions from young, local designers on Saturdays. Find arts, crafts, antiques, and exotic food at Balmain Markets on Darling Street on Saturday and The Rocks Market on George Street on Saturday and Sunday. For a seafood cooking demonstration, don't pass up the Sydney Fish Market on Gipps Street,

Pyrmont. On Saturday try Glebe Market on Glebe Point, and on Thursday afternoon and Friday, Newtown Market on King Street.

- If you're into factory outlet stores, you have plenty of options in Sydney and Melbourne.

- In Melbourne bring home wines from the Yarra Valley, Mornington Peninsula, and Rutherglen regions. You may also want to slip into upscale Australian designer clothes and shoes, keep warm in wool and sheepskin garments, or browse for antiques on Brunswick, Chapel, and Greville streets.

- Bargain like crazy in Melbourne's Queen Victoria Markets on the corner of Elizabeth and Victoria streets any day but Monday when it is closed. On Sunday look for arts and crafts at St. Kilda Markets, along the beachfront Esplanade. Traditional and contemporary ceramics, jewelry, and hand-painted silk at the Victorian Arts Centre Market on St. Kilda Road. Go undercover at Collins Place to browse indoors for Australian crafts, and visit the historic Meat Market Craft Center in North Melbourne for high-quality glass, metal, textile, wood, leather, and cane goods from Australian artists.

- Sip your way through the Canberra district's sixteen cool-climate wineries and buy what your taste buds crave. Then follow the locals to Bungendore, a thirty-minute drive east of Canberra, to shop for wood crafts, antiques, and leather goods. The Wood Works Gallery offers quality products made from native Australian woods.

As I was driving from Port Fairy to Melbourne, just before the Great Ocean Road, I found a farmer with a secondhand shop in his barn, behind a dilapidated row of bluestone Victorian cottages. The cottages were absolutely charming. I could not figure out why this man had his barn full of stuff, hidden off the main road, when he had these beautiful buildings right out on the road. I bought a 1940s armoire (as a gift for friends in Australia) for AU$35. It was in perfect condition. The farmer even let me leave it there for three weeks until I was coming through again.

♦

James E. Martin, accountant

- Along your way to Namadgi National Park, stop at Cuppacumbalong. The craft center in Tharwa sells ceramics, glassware, weaving, woodwork, paintings, and sculpture. Then head out to Gold Creek Village where specialty shops in Federation Square are brimming with ceramics, lace, clothing, and sweets. Next try Ginninderra Village for other Australian gifts, pottery, leatherwork, and wine.

- On Saturday and Sunday in Canberra bargain for arts, crafts, and produce at Gorman House Markets at Ainslie Avenue, and on the first Sunday of every month try the Hall Markets in the Hall Showground. You might also find a souvenir at the Kingston Bus Depot Markets on Wentworth Avenue.

- In Alice Springs in Australia's Northern Territory, look for locally grown dates, hand-carved didgeridoos, Aboriginal arts, and outback wines from The Winery.

- Roam the open-air Riverside Markets in balmy Brisbane along Eagle Street and the Brisbane River for handmade pottery, art, jewelry, painted fabric, and wood carving on weekends.

- In Adelaide buy opals from Coober Pedy and Andamooka, wines from the South Australian vineyards, Aboriginal artifacts, and local chocolate and crafts. The Jam Factory Craft and Design Centre on Morphett Street is a workshop and gallery of local artists and designers.

- In Perth look for Aboriginal handicrafts as well as wine and precious gems and jewelry made from Argyle diamonds, Broome pearls, and Kalgoorlie gold. Try the wines from Swan Valley.

- Don't leave Tasmania without pinot noir or these other special buys: chocolate from the Cadbury Chocolate Factory in Hobart, fudge, local woodwork, gemstones, and hand knits. Don't forget Tasmanian honey.

Country Specialties & Tips

Bangladesh
Specialties: pink pearls, embroidery, jewelry, ceramics, leather goods, jute carpets, brass, tea, wood, metalwork, fine muslin or silk saris and

yard goods, antique trunks, and cane furniture.

- Shop the markets early in the morning to watch the Hindu shop-keepers make their morning *puja*, and catch a drift of the sandal-wood incense as you walk by. In Dhaka, browse in the specialized shops at the DIT (Dhaka Improvement Trust) shopping centers.

- Furniture shops dominate Gulshan–Banani, the market at DIT1, also called Gulshan South Market, but you can also buy spices, toys, clothes, local tea, and coffee. The tailors at DIT1 can make or copy clothes. This market is closed on Friday.

Learn the words for "too expensive." You'll impress the foreign folk and perhaps get a chuckle from them. It almost always worked in Asia.

♦

Lisa Woods, agency bond trader

- At DIT2, the Gulshan North Market on Gulshan Avenue, brass shops, art galleries, and art and craft shops are plentiful. Most shops are closed on Friday.

- Gausia Market is known for a nice selection of dress fabrics from cottons to wedding brocades. The stalls offer a variety of colors and patterns. Bargaining is essential. New Market is across the street from Gausia Market and carries books, clothes, housewares, and more. The area is closed off to the general public so beggars are at a minimum in New Market.

At Aarong Handicrafts in Dhaka on Mirpur Road in the Moham-madpur area, you can buy pillow covers or Christmas stockings decorated with traditional needlework called *kantha*.

♦

*Ruth A. Hoffman,
textiles project manager*

- In the stores on Elephant Road, you'll find upholstery fabrics, jute rugs, and brass. The wedding shops are also along Elephant Road, so if you need some tinsel or glitter, this is the place.

- Women should dress inconspicuously while shopping in the streets.

- Expect street children and beggars wherever you shop. They'll want to help you carry your purchases or just beg for alms.

- For silk, head to the Mirpur District. Go with a local.

- Bargain for pink perls at Cosmic Pearl in Gulshan 2.

- For handmade paper goods, try Creation at 1/69 Eastern Plaza.

- Visit Salesian Sisters at 105/1/A Monipuri Para for embroidered linens. If you want any photo or design copied in embroidery, they can do it for you, but the waiting list is long.

- For cheap clothing seconds, scrounge around Banga Bazaar.

- Browse Kumdini Handicraft Centre at 74 Gulshan, IDEAS International at 20 Gulshan, and Aranya Crafts at 60/E. Kamal Ataturk Avenue for clothing and crafts.

- Leather crafters at Leather Emporium at Gulshan 2 will copy your favorite leather bag or accessory in a few days. Bargain for a fair price and insist on quality work. Inspect items carefully before paying. Do not accept inferior work and point out any problems you see. Most merchants will understand and offer to remake the item.

Cambodia

Specialties: silk, stone and wood carvings, Buddha statues, woven mats and baskets, rattan furniture, chopsticks, sarongs, betelnut boxes

Pink pearls are a popular item to buy when visiting Bangladesh. They are sold all over the city and range from single strands to elaborate multi-strand necklaces. Prices range from ten dollars to hundreds of dollars depending on the quality. The major hotels and DIT2 have a nice variety of styles. Try to get the matching earrings thrown in for free.

♦

Jo Fuller,
community liaison officer

South of Phnom Penh across from Angkor Wat, a complex of temples, people are selling stuff from their homes. Local Cambodians will bring you into their houses. The typical souvenirs are rubbings from the temple on white rice paper.

♦

Apurva Sanghi,
economic consultant

with animal motifs, gold, and silverware.

- Wander around the gem counters in Central Market in Phnom Penh where you can also find silks, souvenirs, silverwork, and more. On the second floor of Olympic Market you'll find additional crafts and gems. In the Russian Market, dig around for old neat stuff. For arts, crafts, and antiques try Samiti House on Street 278.

- At Wat Than on Norodom Boulevard, a training center for Cambodians disabled by land mines, you can watch students learn sewing and woodworking skills. Their gift shop sells small purses, bags, clothes, and frames.

- To observe traditional silk weaving take a ferry to Silk Island or visit the Traditional Silk Weaving Training Center and studio of master weaver Liv Sa Em.

- Pick up a few *kramas*, scarves made from cotton or silk, and use them for shopping in the markets as the Cambodian women do. Quintessentially Cambodian, these scarves also function as totes for carrying babies, chickens, and kittens, and as covers for pillows. Cambodians wind or knot them around their body as protection against the elements. In villages almost each family has a loom to weave them, and each province creates its own patterns, though red and blue checks are common. If you want vibrant colors look for the silks; the darker, more subdued shades are cotton. Wrap them around your head or drape them as skirts, sarongs, or aprons.

Fiji
Specialties: baskets, carvings, wood bowls, spices, cannibal forks, and shell souvenirs.

- In Suva, stop in at the Government Handicraft Centre in Ratu Sukauna House on the corner of Carnarvon and MacArthur streets for an

Be wary of a smiling Fijian greeting you with the traditional *"Bula"* and asking you your name. You may be talking to a sword seller who will quickly carve your name in a small wooden sword and pressure you to buy. A firm "No thank you" as you walk away should end the conversation.

◆

Ruth A. Hoffman,
textiles project manager

overview of local crafts. After looking at the high prices, head over to the handicraft market on the waterfront. When you bargain here with indigenous Fijian vendors ask, "Is that your best price?" With Indo-Fijian merchants you're more likely to have extended negotiations.

- At the Suva Municipal Market on the waterfront try the exotic fruit, taste an Indian sweet, or pick up some spices while you mingle in this multicultural scene.

- Wolf's Boutique on Victoria Parade across from the Post Office houses an assortment of South Pacific handicrafts.

- Export restrictions may apply for artifacts and shell products.

Indonesia

Specialties: Balinese jewelry, carvings, wayang *puppets (carved wood and traditionally clad marionettes), masks, antiques, paper or pierced-leather shadow puppets, rattan, batik clothes, cloth paintings,* ikat *weavings, cotton floral-designed t-shirts, and coffee.*

- With a plethora of handmade crafts, Bali is the place most shoppers think of when traveling in Indonesia. Start looking in Denpasar, the capital, where countless shops will entice you in from the tree-lined streets. I remember a batik, reversible jacket just beckoning me from a shop window. There's too much to buy here, and it's all at irresistible prices, even before you bargain.

- For more great shopping go to the beaches of Kuta and Legian on Bali. If you can draw your eyes away from the topless bathers, wind your way behind

My favorite area of Bali is Ubud and its surrounding villages. I purchased beautiful hand-carved and -rubbed tools. Avoid purchasing "copies" of treasures. Your best bet is to bargain for a car and driver on the main street of Ubud near the local market. A few of the drivers speak enough English to understand your request to visit "out of town" antique dealers or whatever you're looking for. The driver will first take you to his family business. I found that by being polite to the family and driver and purchasing a token piece, the driver would then take me to shop for whatever I could draw a picture of.

◆

Gloria Delaney, importer and wholesaler

the beaches through the maze of alleys and roads in Kuta Bay, about six miles southwest of Denpasar. You'll find shops and village vendors hawking everything from fakes to genuine antiques.

- To discover the cultural center of Bali, head to the hills of Ubud, about thirteen miles north of Denpasar. The local art will captivate you.

- For an inexpensive souvenir of Bali, buy a lightweight cotton nightshirt with a floral-printed design—great and comfortable for those horribly humid nights. I still have mine.

- Explore one or more of Indonesia's 10,000 islands for regional differences in cuisine and crafts. Start with Java, Sumatra, and Lombok.

- In Jakarta, the capital of Java, barter and bargain with the crowds at the early-morning fish market called Pasar Ikan. Most items are more expensive in Jakarta than elsewhere in Indonesia.

- To find more old-time charm and culture on Java, go to Yogyakarta or Yogya (pronounced "Jog-ja") as it's affectionately called. Visit the Yogyakarta Craft Centre, the Agastya Art Institute, and wander into the shops in the alleys in Yogya. This is the city to buy batik and *wayang* puppets, and the suburb of Kota Gede is known for its silversmiths.

> Negotiating for handmade items in Irian Jaya, Indonesia, with a Dan tribesman, naked but for a penis gourd, is a bit of an emotional shake-up.
>
> ◆
>
> *Harriet Begelfer, travel agent*

- Sumatra is a refreshing contrast from congested cities of Java. Check out the clean, wide streets and colonial mansions in Medan, the capital of north Sumatra and Indonesia's third largest city. Then, look for crafts and volcanoes in the relaxing hill town of Berastagi in the Karo Highlands, about 45 miles from Medan.

- For a longer shopping journey, visit Lake Toba with its pine-covered beaches and steep mountains, about 110 miles from Medan. Be prepared to rough it over irregular roads with huge potholes. Despite a backbreaking ride in a beat-up pickup, my trip was worth it for the shopping and the volcanic views. Dig around in the shops in Parapat and you might unearth a unique wood carving and other crafts. For good quality ask for Usman's shop and negotiate prices with him.

- After you shop in Parapat, buy a ferry ride to Samosir, the wedge-shaped island in the middle of Lake Toba where former Batak headhunters and cannibals practiced their rituals.

- On the island of Lombok, go to the weaving factories in Mataram. Watch the weaving and dyeing, and buy handwoven sarongs and *ikat* cloth. The hand looms are foot powered and look ancient. Then visit Sukarara, a village known for basketry and more weaving. Watch traditionally dressed women work the old wooden looms. Just south of Sukarara in Penujak buy hand-crafted pottery made of local red clay and fired in traditional kilns. On the east coast in the town of Sukaraja, find traditional wood carvings.

- Before you leave Indonesia, don't forget the coffee.

Korea
Specialties: leather goods, silk, rice paper, calligraphy scrolls, writing brushes, masks, celadon ceramics, ginseng, and Korean chests.

- In Seoul, browse the markets at Eastgate (Dongdaemun) and Southgate (Namdaemun).

- Haggle politely with a smile in small shops, and merchants may extend a discount.

- In Insadong look for antiques and celadon, a green crackled pottery. Small celadon bowls and vases make great souvenirs and lightweight, take-home gifts.

- Itaewon, adjacent to the Yongsan Army Base, caters to foreign tourists. From fur coats to eel-skin bags, you can find everything here. If you purchase an antique chest or reproduction and have it shipped home, remember to factor in the shipping costs. Vendors here understand and speak English.

- The outlet shops in Seoul are packed with athletic gear and leather bomber jackets, but the quality is disappointing. Most of these stores sell seconds. When I combed the stalls for tennis shoes, I found cheap prices but no comfortable fit.

- Buses leave every twenty minutes from Seoul to the Korean Folk Village. It's a bit touristy, but it gives you an overview of rural life where you can see artisan workshops.

- International credit cards, traveler's checks, and cash are widely accepted. You can try using ATMs all over Seoul and other major cities, but the instructions are in Korean.

Laos
Specialties: silk, handicrafts, weaving, embroidery, ceramics, silverware, cotton, rattan, wood carvings, rice whiskey, and coffee beans.

- The main shopping areas in the capital Vientiane are Pangkham and Chao Anou streets and Samsemthai, Dongpalane, and Setthathilath roads. Look for weavings, silks, ceramics, and embroidery.

- The Morning Market (Talat Sao) has a range of shops selling crafts and antiques. Watch out for the fakes.

- On Manthatoulath Road go to the Art of Silk. Run in conjunction with the Lao Women's Union, this museum and shop sells textiles, clothing, and accessories made by women. It aims to promote and preserve textile production throughout Laos.

- At Saigon Bijoux on Samsenthai Road you can find old and new silver jewelry.

- For an expensive range of pottery, textiles, and jewelry, shop at Lao Phatana Handicraft Centre on Pangkham Street.

- If you want to purchase handwoven silk adaptations of old Lao designs, go to Lao Textiles by Carol Cassidy on Nokeokoummane Street.

- Phengmai Gallery on Nongbouathong Road is a training center for traditional Lao weaving and natural dyeing where you can buy silk, scarves, and clothing. Watch village women weaving here (Nongbouathong Weavers Village).

- In Phontong Village, Camacrafts sells a range of Lao and Hmong handicrafts and will take special orders.

- Prices in the town of Luang Prabang tend to be lower than in Vientiane. Look for the shops selling old and contemporary Lao handicrafts on Phothisalat Road.

- Antiques and Buddha images older than fifty years are not permitted out of the country.

Macao
Specialties: antiques.

- Hop over to Macao from Hong Kong for the day to shop for antiques and reproductions (realistic fakes) at lower-than-Hong Kong prices. Your price often includes freight back to Hong Kong if you ship your purchase.

- Many of the antiques in Macao were made yesterday.

- Bargain fearlessly here.

Malaysia
Specialties: Batik clothing, songket cloth, silk, silver, pewter, brasswork, Oriental carpets, shadow puppets, antiques, and Chinese crafts.

- Chinatown in Kuala Lumpur has lively street vendors and a bustling night market.

- Wander around Jalan Petaling Street for more shopping.

- In the old part of Melaka, Malaysia's historic city, stroll along Jalan Hang Jebat to find Melaka's famous antique shops. Search for Portuguese, Dutch, Victorian, Chinese, and Malay antiques.

- Malaysian prices for designer clothes are at least thirty percent cheaper than in Bangkok and about forty percent cheaper than in Singapore.

- In Kuching, the capital of Sarawak, look for the Main Bazaar. Located opposite the Waterfront in a row of two-story shops that date back to 1846, this market sells an assortment of Bornean and Indonesian arts and crafts. Purchase rattan baskets, Iban *ikats*, Java batiks, plaited mats, carved masks and spears, pottery, bead necklaces, and brassware. Don't forget to bargain.

- Experience *tamus*, tribal gatherings, at Kota Belud in Sabah. At the Sunday open-air market, medicine men, along with traders, artisans, and horsemen get together and hawk everything from tribal crafts to cattle and magic medicine. Visit during May for a wilder time.

Myanmar (Burma)
Specialties: jade, rubies, sapphires, silk, lacquerware, local artist watercolors, traditional clothing and accessories, rattan furniture, and antiques.

- Most markets in Yangon (Rangoon) are open on Sunday and closed on Monday. At night wander the vendor stalls on Yangon's wide boulevards.

- Shop at the Gems Museums and the Gem Mart on Kaba-Aye Pagoda Road.

- Bogyoke Aung San Market (Scott Market), located in the center of Yangon, is a big tourist destination, so expect inflated prices. It's still a good place to buy traditional handicrafts, fabrics, jewelry, and cane and bamboo items.

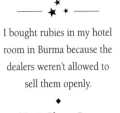

I bought rubies in my hotel room in Burma because the dealers weren't allowed to sell them openly.

♦

*Manju Bharat Ram,
arts patron*

- For Chinese spices and herbs go to Chinatown on Maha Bandoola Road, and the Chinese Market on Bogyoke Aung San Street sells locally made cooking utensils.

- For wood products visit Aung Wood Working Enterprises in Building 91 on 49th Street.

- Buy handicrafts from the Southern Chin Hills at Chin Craft Sales on Shwe Hninsi Road.

- In Mandalay, you'll find bustling markets with handicrafts from Upper Myanmar.

In Burma, we went to the house of our driver's "uncle" who had a small collection of gems. We had tea, talked, studied the gems, and negotiated a price.

♦

Deborah Fallows, writer

Nepal

Specialties: handmade paper products, ceramics, papier-mâché, scarves, shawls, wood carvings, brass and metal ornaments, traditional Nepali and Tibetan musical instruments, and Tibetan crafts.

- The best local crafts are made by Tibetan refugees: jackets, singing brass bowls, bells, bags, prayer rugs.

- Compare prices and quality in the many jewelry stores in Kathmandu before purchasing. Find antique Tibetan beads at Lhasa Gift House. Select your beads and stones at Creative Arts where they will customize your necklace. Look for excellent reproductions in gold and silver jewelry at Vishnu & Sons, and don't miss the Bead Bazaar at Indra Chowk.

- Having revived ancient craft traditions and learned new ones, various Nepali women's groups provide income for their families from the sales of their handicrafts. Buy their work at these shops on Kupondole Road: Nepal Knotcraft Centre, Dhankuta Sisters, Dhukuti, Koseli, Mahaguthi, Wean cooperative, and Sana Hastakala.

- At the Royal Chitwan National Park look for other women's craft shops at Tiger Tops, Temple Tiger, Machan Wildlife Resort, and Chitwan Jungle Lodge.

- Watch women produce handicrafts at Janakpu Women's Development Centre and Kumbeshwar Technical School.

During that first trip to Nepal—which lasted five months—I shopped naïvely, buying a bunch of silly souvenirs and third-rate statues that have moldered in various attics around the San Francisco Bay Area for the past decade, waiting for a cataclysmic earthquake to put them out of their misery.

◆

Jeff Greenwald,
Shopping for Buddhas

- Many fabrics are not preshrunk or colorfast; ask the merchant for advice on extra cloth length for shrinkage.

- South of the Durbar Square in Patan, brass and metal shops line the streets.

- In Bhaktapur, watch potters throw clay and buy your pot in Potters' Square.

- Buy Tibetan carpets in Jawlakhel, east of Patan.

- Bargaining is common in tourist shops and the markets, but haggle politely as a form of social interaction rather than a life or death challenge.

- Wherever you go Nepal, there's no escaping countless brass deities of varying quality and price.

In Katmandu the best buys are pashmina shawls and scarves. Bargain for quality and price. A must: Mike's Breakfast—for great food throughout the day.

◆

Ruth A. Hoffman,
textiles project manager

156

New Zealand

Specialties: Maori carvings, shell jewelry, pottery, bone and jade carvings, and hand-knit woolen sweaters.

- In Auckland, big city shopping is on Queen Street. But for more colorful shopping, visit older suburbs like Parnell, where you'll browse in modern retail stores amid colonial wood buildings and Victorian facades. Shopping in the suburb of New Market is also more interesting than Queen Street.

- On the opposite end of Auckland, the up-and-coming areas of Herne Bay and Ponsonby should provide shopping competition for Parnell and New Market.

- In Wellington, wander the Wakefield Market and Lambton Quay for arts and crafts. Try The Potters Shop and Earthworks Pottery.

- For the best range of quality New Zealand crafts, gifts, and jewelry, go to Cranfields or van Helden Gallery, both on Lambton Quay. For custom-designed jewelry, try the Hanne Andersen Jewelry at Capital on the Quay, Lambton Quay, or Village Goldsmiths on Victoria Street.

- Look for bargains at Consolidated Traders, a sheepskin warehouse on Evans Bay Parade, Wellington, en route to the airport.

- Check out the contemporary New Zealand art scene at the Brooker Gallery, Land Janne Gallery, or Hamish McKay Gallery.

Pakistan

Specialties: jewelry, Afghan tribal and Persian carpets, dhurries, onyx, precious stones, inlaid brass, wall hangings, embroidery, ceramics, leather jackets, wallets and handbags, silverwork, silk paintings, wood crafts, and copper.

- It's customary to bargain in Pakistan's sprawling bazaars. Negotiate with style and good humor. Merchants may invite you in for a cup of tea and small talk before you begin the bargaining game. If you see signs displaying fixed prices or prices marked on goods, ask the merchant if it is his best price.

- When you bargain in the markets in Pakistan offer about twent-five percent less than the asking price. Expect to get about a fif-teen percent discount.

- Western women should wear modest clothes while shopping.

- Find the Karachi markets in Saddar, the city center, and begin your shopping orgy for handicrafts, fur coats, rugs, leather jackets, snakeskin bags, and silk scarves.

- For a wide selection of Pakistani carpets, Persian rugs, kilims, *dhurries*, camel bags, and chemically darkened Afgan tribals, dig around in the Afghan Carpet Warehouse on Chowdry Khaliquzzman Road, Clifton.

- Shop the Zainab Market in Karachi for handicrafts, the Jubilee Market for all kinds of fabrics, and the Madina Market for furniture.

- Look for Marvi Handicrafts at #30 Zainab Market to buy silver, copper, and brass items.

- Wander down Brass Alley off Abdullah Haroon Road. Don't bother looking for the Brass Alley sign, just look for the brass—old and not so old including brass objects from ships.

- Visit Gemstone of Pakistan, a government store in the Pearl Continental Hotel, for jewelry.

- For the best in quality leather bags, stop in at Jafferjee & Co. on Zebunnisa Street.

- In the Old City of Lahore make your way through the parade of vehicles, veiled women, pony carts, and rickshaws to the street vendors. Look for shops specializing in jewelry, onyx, metalwork, fabrics, and carpets on Mall Road, Abbott Road, Commercial Zone, and Nickolson Road. For the adventurous: the Friday Bazaar behind Fortress Stadium.

- In mountainous Quetta, visit the lively bazaars for carpets, marble, and onyx.

- Beware of pirated videos and CDs in Pakistan as it is illegal to bring them back to the U.S.

Papua New Guinea

Specialties: jewelry and body ornaments, ritualistic and ceremonial objects, Buka baskets and purses, masks, carved figures, shields, stools, headrests, musical instruments, clay carved storage pots, and carved wood bowls.

- In Port Moresby wander off to Boroko shopping center and Gordons Market.

- Visit PNG Arts and Handicraft for local handicrafts.

- Woman should avoid shopping in shorts or short skirts.
- Since there's no tradition of bargaining here, don't bother to dicker over the price of a souvenir.

Philippines
Specialties: baskets, ethnic beaded jewelry, wood carvings, shell crafts, embroidered barong *blouses, silver filigree, Palawan pearls, and musical instruments.*

- In Manila, shop at Tesoro's and Balikbayan Handicrafts on Pasay Road.
- Stop in at the museum store in the Metropolitan Museum of Art here.
- In the markets, ask for a ten percent discount instead of bargaining. The vendor will probably quote a higher price for you as a tourist than he would for most Filipinos.
- If you enjoy remote areas find the island of Mindanao and look for the Saturday market where the indigenous T'boli peddle their weaving and brass work.
- Wood products should be treated for possible insects when you return home.

Singapore
Specialties: fabrics, silk, Chinese crafts, Oriental carpets, gold, jade, pearls, and diamonds. Just about anything you want, another shopper's paradise.

- Singapore thrives as a cleaner Hong Kong. Capitalism reigns—especially on Sunday—in this modern city-state with its Asian culture and colonial past.
- It's easy to find ATMs, and credit cards are widely accepted. But bring cash or traveler's checks for bargaining.
- Follow Singapore's elite to Orchard Street. Bring your credit card for these expensive purchases.

In the Little India section of Singapore shops sell everything from peacock feathers to gifts to be burned and sent to heaven for a deceased family member.

♦

*Gloria Delaney,
importer and wholesaler*

- Dodge the temple worshipers and fortune-tellers in Chinatown and explore its old and new shops.

- Look for silk textiles and Indo-nesian batiks on Arab Street.

- Step into Little India at the southern end of Serangoon Road. Navigate your way around Zhujiao Centre market and the surrounding cluster of colorful shops to bargain for fabric, spices, jewelry, and traditional Indian clothing.

Sri Lanka
Specialties: gems, woven baskets, wood carvings, pottery, metalwork, masks, brass, silk, sarongs, fabrics, linen, and spices.

- Former Pearl of the Orient, Sri Lanka is renowned for its gems. Novice gem shoppers be wary: prices may be seriously inflated. Bargain without mercy. For a minimal fee the State Gem Corporation in Colombo will test your gems for carat weight and authenticity at 24 York Street, and examine the metal for purity at 25 Galle Face Terrace 3.

- Jewelry stores abound in Colombo. Visit the twenty-five shops in the Sri Lanka Gem and Jewelry Exchange at Galle Road. Created by the National Gem and Jewelry Authority, this government organization claims only authentic gems and jewelry are sold here. A gems laboratory is on the premises and will evaluate gems for authenticity, free of charge.

- For more jewelry choices try these stores: H. Salie Ltd. on Sir Baron Jayatileka Mawatha, a family business for generations; AMA Careem Jewellers at the Hilton Hotel will create your name in Sinhala script as a necklace; Jewel Qudsi in the Galle Face Hotel Shopping Village and Zam Gems on Galle Road will customize jewelry.

- Visit Craftlink on Iswari Road, off High Level Road for handicrafts. USAID sponsors this women's development project. Purchase pottery, clothes, jewelry, block-printed linens, and batiks.

- Tilak Samarawickrema's Design Gallery on Ascot Avenue features this architect's home designs, which have also sold at MoMA's Design store in New York City.

- Mariposa on Dharmapala Mawatha will custom design clothing in batik fabrics as will Yolanda Collection on Sarasavi Lane, off Castle Street. For exclusive embroidered garments and batiks, try Sheranee Sellamuttu on 13th Lane.

- For more jewelry and crafts, shop around the Fort district and then follow the scents east to the Pettah bazaar district.

- In Kandy, visit the Kandyan Art Association & Cultural Centre to view local crafts.

Taiwan
Specialties: jade, jewelry, silk, dolls, cloisonné, carved jade figures, vases, Chinese crafts, calligraphy supplies, museum reproductions, and clothes.

- Visit Taipei World Trade Center for an overview of products.

- Export or outlet stores stock brand-name seconds. Check quality before you purchase.

- Buy porcelain, bronze, and ceramic reproductions from the National Palace Museum stores.

- Check out the Shihlin Night Market for unusual food.

- Clothes can be made to order, but Hong Kong tailors are less expensive.

- Even though stores may display credit card signs, merchants are reluctant to accept them. Cash is always the preferred form of payment.

- Bargaining is widespread, but the better stores—especially those catering to foreigners—have fixed prices.

- Don't miss Huahsi Night Market, otherwise known as Snake Alley, for a bit of local fun. Pick out your cobra—live, fried, boiled, or pickled.

Thailand
Specialties: Thai silk, gems and jewelry, dolls, bronze, carved wood masks, lacquerware, clothing and accessories, wicker baskets, and rattan furniture.

- Bangkok is another shop till you drop paradise.

- Bargain in the tourist shops, the markets, and before getting in nonmetered taxis. Don't bargain unless you intend to buy. The Thais view bargaining as a satisfying arrangement to both parties, and an opportunity to establish rapport.

- For the broadest selection and the best designs and products in Thai silk, Jim Thompson's Thai Silk Co. is a must. It's hard not to buy all of your gifts here. Shopaholics beware: this is not a place conducive to self-control.

- Mosey around Bangkok's night markets behind Ratchaprarop Road in Pratunam.

- Stock up on cheap, fake designer clothes and souvenir t-shirts in Bangkok.

- Rubies, sapphires, zircons, and garnets are the local natural gems. Many jewelry stores in Bangkok will sell individual stones or set them. The city's gold shops are located in Chinatown. Gold is a good buy and less expensive than in Western countries.

- Stock up on bronze castings of temple bells, gongs, bowls, and Buddha images. S. Samram Thailand Co. on Petchburi Road is a well-established producer of bronzework.

- The Hilltribe Foundation at the Srapatum Palace on Phaya Thai Road sells embroideries and jewelry.

- Hunt around the many antique shops in Bangkok to unearth an old treasure, but beware: making "instant antiques" is a minor industry here.

- Ask shops for a written agreement for a full refund to return merchandise (except jewelry)

I went shopping with friends in Thailand to the marketplace to find a beetle used in cooking that my friend said gave off a flavor somewhat like vanilla. We located the beetles and a lot of other weird foods and spices; snakes, various insects, etc. When my friend asked the merchant if this was a "good" beetle, he took a small straw and stuck it in the bug's anus so my friend could smell to see if it would have a strong enough flavor.

♦

Carole Soden,
international consultant

At Chatuchak, on the outskirts of Bangkok near the airport, the weekend market sells everything from clothes to crocodiles.

♦

Apurva Sanghi,
economic consultant

within ninety days. Shop elsewhere if the store owner refuses
your request.

- Between shopping excursions,
expect to sit in Bangkok traffic
for hours.

- Go north to Chiang Mai,
Thailand's second-largest city
and the heart of its handicraft
industry. Watch skilled crafts-
men work and buy traditional crafts in the shops along the
Chiangmai-Sankampaeng Road. Your abundance of choices
includes: an assortment of jade, lacquerware, celadon, textiles,
hand-painted paper umbrellas, silverware, wood carvings, and
Hill tribe crafts.

- In the evening meander around the central Night Bazaar. Bargain
here without mercy.

> In Chiang Mai at the Night
> Market in the town square you
> can find seconds on Thai
> celadon (*swankalok*).
>
> ◆
>
> *Hilary Richardson, consultant*

Vietnam

*Specialties: Lacquerware, silk, ceramics, ginseng, leather and snakeskin
products, gemstones, jade, amber, stone ornaments, gold and silver jewelry, carpets, brass, embroidered table linen, old coins and stamps,
mother-of-pearl, and orchids.*

- Watch out for fake gemstones, motorbikes, and beggars.

- Ho Chi Minh City (Saigon) is the dynamic heart and soul of
Vietnam. Find the shopping action in the teeming street life.
Cruise the sidewalk stalls, the shops, and the vendor kiosks on
wheels.

- Don't miss the snake market.

WESTERN EUROPE

Does this boat go to Europe, France?

—Marilyn Monroe, in
Gentlemen Prefer Blondes

———————

*A*s a student in Holland, I remember being amazed that stores were not open on Sunday and discovering that many European stores had regular blue laws and irregular hours. As I learned years later with colleagues, these restrictions could wreck the most ambitious shopping plans.

About twice a year a few Smithsonian buyers would travel to Europe for trade shows and product development projects. I looked forward to our excursions to Italy the most and Como specifically. A lakeside resort in northern Italy about thirty miles from Milan, Como—the heart of the silk industry—was a special treat.

With the lake and mountains as background inspiration, we worked with Italian scarf and tie manufacturers. Samples of scarves and ties lay scattered around a worktable where we reviewed colors, film, artwork, photographs, slides, and swatches of fabric. Often we brought transparencies from a museum's textile collection or photos of objects in an exhibition. All of which served as source material for new designs. If we wanted an exact copy of a piece, we'd bring an image of a scarf in the collection. Other times, we'd choose a design element—perhaps focusing on a border from a ceramic plate or a smaller design within a larger fabric—and adapt it for a new tie or scarf. I loved these working sessions with the designers. They allowed a free flow of creative energy, and no one designed better than the Italians.

I always came away inspired by the brainstorming, wired from the caffeine in their espresso, and well fed with pasta and wine. The most fun, however, occurred after we met with the creative team at Ratti, a well-known scarf design house located in a villa overlooking Lake Como. The atmosphere was professional and fast unlike other, more laid-back factories. And always after our meetings we would spend an hour or so shopping in their adjacent retail store.

There, the prices were right even at retail, and often designer- name scarves were a bargain. (Everyone back home got Ratti scarves for presents.) One morning we worked overtime, and as we were gathering our paperwork, we casually mentioned we were ready to shop the Ratti store.

"Better hurry," they said, "only ten minutes to closing."

"Yikes. Only ten minutes?" We asked in a panic.

They shrugged.

We raced out of there and, like four mad women, proceeded to do considerable damage. Within ten minutes, laughing like lunatics at our own antics, I think we opened every scarf on the shelves, looked at every available pattern, color, and style. Our arms draped with silk stuff, we marched up to the cashier and checked out. As we did, I looked back at the havoc we unleashed and the heaps of textiles we left in our wake. The phrase "Ugly Americans" comes to mind now. I think the salesladies are still folding.

General Tips

➤ As a basic courtesy, always acknowledge the shopkeeper in Europe—say hello and good-bye as you enter and leave.

➤ For tasty souvenirs such as jam, mustard, and olives, include the local grocery stores on your shopping sprees.

➤ In Holland, Belgium, and Switzerland, chocolate is a handy, easy-to-pack gift or quick pick-me-up during intensive shopping excursions. Of course, a little cheese and bread and wine will do nicely, too.

➤ In France, Portugal, Spain, and Italy, plan your shopping excursions around lunch. The best thing about shopping in these European countries—especially Italy—is eating. Check out the local olives in summer, savor the flavor, find an olive oil factory to tour, and bring home a few bottles. Visiting vineyards works also.

➤ No matter how adept you are at math (even if you scored 800 on those college boards), always travel with a calculator—especially after six glasses of port.

➤ Take advantage of local, cottage industries in each country. Handmade pottery and

In Lisbon on business, a colleague and I resolved to learn more about port wine while there. Each evening we would visit the Port Wine Institute where we would sample a wide variety of port wines. After three such evenings, we settled on what was indisputably the finest port we had tasted. Now, it is important to say at this point that the virtues of Portugal's low prices had been sung to us by any number of people. And, so we did a quick calculation in our head to determine the price of our 1937 prize bottles of port—$35— and happily purchased a bottle each. A month or so later, on receiving our credit card bills, we learned their true cost: $350 per bottle, still a bargain, but only if one happens to be a connoisseur!

◆

Rebecca Phillips Abbott,
art historian and photographer

glass stores clog back roads and hill towns of Europe where you have a chance to meet the family artists and learn about the craft.

➢ Be careful that the pottery you purchase along the roads is lead-free; otherwise, you should use it for decorative purposes only. Ask. If pieces are not labeled, or you cannot get a comfortable answer, assume they contain lead. The same holds true for being dishwasher- and microwave-safe, which often the pottery is not.

➢ Know your clothing and shoe size equivalent in European countries. (See the size conversion chart at the back of this book.)

I always visit hardware stores in Europe. I have found the "gift" sections to be very reasonable and unique to the country. Also, the hardware stores carry functional gadgets for bathrooms and kitchens not always offered in the U.S.

◆

Joan Chickvary Cavanaugh, businesswoman and voice-over artist

➢ Look for your favorite brand-name clothing in European styles, which may not be available at home. Often designers' European lines have slightly different cuts and fabrics.

➢ Generally, avoid the duty-free stores at airports throughout Europe. Prices are often high, and you only save taxes; there are no bargains except perhaps in Amsterdam.

➢ Though many prices are fixed, always ask for a discount.

➢ Museum stores are getting more sophisticated in Europe. Generally, they are the best place to find accurate museum-quality reproductions and adaptations.

➤ Europe is chock full of flea markets. Having invented the flea in flea market, Paris claims the best.

➤ If designer-brand merchandise is an extremely good buy in the flea markets, you're probably looking at fakes.

➤ Many European stores have sales twice a year—in January and June/July. Time your trips for bargain prices.

➤ In southern European towns, shops often close for lunch and reopen around 3:00 or 4:00 P.M.; then, stay open until about 7:30 P.M.

➤ You may want to use a separate credit card for your European trips. That way you know your credit limit is available, and it's easy to identify your European purchases when the bill comes.

> ───── ✦ ✦ ✦ ─────
>
> *Buying in the flea market in Florence, Italy, with little knowledge of the language, a friend wanted to buy a Gucci pocketbook. The sellers had real Gucci, fake Gucci, and fake-fake Gucci. The real were black market, the fake were leather copies, and the fake-fake were vinyl.*
>
> ♦
>
> *Patricia Engel, homemaker*

➤ Change your money for local currency, not euros. While euros are available, they don't make their street debut until January 1, 2002. Until the notes and coins circulate regularly, don't expect shopkeepers to make change or accept euros for purchases.

About VAT

VAT (value-added tax) is the European version of sales tax on consumer products. It is always included in the price of an item, so you may not even realize you are being taxed. Foreigners are exempt from VAT and are often entitled to refunds (sometimes depending upon the purchase price).

Tips

➢ Check the regulations on VAT and the refund procedures before visiting each country.

➢ Taxes are high—as much as twenty-five percent—so if you are purchasing expensive items, you could get a substantial amount back.

➢ Each country has a different procedure for refunds.

➢ Usually you must apply for a VAT refund before you leave the country where you purchased an item. Contact country embassies, guidebooks, or the European Tax-free Shopping Company (ETS) for specific country information. (See the ETS listing in the Resources & References section of this book.)

When traveling, always ask about local markets. I still use a waffle-weave woolen blanket from Lisbon, a large blue-and-white pitcher from a gypsy market near the beach just south of Porto, and my silver crumb sweeper shaped like a palm leaf from a market in Provence.

◆

Hilary Richardson, consultant

To receive a refund:

➢ Shop at stores authorized to offer VAT refunds.

➢ Ask for VAT forms from stores, airports, and train stations. The form should be signed by the salesperson.

➢ Carry your receipts with you when you leave. Have them readily available.

➤ Look for the VAT window at departure terminals and present your forms and receipts to the official.

➤ Ask the foreign customs officer there to stamp the form upon departure from the country.

➤ Upon returning home, mail the forms to the stores. Depending on the store policy, you may receive a refund by credit card or check.

Country Specialties & Tips

Throughout this section, country shopping tips are generally confined to a few cities and common regions. This is not meant to be a comprehensive listing for every town in each European country. As Fearless Shoppers know, the best buys are often the serendipitous finds when you've veered off course. So, here's my shopping tip for the road: whenever possible head out of town and follow the signs that intrigue you.

Andorra
Specialties: duty-free shopping, especially electronics.

- An independent republic between France and Spain in the eastern Pyrenees, Andorra does not have its own money and uses French and Spanish currencies.

- Shop in this duty-free mecca when you're not skiing. Know comparative prices at home to take advantage of possible bargains.

- Find numerous shops along the main road at the French and Spanish borders.

Austria
Specialties: ski clothes, hiking gear, crystal, dolls, porcelain, embroidered linens, dirndls, wood carvings, jewelry, Christmas ornaments, carved nutcrackers, and one-of-a-kind carved, wood nativity scenes.

- Greet shopkeepers with *Grüss Gott* and leave saying *Auf Wiedersehen.*

- More renowned for music and skiing, Austria is an expensive place to shop. In Vienna, try on luxury clothing and jewelry around Freyung, Graben, Kärntnerstrasse, Kohlmarkt, and Stephansplatz.

- For antiques, peer in store windows around Branerstrasse, Dorotheergasse, Mariahilfestrasse, Plankengasse, and Spiegelgasse.

In western Austria at the small town of Schwaz (near Innsbruck), the Geiger company has a factory outlet that sells their famous wool clothing at clearance prices. These are "end lots" as well as one-of-a-kind prototypes that did not go into the main line production.

◆

Steve Herbaly,
local government advisor

- Attend art auctions at Dorotheum on Dorotheergasse. You can inspect lots in advance.

- Find specialty foods at the Naschmarkt, a large open-air market, where there is also a Saturday flea market from 6 A.M. until noon.

- Vienna's upscale, but spice holders and scented candles are inexpensive souvenirs.

- In Salzburg, shop on Getreidegasse and don't leave without chocolate marzipan.

Belgium

Specialties: lace, antiques, quilts, tapestries, leather, diamonds, Belgian chocolate, cheese, and Ardennes ham.

- Wander Europe's oldest covered shopping area, Galeries Royale St-Hubert near Grand Place in Brussels.

- For antiques go to the Grand Sablon Square every Saturday and Sunday.

- Dig around Rue Blaes for less expensive flea market buys.

- For specialty foods and general goods visit the markets at Place Bara near Gare du Midi on Sunday and Place du Châtelain on Wednesday afternoon.

- If you're shopping around for a diamond, Antwerp is the place to be. It's less expensive to just watch the trading action on

Pelikaanstraat (any day except Saturday or late afternoon Friday) or visit the Diamond Museum for free.

Denmark

Specialties: contemporary jewelry, glass, Georg Jensen silver, Royal Copenhagen porcelain, furs, sweaters, and leather.

- A fairy-tale country and birthplace of the Danish pastry, Denmark is known for high-quality, contemporary design.

- Shop along Copenhagen's long pedestrian mall, the Strøget and nearby streets from Rådhuspladsen to Kongens Nytorv.

- Visit Royal Copenhagen's five retail stores in a Renaissance house dating from 1616 on Amagertorv 6: Royal Copenhagen Porcelain, The Royal Copenhagen Antiques and Georg Jensen Museum, Georg Jensen Silver, and Royal Copenhagen Crystal. For modern design browse around next door at Illums Bolighus.

- At The Royal Copenhagen Antiques & Georg Jensen Museum, a well-stocked antique shop, purchase old pieces of Georg Jensen silver jewelry, cutlery, and rare hollowware. Don't miss the Georg Jensen Museum in the back of the shop.

- Other antique and secondhand shops on the streets off Strøget feature vintage and modern Georg Jensen silver at reasonable prices.

- Museum Kopi Smykker on Frederiksberggade 2, Strøget sells jewelry reproductions from Danish Museums of the Viking era and of the Bronze and Iron ages.

- Warm up in the Sweater Market at Frederiksberggade 15, Strøget with a typical Scandinavian sweater purchase.

- Stop in at any corner bakery and buy a *wienerbrød* (Danish pastry).

- If you are traveling with children, they might want to buy their way through Legoland, the plastic-toy theme park in the town of Billund.

- Foreigners are entitled to a VAT refund of twenty percent (minus a handling fee of five percent) off the price of goods purchased for more than about $44 at a single participating store.

Finland

Specialties: arts and crafts, designer furs, reindeer skins, knitted clothes, glassware, Arabia ceramics, jewelry, rugs, and vodka.

- Browse along Aleksanterinkatu and Esplanadi, Helsinki's major shopping streets.

- If shopping centers draw you in, meander through Forum near the train station, Kiseleff Bazaar on Senate Square, or Itakeskus Eastern Shopping Mall, the largest indoor shopping center in Scandinavia.

- For flea market purchases, antiques, and traditional crafts, scrounge a few outdoor and indoor markets: Market Square, Hietalahti Flea Market, Hakaniemi Market Place, and Kauppatori Indoor Market.

- Purchase ceramic dinnerware and one-of-a-kind pieces at the Arabia Factory Store and Museum. During the summer, ride a free shuttle bus from the Havis Amanda statue in Helsinki to tour the Arabia factory.

- Visit the towns of Iittala, Nuutajärvi, Riihimäki, about a one-and-a-half-hour drive from Helsinki. For two centuries these glass-blowing centers have produced famous glassware.

France

The mere mention of France inspires wild dreams of shopping, and Paris is the guiding light—a cultural blend of shopping, art, food, and romance. So, let's concentrate on this classy, trendy, arty, creative, dynamic City of Light.

Specialties: antiques, designer clothes, secondhand clothing, crystal (Baccarat, Lalique), porcelain (Limoges, Haviland), Quimper ceramics, perfume and other toiletries such as Provençal soap, jewelry, books, collectibles, regional crafts, chocolate, wine, olives, mustard, and cheese.

- Contact the French Government Tourist Office, 444 Madison Ave., New York, NY (212-757-0229) for information. Ask about the Club France membership program for special shopping

Quimper, France, is known for its beautiful H. B. Henriot dishes. The factory runs a nice tour showing how everything is made. And they have a large outlet; however, even then, everything is very expensive.

♦

Dana Lansky, law student

discounts and promotions.

- To conserve your energy, study a map and arrange your shopping excursions by arrondissements, Paris' city zones. (The last two digits in a zip code address indicate the arrondissement, as does a number with a lower-case "e.")

- French laws keep many traditional retail stores closed on Sunday, but you can still find plenty of action: join the locals for antiquing at Village St-Paul, flea market hunting along the Seine, wandering around the Marais, or shopping between doses of art at the Louvre.

- Find the antique dealers at Village St-Paul on the streets between the Saint Paul Church and the Seine (rue St-Paul, 4e); bargain a bit at Le Louvre des Antiquaries, a one-stop source for high quality and reasonable prices (2 place Palais Royal, 1er); or rummage around theme shops at Le Village Suisse near the Eiffel Tower (54 avenue de la Motte-Picquet, 15e).

- Parisian auctions are definitely for the fearless (and fluent in French), or go with a pro. For estate auctions bid at the old Hôtel Drouot (9 rue Drouot, 9e); for specific themed lots, make an offer at the new Hôtel Drouot (15 avenue Montaigne, 8e). These auctions occur every

In Paris, the little prints/sketches are often a good deal. Rue St-Paul is full of good secondhand art—oil paintings, decent Impressionist stuff for $100. If you are into frames, they have some great ones, back when the frames used to be as much a work of art as the paintings. They may not be in perfect shape, but they are easily reconditioned. People at these shops often bargain. I certainly bargain with them. They seldom take credit cards, although they'll run to another shopkeeper who will and get their forms.

Patty Zubeck, filmmaker

There is a great stamp market not far from the Champs-Elysées in Paris. It is only open about one afternoon a week. And it is beautiful, even if you aren't into buying stamps.

◆

Dana Lansky, law student

day, but not on weekends during the summer.

- Find great, old stuff in the many flea markets here. Among the most popular: St-Ouen, Vanves, and Montreuil. If you are in Paris, check out the Wednesday insert in Figaro for flea market happenings. If you read French, pick up a copy of Pariscope for big flea market events. For serious, upscale finds try Marché Biron; for terrific junk buys, dig around Marché Paul-Bert, both at St-Ouen.

- Meander into the trendy shops around place des Vosges in the Marais for funky gifts and clothing. Stop for lunch along rue des Rosiers for kosher deli food.

- Investigate the ritzy antique shops along Faubourg Saint Honoré for high-quality antiques.

- Find fashionable clothing on rue Saint Honoré, avenne Montaigne, place Vendôme, and rue de Faubourg Saint Honoré.

- Shop and have an artful outing at the Louvre (closed Tuesday) and the multiplex underground shopping at Le Carrousel du Louvre.

- St-Germain-des-Prés and boulevard St-Michel are walkable neighborhoods with specialty boutiques and bookstores.

The markets in the south of France are the place to shop. In Nice at the marketplace on Monday, look for antiques, old 78 rpm records, French music, books, and olives. On Wednesday on market day in Arles, you can find jackets, shirts, antiques, and bric-a-brac like old seltzer bottles. The market in Aix-en-Provence is much less expensive than the others.

◆

Leon Klayman,
art and music consultant

Montpellier (between Nice and Barcelona) is a great place to shop for art. Most artists who exhibit for high prices in Paris and Rome, have small studios down there. (It's also a two-hour bus ride from Arles). Bernard Calvet is one of my favorites. Another is Mme. Bertrand, of which I have one of her pieces for $400-$600. If I just shopped in Paris, I couldn't touch gallery artists like them for less than $1,500.

◆

Patty Zubeck, filmmaker

- For hip street fashion visit rue de la Roquette around the Bastille.

- Hang out with the students on the Left Bank (Quartier Latin) and browse for books, music, and cheap clothes.

- Window-shop along the Champs-Elysées, and buy along the side streets.

- Bargain hunt for designer clothes on rue d'Alésia in Montparnasse.

Germany
Specialties: bone china, Birkenstock sandals, traditional crafts such as handblown-glass Christmas ornaments, wood-carved nutcrackers and one-of-a-kind nativity scenes, Bavarian clothes, porcelain dolls, toys, beer steins, and wine.

- For international shopping in Berlin, browse along Kurfürstendamm. Don't miss Berlin's grand store, KaDeWe on nearby Tauentzienstrasse, or it's food hall.

- Specialized neighborhoods in Berlin provide more shopping opportunities: check out the secondhand junk in the Kreuzberg area and wander the fashionable boutiques and art galleries in the Charlottenburg neighborhood.

- Follow the local Berliners to the pedestrian shopping district around Wilmersdorferstrasse and join the flea market crowd on Sunday at Fehrbelliner Platz Market. For collectibles, ethnic crafts, and books, find the Berlin Art and Nostalgia Market at the north end of Museumsinsel on weekends.

- Buy a mug of beer in one of the many beer halls in Munich, the heart of Bavaria, then stroll the pedestrian shopping streets around historic Marienplatz. Find sporting goods and outdoor gear at Sport Scheck and Sport Schuster on Sendlingerstrasse near Marienplatz.

- Munich is the place to buy beer steins and pottery as well as traditional Bavarian clothing such as dirndl dresses and *lederhosen*. Look for department stores along Neuhauserstrasse and Kaufingerstrasse and upscale stores on Weinstrasse and Residenzstrasse. For antiques and books, wander into the shops on Schwabing in the University area of Munich.

- In Bonn, after a visit to Beethoven-Haus in the old town, shop around the pedestrian streets. Then head for the other end of the

tram line to the Bad Godesberg quarter where you can buy typical
wooden toys or roam the Moltkestrasse open-air market on Tuesday,
Thursday, and Saturday morning. Or try the Bonn market on the
Marketplatz any day.

- While in Bonn, visit the Birkenstock sandal factory in Bad Honnef
  and buy pottery in Adendorf between Meikenheim and Bad
  Godesberg.

- In Düsseldorf, window shop along Königsallee and on the cobbled
  pedestrian streets of Altstadt, the old town area. Find typical
  European stores on Schadowstrasse.

- If you're looking for exclusive, elegant, and expensive boutiques,
  shop on Goëthestrasse in Frankfurt.

- In Hamburg, amble around the pedestrian streets, Spitalerstrasse
  and Mönckebergstrasse, in the Jungfernsteig area or part with
  your money in the expensive Eppendorf district.

- Bring home a bottle of eau de cologne from Cologne, of course.
  Splash on a spray of 4711, the famous brand named after the
  house number where it was created. Look for the perfumery of the
  same name on the corner of Schwertnergasse and Glockengasse.

Greece
*Specialties: handmade sandals, gold, leatherwork, copperware, rugs,
tapestries, pottery, museum reproductions, hand-embroidered table
linens, and blouses.*

- A cultural blend of European and Eastern traditions, Greece com-
  bines the best of both for shopping. You can find handicrafts from
  all over Greece in central Athens. Ignore the tacky tourist trinkets.

- The main shopping center between Omonoia Square and Syntagma
  Square in downtown Athens is undistinguished with large department stores, but Omonoia is the hub for the trolley lines to more
  interesting shopping.

- For a touch of the East, head to the Athens street vendors at
  Monastiraki Square, the heart of the old market district, and then
  onto Pandrossou. Everyone seems to know the poet sandal maker,
  Stavros Melissinos at No. 89, who will fit you for sandals and give
  you a poem.

- Dating back to Turkish control and the oldest part of Athens, the

Plaka district expands southeast from Monastriaki Square. Wind your way through the cobblestoned alleys to find clusters of shops. Stroll along Ermou and Mitropoleos.

- Mingle with the Greeks buying produce and meat at the Central Market on Athinas Street.

- The National Welfare Organization of Greece sells handicrafts such as embroidery, tapestries, and rugs at various outlets around the city: at the Athens Hilton, and at 24a Voukourestiou Street, and 135 Vassilissis Sophias Avenue. Sales help preserve Greek craft traditions.

- Thessaloníki, Greece's second-largest city, brims with lively and sophisticated action amid its Roman ruins and Byzantine churches. For handicrafts and jewelry visit Olympic Bazaar at 10 Aristotelous Square, Hellenic Artisan Trade Cooperative at 11 Agias Sofias, and the government-sponsored Handicrafts Exhibition Hall at 90 Megalou Alexandrou, Harilaou.

- Bargain for *flokati* rugs in the Arahova, the village where they are made near Delphi.

- In the summer most shops close at about 2:00 P.M. Some are open again for a imprecise period of time between 5:30 and 9:00 P.M.

Italy

Italy is another shopping haven. Italians have a flair for great design. Along with the old, you'll discover new styles and trends. Whether you seek designer fashions, rustic pottery, or just a bottle of olive oil, you won't find a more artistic country in which to spread around your money. With a surplus of shopping in every city and hamlet, I'll just hit the highlights from Milan to Rome.

Specialties: antiques, silk scarves, shawls, and ties, gold jewelry, hand-made pottery, porcelain, leather goods, Venetian and Murano hand-blown glass, mosaics, cameos, handmade paper, Venetian beads and carnival masks, designer clothes, olive oil, and wine.

- For high fashion and modern design, start shopping in Milan: behind the Duomo in and around Corso Vittorio Emanuele, on Via della Spiga, Via Monte Napoleone, and Via Borgospesso. Bring tons of money or just window-shop.

- For more affordable shopping, head for Milan's other shopping districts and street markets, especially Brera, Navigli, and Buenos

Aires. Wander around the pedestrian-only back streets of Brera and check out its antiques fair on the third Saturday each month. For arty, funky, and junky, you can't beat the shops and studios around Navigli, which also has an Antique Market along the canal on the last Sunday each month. Corso Buenos Aires features value, local color, designer knockoffs, and almost a mile of shopping.

- As usual, it's the out-of-the-way places that are the most fun. Rent a car or take the train from Milan to Como. Shop for silk accessories at Ratti on Via Cernobbio in Como. And if you have the urge for Swiss chocolate, cross the border for a quick snack. On the third Sunday of the month, wander the flea market in Carimate.

- Next stop: Florence, *the* city to combine art and shopping. Ignore the multitudes of tourists and the attendant schlock commercial stuff at San Lorenzo Market and the Straw Market; concentrate instead on the old-world elegance and charm. Comb the side streets and back alleys, then head for the hill towns.

- In Florence, watch out for name merchandise that's fake, especially the leather goods. Roam the Ponte Vecchio, especially on a Sunday, for the action. The jewelers here weigh the gold, but you'll probably get better prices elsewhere.

- For real neighborhood shopping, the San Spirito area near the Pitti Palace offers specialty craft merchants and antique stores. The San Spirito flea market—one of the best in Florence—is on the last Sunday in the month.

PBS did a feature on the Mask Maker of Venice and *National Geographic* had an article at the same time with a map included to find his tiny studio, tucked away off one of the alleyways of Venice. I found myself totally lost, searching for the mask maker and a canal boatman had told me where to get off (a very real expression). After four hours I found him. He opened his doors and took me for a full tour of his studio and introduced me to his apprentices. From that trip, I have treasured Venetian masks—especially the ancient medicine man—hanging on my living room wall.

♦

Gloria Delaney,
importer and wholesaler

- Follow the locals about forty-five minutes outside Florence to the flea market in Viterbo on Sunday. It's worth a look for antique finds.

- For fine china visit, the Richard Ginori museum and factory outlet at Via Pratese 31, Sesto Fiorentino outside Florence.

- Around the hill towns of Tuscany, you'll find families making hand-painted pottery. Stop in the charming town of Faenza, northeast of Florence near Bologna. Visit the Faenza International Ceramics Museum in town and buy pottery along the way. Try these workshops: Cooperativa Ceramisti Faentini at Viale delle Ceramiche 11, Antonietta Mazzotti at Via Firenze 240, Gatti di Dante Servadei at Via Pompignoli 4, Franca Navarra at Via XX Settembre 42A, and Marta Morigi at Via Barbavara 7. You can arrange shipping, but be prepared to wait thirty to ninety days for your order.

- Arezzo boasts the biggest antique fair in Italy. It's on the first Sunday each month and the preceding Saturday, and it is also open during the summer.

- Bargain for a gondola ride in Venice. Then, look for bargains in handblown Murano glass, local crafts, and masks. Don't bother with the stores, just shop the street vendors every-where. Sunday's the best day to tour glass factories in Murano.

- Browse the flea markets all over Italy, but some may close dur-ing the summer months. In Pisa, go to Via XX Settembre on the second Sunday of each month. On your way to Rome stop in Siena, Florence's ancient rival city. The Piazza del Mercato flea market there is on the third Sunday each month.

- In Rome, wander Porta Portese flea market in Trastevere.

- For Rome high style, the side streets around the Spanish Steps and Via Condotti are the Roman equivalent to Rodeo Drive.

> ⎯ ⭐ ⭐ ⎯
>
> I've collected Italian dishes made in Siena for nearly thirty years. About fifteen years ago, when visiting Siena, I wanted to find the maker. No one could direct me. But I followed tiles placed here and there along a street's wall, and I eventually found the house where the ceramics were made.
>
> ◆
>
> *Karen Doubek,*
> *artist's representative*

- Many shops in Rome will send your purchases to the Pope to be blessed. Allow twenty-four hours and arrange to pick up your merchandise at the store or have your package delivered to your hotel.

- Buy museum reproductions at the Vatican museum stores.

- About an hour outside Rome, visit the city of Deruta for its famous hand-painted pottery.

- Skip down to the Mediterranean resort villages and go home with chocolate from Naples and shoes from Capri.

Netherlands

Specialties: Delft china, flowers and bulbs, cheese, chocolate, and diamonds.

- With bike lanes galore and easy tram transportation, Amsterdam is easy to maneuver around for your shopping excursions. When you don't want to walk, hop the trams or rent a bike to A'dam's main shopping areas: the Leidsestraat between the Leidseplein and Spui, and the Kalverstraat and Nieuwendijk, leading from the Munt Tower via the Dam to near the Central Station. There are large stores near the Munt Tower (V&D and Hema), and at the Dam (Bijenkorf and Magna Plaza).

- Check out Waterlooplein flea market around the City Hall and Opera, open daily, for clothes and secondhand items. Pick up a used bike here and join the cyclists in the city.

- Find all the necessities at bustling Albert Cuyp Market on Albert Cuypstraat.

- Look for chic shops in the PC Hooftstraat and in the district near the museums, and find more unique shops on Jordaan and the streets around it.

- Traditionally, shops and markets are closed all day Sunday and Monday mornings. Thursday is late-night shopping until 9 P.M.

- Don't miss the floating flower market on the Singel between the top of the Leidsestraat and the Munt Tower.

- Attend PAN Amsterdam, the annual art and antiques fair with dealers and galleries from the Netherlands and Flanders (formally the Low Countries). Open to dealers and the general public, the fair has a range of prices and items for anyone's budget and tastes:

old master paintings, manuscripts, silver, jewelry, nineteenth-century paintings, clocks, furniture, and contemporary art. Buy a bit of cultural heritage from the Low Countries. All items are subject to strict rules of authenticity, condition, and quality. The fair is held in October each year in the RAI exhibition center. For dates and admission information, contact PAN, Pictura Antiquairs Nationaal, Oude Dieze 17, 5211 KT Den Bosch, or their web site at http://www.pan-amsterdam.com.

- A European art center since the seventeeth-century, Amsterdam has numerous galleries, antique dealers, and antiquarian book-sellers around Rokin, along the River Amstel. In the Spiegel quarter, find more art and antique shops in the streets and side streets around the Spiegelgracht and Nieuwe Spiegelstraat.

- Buy the famous blue-and-white delftware anywhere in Amsterdam, but visit the town of Delft with throngs of tourists to tour the factories. The original factory, De Porceleyne Fles on Rotterdamseweg 196, dates back to the 1650s. Purchase more delft pottery at two smaller and less expensive factories: Atelier de Candelaer on Kerkstraat 14 and De Delftse Pauw on Delftweg 133.

- If you happen to buy milk in the food stores, look for the *blue* cartons; the *red* cartons are buttermilk (*karnemelk*).

- If you're here to buy diamonds, you need a pro's advice not mine.

Norway
Specialties: ski clothing, children's waterproof clothing and boots, knitwear.

- Visit Norway for the panoramic views: the fjords, the mountains, waterfalls, and coastline. If you didn't bring the appropriate clothing or accessories, buy them in Oslo or along the way.

- Crafts made from reindeer skins, wood, brass, pewter, and enamel are available but not cheap.

- Ski clothes are especially good buys during sales.

Portugal
Specialties: Coimbra pottery, azulejos (hand-painted tiles), leather shoes and sandals, antique silver, and jewelry.

- Lisbon, the city that gave us explorers, gives us back an opportunity to explore shopping up and down the hilly, cobblestoned streets. Start in the Baixa district, the center of town. On Sunday, stores are closed, but windowshop with the locals on Rua Augusta, a wide pedestrian thoroughfare.

- Search for jewelry on Rua da Prata in the Baixa.

- Look for antiques in the shops at the upper end of Rua das Portas de Santo Antao and Rua de São.

- Find fashionable shopping in the Chiado area on Rua Garrett, Rua Nova do Almada, and Rua do Carmo. For antique stores in the Chiado, try Rua do Alecrim.

- In the Bairro Alto section hunt for antiques on Rua Dom Pedro V and Rua de São Bento.

- On Tuesday and Saturday in the Alfama district, hang out at Feira da Ladra, the big open-air market at Campo de Santa Clara.

- Buy *azulejos* all over or try the museum shop in the Museu Nacional do Azulejo, or the showroom at Fabrica Sant' Ana at Rua do Alecrim 95. Ask about a factory tour.

- Outside Lisbon, shop in Sintra's town square or bargain for Coimbra pottery and clothes in the street markets of Cascais, a fishing village outside Lisbon. In Cascais, you will also find plenty of shops. I bought pottery in the shops here and had it shipped home easily.

- Savor fresh grilled sardines in Nazaré, a seventeenth-century fishing village, and shopping along the coast.

- Visit Porto in northern Portugal. For old and new silverware and jewelry, try Topazio at Rua do Heroísmo 267 and Henrique Cândido Crux on Avenue Rodrigues de Freitas 194. And, of course, tour the port-wine lodges. Tastings are part of the tours. Buy port in Porto; sip it at home.

Spain

With a Roman and Moorish legacy, Spain offers a wealth of history and culture along with shopping. In between city excursions to art museums, gardens, cafés, galleries, tapas bars, dinner at 10 P.M., gardens, parks, promenades, and more, you'll have ample opportunity to shop. And along your route to castles and coasts, monasteries and mountains, shopping will fit in easily.

Specialties: ceramics, glass, Lladro porcelain, clothes, leather, shoes, olive oil, and wine.

- In Madrid, head for the Serrano, Velázquez, and Goya neighborhoods.

- Join the crowds at El Corto Inglés, Madrid's favorite and largest department store with branch stores throughout the city. The main store is on Calle de Goya 76.

- Find designer clothing in the Chueca area and exclusive Spanish designers on Calle Jorge Juan in Serrano.

- Try on shoes along Calle de Fuencarral, and leather on Gran Vía and Calle del Príncipe.

- On Sunday forage around El Rastro, Madrid's liveliest flea market, hunt around Mola Market at Calle Potosi and Boliva, or scavenge for stamps at Plaza Major. Watch your money; pickpockets work fast in the markets.

- Buy unique museum adaptations at the Prado museum shops.

- Wander into the art galleries around town. Don't be concerned with the high prices of the art on display. Ask to see work of up-and-coming contemporary artists. Prices for their work are quite reasonable. Try Estiarte gallery at Almagro, 44 in Madrid.

On the highway running west from Madrid to Oropesa, the village of Talavera de la Reina is the center of blue-and-white eighteenth century-style ceramics. Shops line the streets there. The ceramics painted predominantly green on beige come from Puente del Arzobizpo, just southwest of Talavera.

Hilary Richardson, consultant

- In Toledo, after you've viewed El Greco's masterpieces, hunt for the ceramic factories. Dust off the dishes and choose your pieces at Talabricense on Calle Marqués de Mirasol 16 or any of the other ceramic shops you stumble across. Pick up an antique ornamental sword or a replica in any shop around Toledo.

- In Barcelona, stroll with the locals around La Ramba along the pedestrian boulevard among the merchant kiosks, flower stands, and artist stalls.

- Barcelona's market days are Monday, Wednesday, Friday, and Saturday at Els Encants flea market.

- In Seville, visit ceramic factories in Triana, a district south of the river.

- Off the east coast of Spain, the Balearic Islands of Majorca and Ibiza are old hippie hangouts and still havens for shopping. On Majorca, search for pottery at Paseo del Borne, shoes at San Miguel, silverware at Plateria San Alonso and La Pirne, and chocolates at La Pajarita.

- In Ibiza, explore the boutiques and funky market stalls in the port area of Sa Penya, and galleries in the old walled town of D'Alt Vila.

- Avoid looking like a casual tourist. Spaniards dress up, so bring nice clothes in which to shop, especially in Madrid.

Sweden

Specialties: Orrefors, Boda, and Kosta glassware, wood-carved folk crafts, ceramics, pewter, sheepskin jackets and coats, fur-lined boots, and Lapp reindeer-skin handicrafts.

- Art and handicrafts are available in most museum stores.

- Find contemporary designed housewares around Hamngatan in Stockholm.

- In Stockholm, Nordiska Kompaniet (NK), the major department store, is in a turn-of-the-century building with separate boutiques.

Switzerland

Specialties: chocolate, watches, cuckoo

I spent three winters in Switzerland teaching skiing to handicapped children and guiding the able-bodied around the glaciers, resorts, and bars. Because I had a vehicle, I used to do the weekly supplies shopping for my friends' businesses at the big supermarket down in the valley. One time my Swiss shopping partner unknowingly dropped the Swiss franc equivalent of a US$1,000 bill in the supermarket. Some mystery shopper handed it to a cashier. The manager found me in the cheese section and while saying "only a foreigner would be stupid enough to lose this" handed me the cash. That's Switzerland for you—chronically honest, unconsciously arrogant.

◆

Anthony Cameron, surfer, ski instructor and sailor

clocks, skiwear, penknives, wine, and cheese.

- Shop the old town section of Geneva—an intriguing maze of antique shops, galleries, bookshops, and cafés.

- Look for the flea market at Pleinpalais in Geneva on Wednesday afternoon and Saturday.

- Buy antique books and prints in Geneva and about thirty minutes away in the ancient town of Nyon.

- In Zurich, explore alleys and antique shops in the Old Town.

- Check out the Zurich handicraft market on Thursday and Saturday, or try the flea market at Burkliplatz on Saturday between May and October.

Turkey

Specialties: towels, carpets, kilims, embroideries, gold, silver, copper, glass, brass, meerschaum pipes, shoes, leather, suede, sheepskin jackets, local wines and liqueurs, hookah pipes, ceramics, antiques, jewelry, spices, and aphrodisiacs.

- A purchase is not a purchase in Istanbul without tea drinking, bargaining, and socializing.

- The legendary place to find it all: Kapali Çarsi, the covered bazaar in the Old City of Istanbul, a labyrinth of more than 4,000 shops and 2,000 workshops. Similar traders are grouped together in their own areas. Always bargain.

- If all Kapali Çarsi is overwhelming, ask the local traders to help

In Turkey, I discovered the world's most useful Turkish phrase. Get yourself an English-Turkish dictionary to look up the name of whatever you want and add varma. Ask, "(name of thing) *varma?*" and, behold, the merchant will give you one of only two responses: *yok*, which means "We do not have what you request," or *var* which means "we have it, and here it is." Walk into a teahouse and say "*Chai varma?*" and a glass of sweet Turkish tea will arrive; "*Ekmek varma?*" will provide you with fresh, warm, and delicious Turkish bread; "*Oda varma?*" will get you a room. It never fails, but be prepared for a torrent of Turkish because they'll assume you are fluent. I just silently sip my tea and look enigmatic.

◆

Anthony Cameron, surfer, ski instructor, and sailor

you find May, a shop run by Mr. Ercan May. From handpainted ceramics and traditional rugs to handwoven kilim-covered backpacks and clothing, you'll find all your souvenirs in one place.

- For arty shopping, try the Ortaköy district along the Bosporus where artists display their work; for chic fashion, head to the Nisantasi area.

- If you crave Turkish market food and local color, cruise the stalls at the Spice Bazaar, Misir Çarsi, and the fish market, Galatasaray Balikpazari.

- Hunt for traditional Turkish craft antiques as well as European furniture in the many antique shops around the city. Wander around Cukurcuma district on the back streets of Beyoglu. Try Antikhane, a warehouse with nine floors of Islamic and Oriental arts, books, maps, prints, Turkish and European paintings, and furniture.

- Küsav, a foundation for the promotions of culture and Arts, holds twice-monthly antique auctions.

United Kingdom

Along with interest in the royal family, shopping is a national pastime. You can buy anything in this nation of shopkeepers. If you can't find it in the U.K., it probably hasn't been invented yet. Regional shopping is easy. Just pick a destination, and the shops will find you. So, I'll focus mainly on London.

Specialties: contemporary design, crafts, antiques, clothes and accessories, music and books, Waterford crystal, Wedgwood, beer and scotch, Irish linens, lace, smoked salmon, and whiskey.

- No trip to London is complete without shopping at Harrod's, especially the Food Hall. If you've never visited, make time for the other famous names: Marks and Spencer, Fortnum & Mason, Liberty, Harvey Nichols. Even if you've been before, it's always fun to see what's new. But I prefer the street action, and London's various neighborhoods and markets promise all kinds of treasures.

- Chelsea is now chic bohemian, so expect pricey shops. Walk around trendy South Kensington for museums and shopping. Find vintage clothes at Kensington Market.

- Thanks to Hugh Grant and Julia Roberts, Notting Hill's Portobello Road is even more famous than it was. Will that make it better or worse? More in vogue or less? Stop by and see for yourself.

- Rivaling Portobello for funky, lively atmosphere and crushing crowds, Camden Markets take first place. Five markets sprawl over the neighborhood. Start with Camden Lock Market for trinkets, used clothing, bootlegged items, and groovy old stuff. Check out the other markets here for more cool junk, heaps of old toys and clothing: Camden Market, Camden Canal Market, Stables, and Electric Ballroom.

- Meander down Camden Passage, a narrow alley of antique shops. In the street market here, find more antiques as well as books, prints, crafts, and jewelry.

- Watch the buskers for free on the square in Covent Garden; wander the pedestrian streets and browse the boutiques for antiques and crafts. It's a bit touristy but entertaining nonetheless.

Entering Harrod's for the first time while on a business trip, I was surprised to find myself in the middle of their once-yearly sale. People were wall to wall and bobbies were directing traffic *inside* the store. As a neophyte shopper, it was an overwhelming sight. Only the endless array of foodstuffs kept me inside the store.

◆

Jeff Brady, business analyst

- Hunt for used CDs, cheap clothes, and knickknacks on Berwick and Rupert streets.

- Claw your way through the crowds on East Street, south of the Thames, and listen to merchants shout out the bargains of the day.

- For arts and crafts lovers, spend weekends at the Greenwich Arts and Crafts Market, the Merton Abbey Mills Riverside Craft Village, or visit the Bayswater Road Art Exhibition on Sunday.

- At St. Martin-in-the-Field Market, dig around for ethnic jewelry and art on Adelaide Street where the cool stuff is hidden.

- For antiques, hang about Bermondsey Market on Fridays from 5 A.M. until noon.

- If you are into numismatics or philately, get to Charing Cross Collectors' Fair on Saturday for medals, coins, and stamps.

- Following the lead of U.S. museums into big-time commercialism, museum shopping is reaching high art in London. For the best, visit the British Museum and the Victoria and Albert. Don't forget the Tate Gallery. There's even a nonaffiliated museum shop in Covent Garden with reproductions and related stuff from museums worldwide.

- Contact The British Antique Dealers Association for information and dates on its annual fair: The BADA Antiques Fair, 20 Rutland Gate, London SW7 1BD or e-mail info@badaantiquesfair.demon.co.uk.

EASTERN EUROPE

On our way back from the Merry Cemetery in Sapinta, Romania, my friend Gloria—an audaciously Fearless Shopper—noticed a young boy of about seven walking with his mother and other women. There's no stopping her when she sets her sights on something, so she tapped the woman on the shoulder and explained by pantomime that she wanted to buy the young boy's cone-shaped hat with the tassel. Words and gestures followed the mother's exchange with her son. The boy burst out crying and screaming and would not let go of the hat. After a while the mother coaxed the hat from the boy, who clung to his mother's leg. He would not look at Gloria, though she tried to befriend him to ease his parting with the hat. Gloria paid the women for the hat and gave her a child's ski parka (one of the many used clothing articles from home that she often doled out on her trips). She felt awful, however, as our translator explained that the mother was playing a joke on the boy, saying she was going to sell the child with the hat.

General Tips

➤ Most Eastern European countries still have much to learn

regarding basic Western services and amenities. Hungary, Czech Republic, and Poland are more accustomed to American tourists. Countries like Romania and Bulgaria have a long way to go, so expect to rough it when it comes to customer service.

➤ In some Eastern European countries, you may need a basket or small cart to enter a store and shop. Carry your own tote bag.

➤ The best buys are the folk crafts, particularly in the less-Westernized Eastern European countries. You can also barter or offer dollars in the countryside for local arts.

➤ Eastern European folk music recordings will transport you, and they make affordable souvenirs and gifts.

➤ Gone are the days when you could get about five times the official exchange rate on the black market in Eastern European countries. Without government restrictions on free currency trading, there's no need. The most you'll get is a few percentage points above bank rates except in Romania where you might get ten to twenty-five percent more. In any case, changing money on the streets is illegal, though no one really cares, and risky—you are a target for thieves who know all the scams to rip you off.

➤ Find out what might be illegal to export before you buy. Get a receipt for anything you buy in hard currency. You may not have to pay duty on those purchases when you leave.

➤ Bring a bag of old clothes from home, especially outgrown children's clothes. They make great giveaways or barter items, especially in the rural towns.

Country Specialties & Tips

Although the products of Western capitalism and pop culture swept through Eastern Europe the instant Communism fell, the internal commercial marketing of each country's own merchandise has been uneven at best. Quality goods are not always available, and political instability in certain regions makes shopping excursions questionable. So, I've included the countries with easy access and relative stability.

Bulgaria

Specialties: embroidered blouses and dresses, vials of rose perfume with painted wood tops, costumed dolls, silver filigree jewelry, woodcarvings, lace, kilims, old musical instruments, watches, pottery, silk shirts, and leather.

- In Sofia, windowshop along fashionable Vitosha Boulevard near the National Museum of History. Stop in at K. Bakalios-Kricket at 55, Vitosha Boulevard for leather coats and jackets, shoes, and handbags.

- Shop at the Sunday Women's Market for hand-tooled wooden spoons and locally made cheap clothes. Find jeans for about fifteen dollars and heavy, wool crocheted sweaters for about ten dollars.

- Buy souvenirs and Bulgarian handicrafts at the Guild of the Craftsmen of Folk Arts and

At the Samokov museum, they seem to have the largest collection of antique woodcuts in the world, or at least Eastern Europe. They have made posters using these woodcuts, usually in two colors advertising some historic time. I bought one that is 43 cm by 59 cm. The woodcut, made in 1935 and the poster in 1971, depicts a marvelous Bulgarian horseman on a fully decorated horse. Done in black and rust, it is a magnificent piece of art—for about fifty cents.

♦

Marilynne B. Davis,
senior resident advisor

Crafts at 14, Vitosha Boulevard; the Shop of the Union of
Bulgarian Artists at 117, G. S. Rakovski Street; Sredets Souvenir
Shop at 7, Legue Street; and the Bulgarian Folk Art shops at 11,
Dondoukov Boulevard and at 86, G. S. Rakovski Street.

- Look for small shops selling crafts, costumes, and musical instruments from all over Bulgaria in the former Royal Palace on Tsar
Osvohoditel Blvd to benefit the National Art Gallery and the
Ethnographical Museum on Moskovska St.

- In Varna, a city on the Black Sea, check out the shopping
on Knyaz Boris I, Vladislav Varnenchik, and Slivnitsa boulevards
and Preslav and Tzar Simeon I streets.

Czech Republic
*Specialties: garnets, folk crafts and ceramics, wooden toys, handblown
glass ornaments, Bohemian crystal, porcelain, contemporary art,
ceramics, paintings, and beer.*

- Pick up a shopping basket at the
entrance of most stores. You may
need one to get into the store.
Many shops control their store
traffic flow by limiting the number of available carts so you may
have to wait on line to get one.

- For a pedestrian-friendly, historical, and architectural tour,
browse around the Castle
District (Hradcany), the Small
Quarter (Mala Strana), the Old
Town (Stare Mesto), and
Wenceslas Square (Václavské
námestí).

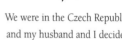

We were in the Czech Republic,
and my husband and I decided
to start collecting beer glasses.
Since I was the only one with
any useable language skills
(German in this case), it fell to
me to explain our mission and
negotiate a deal in every pub
or restaurant we entered.

◆

Deborah Fallows, writer

- Stroll down Prague's fashionable
boulevard, Václavské námestí, with the local residents.

- Between the Old Town Square at Staromestské námestí and
námestí Republiky, wander into shops from Karlova to Celetná.

- Find folk ceramics at Keramika, a shop inside the passageway of
Václavské námestí 41.

- For Bohemian crystal go to the glass shops in the Alfa Cinema

Arcade at Václavské námestí 28.

- Although souvenirs are exempt, export duty on your purchases may be as high as twenty-two percent if you spend more than $1,000.

- A musical, intellectual, and literary capital, Prague is the Paris of Eastern Europe and the place to hang for thousands of American college graduates. Jazz it up or rock with the youth culture after you shop.

Hungary

Specialties: embroidery, folk music, Herend porcelain, dolls, ceramics, painted wood toys and boxes, wall hangings, baskets, glass, and wine.

- In Budapest, look for food and folk crafts at Nagycsarnok, the central market hall on Ffivám tér. Go upstairs to the stalls at the back where the vendors sell dolls, embroideries, painted eggs, and other folk art.

- For an overview and one stop for gifts at fixed prices, go to the Folkart Centrum at V Váci utca 14.

- Buy more crafts at Moszkva tér, in the street markets, or in the Buda District XI market at Fehérvári Út and Schönherz utca.

- The Ajka (Oika) Crystal factory has an outlet in the small city of the same name about one-and-a-half-hours west of Budapest.

Hungarian embroidered textiles and ceramics command top dollar in Budapest, on the street or in a store, but if you make the effort to get out of town, prices drop dramatically. Esztergom, less than two hours north by inexpensive public bus, is worth the trip as prices are half what they are in Budapest.

♦

*Ann McClellan,
marketing director*

In Eger, Hungary, in the park outside of the castle, is a man who sells goose eggs into which he has cut out traditional folk patterns. He uses a dental drill to cut the designs into the shells. They are magnificent renderings of the patterns and very authentic. He was there the entire three years that I lived in Hungary, and I assume that he is still there.

♦

*Marilynne B. Davis,
senior resident advisor*

They have seconds, export quality, and one-of-a-kind pieces as well as "end lots" for several world recognized brand name companies and chain stores that specialize in imports to the West.

Poland

Specialties: amber and silver jewelry, Krosno glass, embroidered place mats and napkins, traditional wood crafts, paper cuts, paintings on glass, Boleslawiec pottery, crystal, vodka, ice skates, and sheepskin rugs, hats, and slippers.

- Find Cepelia handicraft stores in most of the major cities. You can purchase traditional Polish wood carvings, paper cuts, hand-painted boxes, and pottery along with contemporary local artisan work.

- Shop for amber jewelry in Warsaw and Gdansk in commercial galleries and jewelry stores. You can find it in the Cepelia stores and other places. Price varies with the quality of workmanship and the actual pieces of amber used. A piece of this fossil resin with an insect inside may be even more valuable.

- Bring home a Polish poster as a decorative souvenir of Warsaw or Kraków. Look for them in art galleries along with paintings and prints.

- Spend a leisurely shopping day around Market Square, the focus of Kraków city life for 700 years. Treasure the surroundings: wander into a store or art gallery, a church or courtyard, follow the passageways and listen to the trumpeter from the Mariacki Church tower sound his call four times each hour.

Romania

Specialties: traditional folk crafts, painted wood furniture, pottery, sheepskin vests and gloves, embroidered leather clothes, folk music, painted wood eggs, and antiques.

- In the Piata Unirii section of Bucharest, shop at the Unirea Department Store and the surrounding shops and vendor stalls. But to find great folk crafts, leave the city and wander the countryside villages and cities.

- Visit ceramic artisans in Horezu: Eufrosina Vicsoreanu at Strada Olari 99; Ion Biscu at Strada Olari, 198; Gheorghe Iorga at Strada Olari 92.

- In Avrig, watch weaver artisan Ispas Rodica at Strada Ceferistilor 37.

- Bring a photo from home and let potter Nicolae Diaconu create a clay figure resembling a family member. Visit him at Strada Pietei 14, Codlea, Brasov County.

- Buy woven blankets from Turda Irina and Turda Gheorghe at Com. Sapinta 84, Maramures County, in Sapinta.

- Watch famous potter, Colibada Florin, create traditional pieces with geometric and floral designs as well as Byzantine-inspired ceramics at Strada Primaverii 11, Radauti, Suceava County.

- For leather and fur jackets and accessories, visit Bacea family at Sat Tureac, Strada Principala 63, Com. Tiha Birgaului, Bistrita Nasaud County. Nearby, watch weaver artisan, Lucia Todoran at Com. Salva 700.

- Visit the city of Sibiu for shopping and don't miss the Astra Museum, an open-air museum on 200 acres.

- If you're looking for a break from searching for crafts, hitch up your boots and hike in the Carpathian Mountains. In the fall, no fashion color palette can match the lush leaves in the Romanian forests. The walnuts are free gifts from the trees.

Slovakia
Specialties: costume jewelry, ceramics, lace, embroidery, Bohemia garnets, and crystal.

- In Bratislava, wear low heels and thick-soled shoes for walking on the cobblestone streets while you shop.

- Buy traditional handicrafts at Folk Folk at Obchodná 10 or Ul'uv at nám SNP.

- For folk ceramics check out Keramika on the corner of Hurbanovo and Oupné nám.

RUSSIA & CENTRAL ASIA

If you see it, buy it because you
won't see it again.

— *Moscow Rule of Shopping*

———

*I*n Russia six months before Communism fell, I witnessed those infamous empty shelves and endless lines. Grocery stores offered no choice, and throngs of people were lucky to get butter, milk, and eggs there. At GUM, the major department store in Moscow, crowds filled each floor, but there was nothing to buy. In the china and crystal departments packaged sponges replaced dinnerware as the main merchandise offering.

I was in the former Soviet Union trying to buy for a special exhibition shop at the Smithsonian that coincided with a traveling museum show. Finding enough product became an act of prestidigitation: we went in search of traditional crafts, and the trick was making something appear out of nothing. It was the first time I ever worried that we'd come home from a buying trip empty-handed. The obstacles were beyond belief. We not only ran into empty shelves, but also a bureaucracy and a currency that left us little real negotiating room.

But even then, commerce and early entrepreneurs were gaining, and there was no turning back. One afternoon at the brink of this consumer-driven society, a Russian woman, who appeared to be an old-line bureaucrat, invited me and a colleague to meet jewelry artisans. Our hostess's spacious apartment contained a curious mixture of political memorabilia, trinkets, luggage tags from around the world, a few treasures, and numerous photographs of herself with heads-of-state such as Castro and Khrushchev. Now a patron of the arts, she encouraged us to buy from her friends who viewed us as their savior. Dashing their hopes of a hard-currency windfall, we placed a small order and returned the following week when another group of her friends—men from the Cossack Museum—appeared with their goods for sale. These souvenirs were tacky, however. Diplomatically, we explained that their merchandise was unrelated to our needs. They pressured us anyway, and our once gracious, now distant, hostess simply could not understand how we could buy from one set of friends but not another.

At other times we found the best places to buy were in the street market in Moscow and a retail craft store in Ukraine where an industrious manager took the initiative to give us a discount for quantity. Our driver—who for a few packs of Marlboros would miraculously fill his trunk with precisely the crafts we were looking for—supplied us also. We bought in private homes where families literally sold things off their walls. Several times gracious hosts offered us meals and more.

One night after a dinner of sardines, beets, black bread smothered with bacon fat, and free-flowing vodka, we admired their kitchen wall adorned with *Khokhloma*—painted lacquerware bowls, spoons, trays, and vases—and asked where we might get a supply. At which point they gently persuaded us to buy from them in dollars so their son, a budding rock star, would have enough money for a keyboard. In other homes we purchased *matryoshka* (nested dolls) directly from the artist who painted them in elaborate detail and with considerably more talent than what we saw in the street.

I suspect the best buys are still in private homes, and if the Fearless Shopper were lucky enough to be invited to a meal, do not be surprised if your hosts, even today, offer a bit more than food. Though the command economy has changed and goods are generally available for sale, the rule of the streets still applies: If you see it, buy it. You may never see it again.

General Tips

➤ Bring a sense of adventure with you. You are entering what the Wild West must have been like.

➤ Communism is dead but in it's place is an unruly land, run primarily by former bureaucrats, unprincipled businessmen, out-of-control gangsters (also known in the Western press as the Russian Mafia), and petty black marketeers who are adept at con games. With legal currency exchange now, avoid anyone on the street who offers to change your money.

➤ Knowing how to bribe your way around is still helpful. Bring small gifts from home: postcards, pens, American chewing gum, key rings, bottle openers, cheap digital watches, chocolate, t-shirts with Western logos, crayons, baseball cards. And U.S. dollars still work, as do unopened Marlboro cigarette packs, if your conscience permits.

➤ Familiarize yourself with the Cyrillic alphabet so you can decipher some signs on your shopping excursions.

➤ Capitalism reigns today, but concepts of the relative worth of items are still a mystery to many in the former Soviet Union. Always bargain.

➤ Permission to export antiques—anything made before 1945—must be cleared by the Ministry of Culture, and there is an excise tax of 50 percent of the antique's value. Old religious icons are illegal to export.

➤ The lines are gone for the most part and the shelves are fuller, but tourism is still in its infancy in most of the former Soviet Union—especially outside major cities. Have patience at state-run stores and possibly others. Often they operate on the old *kassa* system. Which means several trips to different counters to select, pay, return, pick up.

Russia

Specialties: matryoshka *dolls,* Khokhloma *handicrafts, painted Russian lacquer boxes and eggs, porcelain, antiques, silver, amber jewelry, samovars, amber, wooden folk toys, Central Asian rugs, Soviet-era memorabilia, caviar, and vodka.*

- In Moscow, visit GUM—a lavish architectural structure with three arcades of shops under a glass roof—for department store shopping around Red Square.

- The best antique shops and souvenir stands are around Arbat Street. And the Fearless Shopper should venture to the Sunday flea market at Izmaylovo Park to bargain for matryoshka dolls, antique silver, jewelry, samovars, Soviet memorabilia, and more.

> I went to Moscow and found folk art items at little cost. I had to buy an extra suitcase to get it all home.
>
> ◆
>
> *Aviva Kempner, filmmaker*

- Take advantage of the cultural opportunities in the cities—the museums, the ballets, the circus in Moscow—along with the shopping.

- Watch out for potentially poisonous bootlegged vodka. Look for an official pink tax seal on the top, and don't buy it in the streets.

- The Hermitage is the attraction in St. Petersburg, but the city itself is a gem with elegant buildings along the Neva River. Filled with history from czarist Russia, St. Petersburg is lovely to stroll around. Start at Admiralteysky and wander down Nevsky with its mix of art galleries, shops, toy stores, perfumeries, and more. Watch out for the purse snatchers.

- Head over to St. Petersburg's indoor Kuznechny Market in the Vladimirskaya area for a good old time and a few shops. Buy Fabergé eggs at Ananov in the Grand Hotel Europe. Check out the artists' market near Nevsky Prospekt metro station entrance on ulitsa Mikhailovskaya. For pricey artwork, try the Exhibition Hall at the Union of Artists at ulitsa Bolshaya Morskaya 38.

- Finely detailed, miniature paintings on painted wood or papier-mâché lacquer boxes and eggs are almost national treasures. Based on Russian fairy tales, they are collectible works of art. But look carefully at range of talent and prices before buying. Many are crudely conceived. The best are exquisitely painted, expensive, and made by artists in the villages of Palekh, Fedoskino, Kholuy, and Mstera.

- Many folk crafts are affordable and available in the street markets where you can haggle for the best price. Your best bets in the hinterlands are indigenous crafts.

Country Specialties & Tips

Belarus
Specialties: hand-crafted ceramics, textiles, and wood carvings.

- In Minsk, for a good selection of ceramics at great prices visit the Suveniry shop at vulitsa Valadarskaha 23 near Hotel Svislach. Try Magazin Charaunitsa Skaryny 13 for procelain and wood products, and Paulinka gift store Skaryny 19.

- Visit the museum shop in the Belarussian State Art Museum to purchase ceramics.

- For more gifts and art go to vulitsa Maxima Bahdanovicha 21 to the art gallery and for antiques try the Art Palace upstairs.

Estonia
Specialties: jewelry, amber, ceramics, and leather.

- In Tallinn, at Town Hall square (Raekoja plats) in Old Town shop for gifts at affordable prices.

- East of the Old Town center on Viru väljak, visit Tallina Kaubamaja, a department store, to get an overview of handicrafts from the area.

Georgia

Specialties: Caucasian carpets, woven wall hangings, ceramics, Soviet memorabilia, wine, silk, and hand-forged daggers (kinjals).

- This region claims to have produced wine for well over 2,000 years.

- Visit the daily Art Market, under the Dry Bridge next to the river. The best day to go is Saturday between 11 P.M. and 6 P.M.

- Scrounge around the flea market on the river (near the Art Market) for Soviet memorabilia, china, crystal, old photos, and stuff.

- Check out the hand-painted silk scarves, wall hangings, and pillowcases at La Maison Bleue (Gogebashvili Street) and Manana's Art Salon (near the Metechi Bridge).

Kazakhstan

Specialties: fur hats and Kazakh carpets.

- Visit Salon Bahyt at 56A Abai

Wine is sold throughout the country, and every Georgian makes his own. Even apartment dwellers grow grapes up their balconies. If you want to buy, stick with the big name labels that have a certain amount of predictability in their bottling. Mukuzani and Saperavi are reds similar to Zinfandel. (Look for those bottled by GWS.) Most Georgian white wines are sweet. Try Zsanandali or the Old Tbilisi White (also bottled by GWS).

◆

Mari Radford, embassy community liaison officer

Some crafts available in Alma-Ata can be found at the Oner Gallery located on Furmanov and Chevchenko. Store hours are Monday through Saturday 10 A.M. – 6 P.M. Another location to find antiques and carpets is Antique and Mod-ern Varieties of Carpets Shop, 65 Kazybek bi (ask for Akyl).

◆

Lynda Delaney, embassy community liaison officer

Street in Alma-Ata for regional crafts.

- In the Kaskelen Area (9 kilometers outside Alma-Ata) go to Sheber Aul Artisan Village at GES 2 Kok-Shoky Village.

Moldova
Specialties: Jewelry, pottery, local paintings, Soviet memorabilia.

- In the capital city of Chisinau, the main shopping street is Stefan cel Mare Boulevard, named after a local folk hero.

- Bring your own shopping bag to the Chisinau flea market.

- Bargain in the daily arts and crafts fair on Stefan cel Mare Boulevard.

Latvia
Specialties: fur hats and coats, amber, leather, and red and black caviar.

Check out the vendor (dressed in his Soviet military uniform, full of medals) by the main entrance of the Chisinau Tolchuk to buy old Soviet-era coins and pins. (Tolchuk is the Russian word for "push," and it's the name of the city's largest flea market. And, yes, lots of crowds and pushing!)

♦

Nancy Ilgenfritz Horton, embassy administrator

- Bring waterproof boots to slosh down Riga's cobblestoned streets when you shop here in the winter.

- For a local cultural experience, trek over to the main market, Centralais Tirgus, near the train and bus stations.

- If you are less bold, try Vidzemes Tirgus, a smaller market on Brivibas or the street market on Filharmonijas Square.

- Find Soviet memorabilia in any antique store in Riga.

- For handmade leather goods try Tine at Valnu 2 and buy amber at A & E at Jauniela 17.

Lithuania
Specialties: amber jewelry, fur coats, glass, pottery, antiques, silverware, vodka, and caviar.

- In Vilnius, find arts and crafts at the handicraft market on Pilies in the Old Town.

- The central shopping area runs along Gedimino Prospektas.

- Buy your fur coat from Nijole at Gedimino 3a.

- Look for Soviet memorabilia, antiques, silver, and jewelry in the Stikli/Dominikon area of Old Town.

- On Saturday and Sunday mornings in the summer, search the farmers market at Kalvaarij 61.

- Check out the Garlinai flea market for more surprises just off the highway from Vilnius to Kaunas.

Ukraine
Specialties: carved and painted wooden souvenirs, folk art, painted eggs, antiques, amber jewelry, embroidery, caviar, and vodka.

- Barter or bribe with small gifts—chocolate, chewing gum, t-shirts and U.S. dollars.

- Bargain at the souvenir and craft markets.

- Ukrainsky Souvenirs, a chain of gift stores, stocks a variety of ceramics, embroideries, and other crafts. Quality varies at the different outlets. Check out the one in Kiev and Odessa.

- Find souvenirs in the department stores in the larger towns. Try GUM and TsUM.

- Look for crafts at small state stores, known as *khudozhestvenny salon*.

- Search the craft markets wherever they pop up around various parks. Try Andriyivsky uzviz in Kiev, around the Opera House in L'viv, near Ivano-Frankivsk in Kosiv on Saturday.

Uzbekistan
Specialties: felt handicrafts and ceramics.

- In Bukhara, find regional crafts at Bukhara Artisan Center Craft Shop on B. Nakshband Street, 100.

- Operated by the Businesswomen's Association of Bukhara, the Zebiniso Artisan Gallery on Mehtar Anbar Street sells handicrafts.

- In Samarkand, visit the displays at Meros Handcraft Center Sales and Exhibition Hall, State Museum of History, Culture and Arts in Registan Square.

- In Tashkent, look for handicrafts at Zumrad on 41 Afrosiyab Street.

SOUTH &
CENTRAL AMERICA

Much have I traveled in the realms of gold,
And many goodly states and kingdoms seen.

— *John Keats*

———

*O*utside Gutemala City off the main highway, my colleagues and I drove up a dirt road to visit a community of women weavers whose festive clothes and
beautiful smiles belied their impoverished state. They took
us into their lean-to shacks for hot chocolate and cake.
Then, the women took turns displaying their handwoven
garments and accessories created on back-strap looms.

Traditional Guatemalan textiles are well known for their
intensity of color and design, and many Guatemalan Indians
spin and dye their cotton then weave their own clothes.
Hand weaving on back-strap looms produces narrow strips
that are sewn together to make blouses and pants. Generally,
men operate foot looms and women work back-strap looms,
on which they weave after tying one end to a tree or post
and the other around their waist.

I wondered how these women survived on the few dollars
these textiles brought them. Nonetheless, our orders would
feed many families from this cooperative. We struggled to balance our desire to help these woman with our responsibility
to get the best possible price for the Smithsonian. None of
these women had heard of the Smithsonian, much less the
concept of a museum shop. They only knew we appreciated
their detailed handiwork and were willing to pay for it.

Intricately woven with multicolored designs, these textiles enhance the market culture in Guatemala: women wear handwoven cotton *huipiles* (blouses), embroidered with flowers, plants, and geometric designs. Part of the native dress, the *huipil* is typical among the Indian women in every town, often distinguished by colors specific to each village. They wrap their ankle-length skirts at the waist with blue embroidered and striped sashes. *Tzutes* (head cloths) cushion their baskets and water jugs. Young women, barefoot on the dirt, saunter down the market paths, nestling babies slung in *parrajes* (shawls) wrapped around their bodies. Men carrying crocheted tote bags traipse around the market in tire-tread sandals, wearing loose pants, stitched together in a patchwork of hand-loomed and decorated cloth.

People weave in and out of the markets like the intricate embroidery on each *huipil* and this human activity resembles a colorful appliqué that reflects the past—an intermingling of Indians and Spanish descendants. When the Spaniards conquered Guatemala, introduced Catholicism, and forced cultural change, they patterned the villages on the Spanish plaza with clusters of trading posts. Although the natives mimicked the dress of Spanish women and officers, each village developed its own identity through textiles and color: red in one town, blue in another. Today, in a mix of Spanish and their native Quiche, peddlers—men, women, and children—trade their handicrafts, filling the market in Chichicastenango and elsewhere, with textiles and produce much the same as they have for centuries.

In the western highlands, north of Lake Atitlán, Chichicastenango is the market to see with handicrafts from all over the region. Not only do I love the sound of the name Chichicastenango, but it's also my favorite place in

Latin America to bargain. Prices start a bit higher here, but the native color and the lively marketplace make bargaining more fun. Almost anywhere you go in Latin America, you'll run into a major market or makeshift street stalls where the local action is far more exciting a place to shop than traditional retail stores. And Fearless Shoppers will undoubtedly find their favorite, too.

General Tips

Many major cities in Central and South America have pedestrian shopping promenades, department stores, market squares, small handicraft shops, and upscale boutiques. Some, like Buenos Aires, have a sophisticated European flavor; others have modest or run-down commercial centers. You may find more than you could possibly afford or nothing at all. By all means search the normal retail stores, but the closer you get to the native culture the more intriguing the shopping is. So many tips listed here for Central and South America apply to market cultures, and for that reason I've included Mexico. Although technically a part of North America, Mexico has a market sensibility that is decidedly Latin in nature.

➤ If you speak the language, you are less likely to be taken advantage of. So, bargain like a native. Even if you don't know Spanish, learn a few key phrases like *Cuanto cuesta?* (What's the cost?), *demasiado* (too much), *No soy turista*, (I'm not a tourist), *solo mirando* (just looking), and *No, me diga* (Don't tell me). The latter should be uttered with extreme astonishment at the outrageously high price just quoted by the seller, especially in Mexico.

➤ Don't miss the opportunity to shop where a little culture and history are woven into every fabric you buy. The markets of Guatemala, Mexico, Peru, and Ecuador especially are great places to buy inexpensive scarves, bags, belts, hats, and one-of-a-kind textiles. When you find something you love, buy several as gifts.

➤ Whenever possible, find native cooperatives where you can buy crafts and pay fair prices to artisans—often women who are eking out a living. Many of these co-ops are organized by outside nonprofits whose goal is to create self-sustaining communities.

➤ Bring a Polaroid camera with you. While many indigenous people will not want their picture taken, others will have no problem with it and often request that you send them a copy. If you travel with a Polaroid, you make instant friends. Children especially love this as a small gift.

While visiting a local village around Lake Atitlán, Guatemala, I saw a workman dressed in the most beautiful embroidered pants—a woven stripe with embroidered birds of all colors and varieties on top of the stripe. I loved them. I gestured that I wanted his pants. He understood my desire. In response, with hand gestures, he expressed his desire for my Levi's. I removed my jeans in the van and passed them through the window to him, and he handed me his embroidered pants caked with mud from the fields. He invited me to his home to meet his wife, mother, and daughter who made his work clothes. On the fence in front of their home two pairs of embroidered pants were hanging in hopes that a tourist would come along and buy them. I couldn't resist.

◆

Gloria Delaney,
importer and wholesaler

207

➤ Indigenous people may ask for a tip to pose for your picture. Give them local currency or a small token from home: pen, lapel pin, patch, hat.

➤ Take several cotton t-shirts with you. They are comfortable for hot climates, easy to sleep in, and make great gifts. Or barter them for a craft you crave.

➤ Keep small bills handy in the markets.

➤ Bring credit cards, ATM cards, and cash. To my surprise it was hard to find a bank that would exchange traveler's checks in Lima, Peru. It may also be difficult to change them in Columbia and Argentina, and the farther you get from major cities. Local banks may charge as high as ten percent commission to change money, and hotels and shops may also charge a surcharge of about five to ten percent for credit card usage.

— ★ ★ ★ —

Having neared the end of our Guatemalan tour and just about out of local money, we stopped for gas. Children around the station were selling decorated pens and woven baskets. A young girl approached me to purchase a small, lidded hanging basket adorned with a plastic poinsettia. She wanted the equivalent of fifty cents, but the true fact was I only had twenty cents left. She thought about this, left the scene, and returned with the plastic flower removed from the lid. Now, it was available. Above my sink at home, this little basket serves as a garlic holder and a memory of a "win-win" sales negotiation.

♦

Kathy Carpenter,
international insurance agent

➤ If you plan a trip to the high mountain regions, be prepared for altitude sickness. Consult your doctor before you go. If you're shopping in the Andes mountains, there are local homeopathic remedies: buy tea made from cocoa leaves in

Peru and Bolivia to relieve symptoms. Also, chewing on these leaves with bicarbonate of soda can be a mild stimulant. Indians have been practicing this for centuries. You can buy these leaves legally in small stores, but don't bring them into other countries.

➢ Beware of thieves, especially in Brazil and Guatemala, but pickpockets and bag-slashers work many of the markets no matter what country you're in.

➢ Bargaining is common practice in almost all artisan markets. In stores and hotels, try asking for a discount or better price.

➢ If you take a taxi without a meter, negotiate your rate before you get in.

➢ Handicrafts are abundant in many Central and South American countries. Don't pass up the opportunity to visit craft workshops or stop on the road to watch a weaver at a handloom or an artisan create a design on pottery. Shop as close to the source as possible. You will get the best price and the artist will benefit directly.

➢ The export of pre-Columbian artifacts is prohibited in most countries.

Country Specialties & Tips

Argentina

Specialties: leather, shoes, antiques, ponchos, hand-tied rugs, blankets, jewelry, red onyx sculpture, baskets, and wool clothing.

• Bring cash or credit cards, not traveler's checks.

• In Buenos Aires, find the main shopping areas along Recoleta, Avenida Santa Fe, and Florida. Funky and fashionable shops are everywhere.

- Ask for discounts for cash and bargain in the leather shops in Buenos Aires as well as the artisan markets (*ferias*).

- For handicrafts, go to Mercado Nacional de Artesnaias Tradicionales Argentinas on Defensa 372, Artesanias Argentinas (ARAR) at Arenales 1239, San Pedro Nolasco de los Molinos at Sulta 1039, or AIDECA, an artisan association at Uruguay 263.

- On Sunday let mimes entertain you while you browse around Feria de San Telmo, the flea market on Plaza Dorrego from 10 A.M. to about 5 P.M. Find good antique shops nearby.

Bolivia

Specialties: fine traditional weavings, embroidery, textiles, ponchos, masks, Andean music cassettes, musical instruments, antique silver.

- Search the markets in La Paz for everything from regional handicrafts to ordinary goods.

- Bargain in Mercado Negro, in the area around Graneros, Maximilianos, and Buenos Aires avenues, for clothing and household things.

- Look for weaving in Sica Sica, a dusty village between La Paz and Oruro.

- In the southwest city of Oruro, buy Diablada masks, costumes, and other devilish paraphernalia in shops on Avenida La Paz.

- Shop the Sunday market in Tarabuco near Sucre. It's popular for tourist souvenirs, but you'll find colorful costumes, handmade weavings, and beautiful ponchos.

- If you need a remedy for an illness or seek protection from an evil spirit, check out Witches Market (Mercado de los Brujos) near Calles Santa Cruz and Linares. Find loads of street vendors and handicraft shops nearby filled with Bolivian weavings, silver antiques, and musical instruments.

Brazil

Specialties: gemstones, mineral specimens, fine jewelry, handcrafted leather, native musical instruments, and bikinis.

- Do not let your credit card out of your sight. Be alert for scams when exchanging money. Count your change. If you discover a mistake and the teller acknowledges the mistake, count your money again when the mistake is "corrected."

- Brazil is the place to buy amethyst. For jewelry and a wide variety of other natural gems and mineral specimens, H. Sterns has branches everywhere. But for equal reliability and great quality go to Amsterdam Sauer, a worldwide wholesaler with a retail location at Rua Garcia D'Avila, 105 in Rio de Janeiro.

- When bargaining for goods or accommodations use key Portuguese phrases: *"Pode fazer um melhor preco?"* ("Can you make a better price?"), *"Tem desconto?"* ("Is there a discount?").

- In Rio de Janeiro, shop for Indian handicrafts at Trem De Minas on Rua Cosme Velho 433-Loja D, the FUNAI Craft Shop, the Pé de Boi shop, and in the local market.

- Shop around the craft fairs on Sunday: Hippie Fair at Praça General Osório in Ipanema and Nordeste Fair at the Pavilhão de São Cristóvão. Find trinkets, cheap clothing, and cowboy hats.

- In São Paulo, hang out at the Sunday street fair at Liberdade in the Oriental district and with the crowds at Praça da República. Any weekend wander the art and craft fair in Embu near São Paulo.

- In Recife, check out the craft and gift shops in the renovated Casa da Cultura, a former prison.

- Climb the hills overlooking Recife to colonial Olinda, Brazil's first capital. Wander Rua Bernardo de Melo there until you get to Mercado da Ribeira with its art galleries and artisan shops.

- If you're in Amazonas to arrange a jungle expedition or a rain forest excursion, see the exhibitions in the Museu do Indio in Manaus. FUNAI runs an craft shop in the museum with indigenous items from the Tikuna and Wai Wai Indians. Near Teatro Amazonas, the opera house, find more crafts at Art-Com Souvenir. While you're there, pick up a few magic berries (*guaraná*).

Chile
Specialties: copper, leather, lapis lazuli, woven goods, baskets, ceramics, carved wood sculptures, woolen crafts, silverware, and wine.

- In Santiago, artisan markets (*ferias*) sell quality crafts. Check out the weekend craft market on Pío Nono in the Bellavista suburb.

- Craft stores and galleries in Santiago also offer a variety of goods. Visit Cooperativa Almacén Campesino at Purísima 303 in Bellavista, and try the shops in the gallery at Moneda 1025.

- Feria Artesanal La Merced is a well-stocked store for Easter Island carved wood, lapis, pottery, and copperware.

- In an old convent at Portugal 351, check out Claustr dell 900 for gift shops.

- Buy Andean music at Cassetería Altiplano in the Arteferia Santa Lucía, Alameda 510.

- Tour the wineries around Santiago and take home some Chilean wine for gifts. Try Vía Cousiío Macul and Vía Santa Carolina.

- Watch master potters in Pomaire, a dusty village near Melipilla, southwest of Santiago. Prices are great and worth the trek. While you're on the road to Melipilla, stop in at Vía Undurraga for more wine cellar visits.

- On the coast near Valparaiso head for the artisan market in Vía del Mar, a beach resort.

- Hop over to the village of Dalcahue on the island of Chiloé. The Sunday market, Feria Artesanal, is filled with crafts from local artisans and nearby islands. Find woolen goods, baskets, and woodwork.

Colombia

Specialties: gold, leather and suede jackets, handbags, pre-Columbian reproduction jewelry, copper, emeralds, and coffee.

- The streets in the cities can be dangerous especially at night or if you are alone. Leave your valuables at home, but carry your passport with you. Police tend to check documents. If you are stopped by a plain-clothesman claiming to be with the secret police, ask to see his credentials first.

- In Bogotá, visit the Museo del Oro, a great gold museum. Then, buy museum-quality jewelry reproductions from Galeria Cano y Accesorios Cano.

- Purchase artisan handicrafts at Artesania El Zipa.

- Browse the Sunday flea market, Los Toldos de San Pelayo, at Usaquen Park north of Bogotá.

- In Cali, find handicrafts at Asociación Mujeres Cabeza de Familia at Apartado Aereo 12-54.

Costa Rica

Specialties: banana leaf fiber products, ponchos, ceramics, jewelry, pre-Columbian reproductions, embroidery, basketry, rain forest products, and wooden bowls.

- In San José, find plenty of shops, but the bustling action is in Mercado Central from handicrafts to live fowl.

- Save your money for the crafts center in Sarchí, the place to buy crafts in Costa Rica.

- After you've walked the butterfly garden in Monteverde, head for the art galleries.

- Listen to reggae and buy handicrafts on the Caribbean coast in Puerto Viejo de Talamanca.

Cuba

Specialties: cigars, palm leaf dolls and hats, wood boxes, and guayabera shirts.

- U.S. dollars are widely used, but souvenirs and gifts are limited.

- Sunday is the best day to visit the artisan market on the Malecón near the Melia Cohiba Hotel in Havana.

- Find souvenirs at the street stalls around the cathedral in Old Havana.

Ecuador

Specialties: Panama hats, embroidery, tagua nut souvenirs, woolen and woven goods, Otavaleño ponchos, leather goods, musical instruments, and colorful wood birds.

- In Quito, wander around the shops on Calle Juan Leon Mera and stop in at Galería Latina for a wide range of Latin American crafts.

- Nearby, find tourist shops on Calle Amazonas. Look for the famous La Casa del Sombrero, the place to buy your Panama hat. A finely woven Panama hat can be rolled up and passed through a ring.

- On Sunday on the south end of Calle Amazonas, gaze at paintings and handicrafts in the market in El Ejido park.

- Roam the Indian markets in the villages of Otavalo and Cotacachi, about two hours from Quito for woolen and leather goods, rugs, and baskets. Bargain away for whatever you want.

- Visit Cotacachi and Ambato for leatherwork.

- Travel to San Antonio de Ibarra, a famous woodworking center in Ecuador, about twenty minutes north of Otavalo.

El Salvador

Specialties: ceramics, textiles, masks, colorful woodwork, embroidery, and baskets.

- Shop at Mercado Ex-Cuartel at the corner of 8a Avenida Norte in San Salvador.

- About five miles southwest of San Salvador on the Interamericana Highway, find Mercado Nacional de Artesanías for another selection of local handicrafts.

Guatemala

Specialties: textiles, huipiles *(embroidered blouses), woven clothes, dolls, embroidered t-shirts, weavings, masks, leather, wood carvings, and metalwork.*

- Exercise personal security precautions and do not travel alone at night.

- In Guatemala City, head over to Mercado Central, the Central Market. Then head up to the upper-level stalls for baskets, pottery, and textiles. Wander the entire market and the nearby street stalls. Most of the vendors are middlemen who buy from the country artisans.

- Catch any bus marked "Terminal" and check out the action around the Bus Terminal in Zone 4. From butchers to merchants hawking tropical birds and handicrafts, the scene at Terminal Market is worth the time.

- Drive about a half hour from Guatemala City to Antigua, the old colonial capital with cobblestone street. Find plenty of textiles and other native crafts in the central square on weekends, at the shops around town, and in the village of San Antionio Aguas Calientes. Find the market in Antigua at the bus terminal.

- Travel into the western highlands for the best prices and the most colorful markets. Check out the markets in all the villages you pass through, especially in Patzún and the lakeside towns around Lake Atitlán: Chichicastenango, Panajachel, Quezaltenango, Solalá. In many villages you'll find informal street bazaars. Have a look.

- Tuesday and Friday are market days in Solalá. Weave around the local crowds at Chichicastenango market every Sunday and Thursday.

- Always bargain in the markets. Ask for cash discounts in stores.

Haiti

Specialties: native folk art, voodoo drums, wood carvings, and fabric.

- Shop local markets in Port-au-Prince and the artisan shop on Rue 3.

- French is the official language, but English is widely spoken.

- Check out crafts at Gingerbread in Petionville (outside Port-au-Prince).

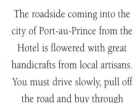

The roadside coming into the city of Port-au-Prince from the Hotel is flowered with great handicrafts from local artisans. You must drive slowly, pull off the road and buy through your window!

♦

*Gloria Delaney,
importer and wholesaler*

Honduras

Specialties: traditional musical instruments, basketry, ceramics, wood carvings, textiles, and leather.

- Buy arts and craft souvenirs in Valle de Angeles, about thirty minutes outside of Tegucigalpa.

- Have an inexpensive copy of your favorite dress or suit made at tailor shops in Tegucigalpa.

- Local artists display their paintings around Plaza Maràzan in the center of town.

- Find more handicrafted ethnic pieces at the Bridge entrance to the public market in Tegucigalpa.

Mexico

Specialties: huipiles *and woven goods, silver,* retablos, *onyx carvings, tin work, pottery, masks, piñatas, silver jewelry, beaded masks,* Dìa de los Muertos *(Day of the Dead) craft figures, wood carvings, and ceramic tiles* (azulejo *Talavera*).

- Mexico is diverse and vast with an indigenous craft culture to match. Just about anything you want is in Mexico City at the markets and the retail stores. But if you want the best buys and a taste of local culture, get out of town. Different states offer distinct crafts so plan your excursions to match your desires.

- In Mexico City, stop in at Asociación Mexicana de Arte y Cultura Popular (AMACUP) on Río Amazonas 17 Colonia Cuauntemoc and Solidaridad Artesanal Mexicana at Tabasco 262-101 to purchase handicrafts.

- Buy silver at the silver market in the Zona Rosa in Mexico City.

- Loaded with artists and expatriates, San Miguel de Allende is fun to visit and a charming city for shopping, though a bit touristy. Start at Casa de Sierra Nevada on Calle Hospicio. Wander around Calle Canal and Calle Umarán.

- In the state of Guanajuato, find ceramics, papier-mâché, tinware, wall hangings, and wooden horses. Nearby in Dolores Hidalgo buy the famous Talvera tiles on Calle Puebla. Stop in at the Vazquez factory and showroom to watch artists paint tiles. Buy tiles, dishes, and accessories at Talavera San Gabriel, a factory and showroom on Carretera Dolores.

- Be aware that most pottery in Mexico contains lead and should be used for decorative purpose only.

- Don't miss the street hawkers, exotic birds, snakes, and crafts around Cinco de Mayo, a pedestrian mall in Puebla. Shop for antiques in Plazo los Sapos and ceramics along 18 Poniente.

- In the state of Guerrero, look for masks, painted bark paintings, and silver jewelry.

- For handblown glass, burnished stoneware and ceramics, clay miniatures, tinware, leather, and brass, go to the state of Jalisco.

- Visit the state of Oaxaca for a magical, mystical tour, and plenty of crafts. Those colorful, carved wooden animals are carved here, and Dìa de los Muertos figures hang around too. Try the shops on Calle Alcalá. Fonart on Manuel Bravo 116 is the state craft source. Artesanías Teresita at Alcalá 401A sells the Oaxacan wood animals. Check out the strip of shops on Cinco de Mayo and the daily markets 20 Noviembre and Benito Juárez.

- For an amazing variety of crafts try ARIPO, an organization of traditional crafts from seven regions of Oaxaca, located on Garcia Vigil 809. They also have a outlet in Mexico City, Arte Indigena Oaxaqueño, at Londres 117 in the Zona Rosa.

- For high-quality Zapotec woven rugs and great chicken molé, stop at Artesanías Mendoza on Avenue Juárez No. 39 in Teotitlán del Valle Oaxaca. (Proprietress Emiliano Mendoza Martínez will show you her traditional and contemporary designs, then her sister Abigail Mendoza Ruiz will cook up lunch.)

- In the state of Chiapas in San Cristobal de las Casas, find weavings and other crafts at Na Bolom on Vincente Guerrero #33, Barrio del Cerrillo.

- San Cristobal de las Casas is remarkable for it's landscape as well as its crafts. While you're there, visit San Juan Chamula market, and do not miss its most ordinary, but extraordinarily spiritual church with hundreds of flickering candles. Nearby, stop in at San Jolobil Coop, museum, and store in Zinacontán Village.

- Pretend you're not gringo in the markets. Bargain as if you were a native.

- Buy Mexican mangos in the food markets; they're heaven sent.

Nicaragua
Specialties: cowboy boots and hats, hammocks, pottery, embroidery, and primitive paintings.

- Negotiate with the taxi drivers for the price of the trip before you go anywhere.

My travel companion and I were hiking in the Sierra Madres in northwest Mexico near the Tarahumara—an indigenous tribe who weave intricate pine needle and agave baskets. One day a mother-son team set up a blanket on a rock about fifty yards away from us and started to weave. I did not know what to make of this behavior. Eventually, we approached them, chose baskets, and asked the craftswoman her price. The amount was more than we had expected—similar, in fact, to shop prices in Creel. When we tried to bargain, she would not budge, and we felt uncomfortable asking for much less, knowing she was poor. In the end, we paid her price and were pleased with our purchases, but it was a unique experience for a low-income artisan not to apply pressure or bargain with us.

♦

*Nina Smith,
nonprofit executive director*

- Shop for crafts at the central market, Huembres, in Managua or on the first Saturday of every month at the Centro Cultural Managua.

- South of Managua, traders sell crafts from all over the country at the central market in Masaya.

- Do not buy turtle shell products. The U.S. and other Western countries have import restrictions on shells from endangered species.

Panama
Specialties: molas *and* guayabera *shirts.*

- Panama claims the longest shopping street in the world. Check it out from the cheap end at Avenida Central to the upscale Vía España.

- Buy crafts and museum shop products at Smithsonian Tropical Research Institute.

Paraguay
Specialties: Paraguayan lace (ñundutí) *and tea* (maté)*, ponchos, hammocks, and Indian handicrafts.*

- In Asunción, buy handmade crafts at Artesanía Viva, Artesanía Hílda, and in the open-air market at Plaza de los Héroes.

- Avoid products made with feathers as they may be subject to endangered species U.S. import regulations.

Peru
Specialties: textiles, embroidery, retablos, *reverse glass painting, ceramics, colonial antiques, musical instruments, painted wood furniture, carved gourds, pottery, alpaca sweaters, rugs, blankets, and scarves.*

- Lima has numerous markets, but the place to feel the native culture and buy indigenous handicrafts is in the Indian markets in other parts of the country like Cuzco, Pisac, Ayacucho, Huancayo, and Arequipa.

- For an overview and wide selection of indigenous crafts available in Lima, go to the north side of Avenido de la Marina for the Indian Artisan Market. But shop carefully because the prices and quality vary.

- Wander Lima's main market for almost anything. It's on the corner of Ayacucho and Ucayali.

- If you're in the mood for more westernized shopping, head over to Centro de Comercial on Camino Real.

- Better stores for alpaca and upscale arts and crafts are in the Miraflores and San Isidro suburbs. Try Proart on Berlin 1491 in Miraflores.

- Visit the showroom of Makiiwan on Navarra 174, Higuereta for pottery and special ceramic art pieces.

- For funky crafts and colonial antiques, go to Barranco. Antigüedades Antiques on Domeyer 109 Esquina Bajada de Baños is a reliable source for quality antiques and artifacts— silver, colonial wood furniture, etc. Vivian and Jaime Liébana are proprietors. If you ask and you're lucky, you might get to see their private collection.

- In Cuzco, buy Indian crafts on Plaza San Blas and the streets around it. In the evening scout around under the arches of Plaza de Armas and Regocijo. The best quality alpaca scarves are in the shops there, but they're pricey compared to the stuff hawked on the square. Visit the Mercado Central for a bit of local color, produce, and lots of hanging meat carcasses.

When we were importers we ordered several hundred of those great little wood and gesso nativity *retablos* from the artisans in Peru. You know the kind with the lower level full of Mary, Joseph, the Christ child and several sheep and cows and the top level with angels and cherubs. In all of our shipments, the child was unaccountably missing. I suppose they forgot to glue him in or they put wings on him and made more cherubs. Anyway, when I protested I got back an amazing grace sort of answer. Oh, they said, "He's not missing. He is in your heart."

♦

*Clare Brett Smith,
nonprofit president*

Uruguay

Specialties: mineral specimens, gemstones, jewelry, leather bags, and shoes.

- In Montevideo, shop for crafts at Manos del Uruguay with branches at San José 1111 and Reconquista 602, and at Mercado de los Artesanos on Plaza Cagancha and at Bartolomé Mitre 1367.

- If you are a rock hound, visit Hector Polleri Mullin on Sarandi 556 in Montevideo. He sells amethyst, agates, citrine, quartz, and other specimens at reasonable prices and reliable quality.

- Hang out with the young crowd and bargain a bit at the crafts market on Plaza Cagancha.

- In Colonia, browse the Sunday market at Plaza Mayor.

- After you check out the beaches and mansions in Punta del Este, shop at Feria Artesanal at Plaza Artigas and the Manos del Uruguay branch stores.

Venezuela

Specialties: shoes, women's clothes, gold jewelry, and indigenous crafts from Amazonas Indian tribes.

- Stroll and shop along the Boulevard de Sabana Grande in Caracas.

- Visit Ateneo de Caracas, a cultural center in new Caracas with an art gallery, theater, concert hall, cinema, bookstore, and café.

- In Caracas, workshops will custom design jewelry for you. Ask for recommendations in the jewelry stores in town.

- In Puerto Ayachucho, the capital of Amazonas State, view the exhibits at Museo Ethnológico for an overview of Indian culture in the region. Then, seek out their crafts at Mercado Indígena, a Sunday-to-Thursday market on the square. Find special pieces at the local handicraft shops, Bazar Corotería La Colmena and Artesanías Amazonas.

NORTH AMERICA

What's great about this country is that America
started the tradition where the richest
consumers buy essentially the same
things as the poorest.

—*Andy Warhol*

———

"The Frenchies are coming," a friend announced.
"Who?" I asked.
"My French cousins from the south of France. They
come here a couple of times a year just to go shopping in
New York City. They think the prices are really cheap."

Indeed, Americans and the French are not the only consumers looking for bargains. I have friends in Japan and
England who say the same thing: "Your prices are so good."
We have an abundance many find appealing. If as Napoleon
suggested Britain is a nation of shopkeepers, then America is
a nation of shoppers, and the rest of the world wants to join us.

In *America: A User's Guide*, Simon Hoggart writes,
"Americans are fascinated by their own love of shopping.
This does not make them unique. It's just that they have
more to buy than most other people on the planet. And it's
also an affirmation of faith in their country, its prosperity,
and limitless bounty. They have shops the way that lesser
countries have statues."

Shops, department stores, outlet malls, and more. In this
land of opportunity, we have it all. But Americans also love
to discover unique places, mix culture and art, history and
shopping, and we love to forage along the way. Stopping at

historic sites, fairs and festivals, museum stores, and places off the beaten track make shopping fun on the road. Include them in your travels and enjoy the search.

Fairs & Festivals

Once or twice a year, my favorite cultural shopping trek—to New Mexico—felt as exotic as any foreign jaunt. My buyers and I would fly into Albuquerque, rent a car, shop the historic districts, and make the rounds of pueblos like Santa Clara, Acoma, Zuni, and San Ildefonso. Eventually, we'd get to Santa Fe, sometimes via the old Turquoise Trail through the town of Madrid where every shop is a must stop. This route is slower than the highway, but the scenery and the one-street town of Madrid (pronounced Ma' drid) is worth the extra time. After Santa Fe we'd make our way north to Taos for local arts and crafts, detouring through Chimayo—the heart of Hispanic culture in New Mexico—to purchase traditional weavings and wood carvings.

As their license plates suggest, New Mexico is indeed a land of enchantment—360 degree vistas, odd rock formations, juniper and piñon forests, mountains and desert, a crossroads of history and culture, and a place whose light inspired artists and writers such as Georgia O'Keeffe and D. H. Lawrence. With shops, galleries, fairs, museums, pueblos, native cooperatives, and street markets, it's a cultural shopper's dream and one that offers a blend of histo-

> It's something that's in the air.
> The sky is different, the stars are different,
> the wind is different.
>
> ◆
>
> *Georgia O'Keeffe*

ry and tradition. Here the lines between commerce and culture blur.

Boasting the oldest seat of government in the U.S., around 1610, Santa Fe is a historic center and a cultural mix of Anglo, Indian, and Hispanic heritage. Under the portals of the seventeenth-century Palace of the Governors and around the plaza, almost any day, Native Americans spread out blankets and settle in for the day to hawk rugs, beads, pottery, and turquoise jewelry. During high tourist season two markets raise the commercial level of activity here along with the prices: Spanish Market in July and Indian Market in August.

Indian Market is a well-known collectors' market for Native American crafts and jewelry, and this is the time when artisans have their largest selection. New Mexico overflows with alternative buying adventures, but other cultural shopping opportunities abound throughout North America: craft fairs, art festivals, museums, zoos, aquariums, and performing arts centers. All offer "edutainment"—that unique blend of education, culture, and shopping.

General Tips

➤ In the U.S. and Canada, most states have local or regional art and craft fairs, and many have events and activities for collectors.

➤ Contact state visitor bureaus or a city's Chamber of Commerce. Request free

I like shopping when I don't need anything in particular and can visit arty, funky places, and only buy if I see something I can't live without. It's the process, not the goal that is important.

♦

Claudia Minnicozzi, artist

223

brochures and information on local events and museums. Most states also have web sites.

➤ Check local papers, magazines, or consult hotel concierges for events happening while you're in town.

➤ While prices are set, many artists are willing to negotiate. Try asking for the best price or bargaining if you are buying several pieces, but don't insult the artist by offering an unreasonable amount.

➤ If you loved the fair and plan to return again, book your hotel before you leave. Hotels at many popular destinations fill up quickly, and you will lock in the price of your room for a year.

➤ Stop along your route to investigate shops in nearby villages and towns. You may discover unique stores and antique treasures away from the main tourist areas.

➤ Numerous museum and craft organizations sponsor high-end, juried craft shows in different cities. Featured artists sell decorative and functional art including fiber arts, jewelry, ceramics, glass, and more. Contact the American Craft Council (ACC phone: 1-800-836-3470) for locations and dates of the ACC Craft Markets open to the public in various cities around the U.S.

> When buying anything hand-made from its maker, ask about the process and materials and understand pertinent traditions. Don't belittle the craftsman if the merchandise isn't for you.
>
> ◆
>
> *Lloyd Herman,*
> *art exhibit consultant*

Museum Stores &
Cultural Outings

On one of my first buying trips in California, I happened into a kite store to scout the competition and look for trends and new sources. I noticed colorful, handmade kites that were quite a bit more expensive than we were used to selling at the National Air & Space Museum Shop, but I was intrigued with the quality and uniqueness. So, I phoned

Look till you drop, then shop.

♦

Susan Stamberg,
as heard on Museum Gift
Shops, NPR News

the maker and placed an order, which sold out once it hit the shop. I reordered the kites many times after that. On one occasion when I called in a reorder, the craft person thanked me and said, "You've taken us off welfare."

Another time we were buying for a special exhibit shop for a related show on the Hispanic culture in New Mexico. We met with loggers who, to pass the down time in the off-season, whittled cultural folk toys and objects. We left them what was for us a small purchase order totaling $1,000. They were thrilled to have the work and enough money to buy necessities that would help carry them through the season.

To contribute positively to someone's life is an obvious reward for a museum store buyer, and it's also pleasant to hear customers say, "I love shopping at museum stores." Indeed, spending money at a cultural or educational institution has a feel-good quality for any shopper. Not only are you helping to fund and maintain the educational mission of an organization, but, hey, you get a memento of your visit.

A favorite *Calvin and Hobbes* cartoon shows Calvin pointing out that the museum has a gift shop, then pleading with his mom to buy him dinosaur memorabilia. When she says he has enough dinosaur stuff, he counters with, "But, Mom, it's all educational. You want me to learn, don't you?"

In the next frame, clad in a dinosaur hat, his arms laden with dinosaur toys, Calvin emerges triumphantly from the museum.

"Boy, she fell for *that* one," Hobbes says. Calvin agrees.

"I'll say! I wonder if we can get any Batman junk this way."

In a different cartoon in *The New Yorker,* two women discuss the advantages of one museum store over another: "For the big, important things, it's the Met and the Modern, of course—but the Whitney is great for stocking stuffers."

When shopping cultural institutions becomes mainstream in the comics, it's hardly a fearless task to shop these venues anymore—unless you count braving the crowds at blockbuster shows to buy your reproduction van Gogh mouse pad or Rodin "thinker pasta." Still, mixed in with souvenir mugs, key chains, and ubiquitous t-shirts are reproductions and adaptations worth owning and missions worth supporting.

So, whether you buy a t-shirt, plush dinosaurs, crafts, or a reproduction of the Hope Diamond, you might make an artisan happy, support research, or help subsidize an organization. And I have often thought that for every 1,000 toy gyroscopes or freeze-dried ice cream packs we sold to a child, there was a budding scientist or astronaut who might make a difference.

General Tips

➤ Every state has multiple museums and other cultural nonprofits, most of which have at least a kiosk, if not a full-fledged retail operation. Patronize them. The sales support the chartered mission and educational goals of the organization.

➤ Ask to be put on the mailing list of those institutions with catalogs. If you loved the museum, you'll have the opportunity to purchase and contribute more even if you live out of state.

> I usually avoid malls, but one holiday season I was determined to make it easier so I decided to buy all the gifts in one store. It was one of those museum stores, and I was actually able to find everyone gifts within two hours.
>
> ◆
>
> *Carol Newmeyer, sculptor and jewelry artist*

➤ Before you visit a different area, check the web site or call the local tourist bureau to request a guidebook.

➤ If you travel with children and want to limit their purchases, give them a budget for their own souvenirs before they go into the museum store. Buy related books and art material in the museum shops which are usually well-equipped with pencils, crayons, art supplies, exhibit-related traveling games, or activity kits. Discuss the exhibits with your children and encourage them to research what interests them. Have children keep a journal of or draw what they saw.

> I love museum shopping and look upon it much as the joy of a museum.
>
> ◆
>
> *Barbara Silverstein, jewelry designer and artist*

➤ If your family separates to
follow their individual interests, use the museum shop
as a meeting place later.
Shop while you wait for
each other.

➤ Avoid museum store crowds
by shopping between 10:00
and 11:00 A.M. when most
museums first open or in the
evenings between 5:30 and
7:00 P.M. if the museum stays open late.

➤ If you hate the commercialization of art, but love museums,
at least buy the postcards—great inexpensive souvenirs
especially if you've forgotten your camera.

➤ Every purchase, no matter how small, increases revenues.

Country Specialties & Tips

CANADA

*Specialties: Inuit crafts, smoked and fresh salmon (packaged to take
home), maple syrup, wood and stone carvings, contemporary art and
crafts, leatherwork, British Columbian jade, Hudson Bay blankets and
coats, outdoor clothes, and camping supplies.*

Toronto & Ontario
• Toronto and its neighborhoods are filled with ethnic shopping
opportunity. Stroll around Chinatown, Cabbagetown (Irish),
Danforth (Greek), Little India, Corso Italia; all offer specialized
shops and distinctive atmosphere.

• Once the haunt for the counterculture, the Yorkville area now
sports upscale boutiques, art galleries, outdoor cafés, and other

hot spots. For Inuit art, check out Inuit Gallery on Prince Arthur Avenue. Browse through Hazelton Lane Shopping Centre for expensive merchandise in exclusive boutiques.

- "Don't just stand there, buy something," beckons the sign at Honest Ed's store at the corner of Markham and Bloor streets. For good, cheap buys on a variety of clothing and household items stand in line at Honest Ed's. Then browse around the area for specialized galleries, bookstores, and boutiques.

- After touring museum exhibitions, wander into the Gallery Shop at the Art Gallery of Ontario on Dundas Street West, the Gardiner Shop at the Gardiner Museum of Ceramic Art and the Royal Ontario Musuem Shop, both on Queen's Park.

- Around Queen Quay's terminal at the Harbourfront, look for renovated warehouses with more shops and visit the Power Plant to view contemporary art. Tuesday through Sunday hunt for junk or collectibles at the Antique Market shops along the pier. On Sunday the market extends outdoors.

- Also on Sunday, check out the flea market at St. Lawrence Market, 92 Front Street East. For more lively fare, bargain at Kennsington Market. On weekends try Dr. Flea's Highway 27 & Albion Flea Market for collectibles, antiques, and new merchandise. From Toronto take Highway 401 to Dixon Road to Highway 27 North and look for the 35-foot-tall flea on the roof of the building.

- Don't miss the historical sites, most of which have shops attached. Watch craft skills of olden days at Black Creek Pioneer Village and bring home baked goods.

- In May attend the Toronto International Powwow and buy Native Indian crafts. At the Canadian National Exhibition in August participate in events, listen to music, watch craft demonstrations, and purchase related festival merchandise. Throughout the summer join in the other fairs and festivals and pick up souvenirs from music CDs to crafts.

- For great outdoor gear try Tilley Endurables at 900 Don Mills Road or at the Queen Quay branch. Rent a tent or buy your camping and hiking supplies in Europe Bound at 49 Front Street. Comparison shop nearby at Trailhead (41 Front Street) and Mountain Equipment Coop (61 Front Street).

Montreal, Quebec

- Vieux Montréal, Old Montreal, is the place to wander narrow cobblestone streets and shop the atmosphere.

- To purchase collectible stone carvings try Galerie Yves Laroche at 4 Rue Saint Paul Est.

- Visit the farmer's market at 350 Rue Saint Paul Est in the Bonsecours Market building. Buy maple syrup from the farmers at Atwater Market on Avenue Atwater at the Lachine Canal.

- Visit Vieux-Port, the old Port waterside district. Look for the handicraft center at Quai Jacques Cartier.

- Mingle with the locals and check out the funky shops along Boulevard Saint Laurent and the Plateau area. If you're looking for offbeat street fashions, try the secondhand shops along Avenue du Mont Royal to Boulevard Saint Laurent. Find upscale boutiques on upper Saint Laurent and to the south on Rue Laurier. North of the Plateau region wander around Jean Talon Market in the Italian district.

- For Inuit carvings and prints try the Canadian Guild of Crafts at 2025 Rue Peel.

- In the winter escape to Montreal's vast underground shopping and entertainment in the city center connected by the Métro—without ever going outside.

- Don't miss the Montreal Jazz Festival around late June or early July for hot music buys.

- On Brossard check out Super Mercado, a great place to shop for just about everything Thursday through Sunday.

- For action-packed Sunday shopping scrounge around Marché aux Puces de Saint Eustache, just north of Montreal on Road 640 West. For a broad array of crafts, antiques, furniture, stamps, coins, and other collectibles visit on quieter days. This market is open Thursday through Sunday.

- Travel through the eastern townships, L'Estrie, stopping in the villages for antique shops, art galleries, craft shops, and maple syrup.

Quebec City, Quebec

- Wander around the old, historic walled city.

- Find galleries and stores around Place Royale. Northwest of Place Royale on Rue Saint Paul look for numerous antique shops.

- Along the waterfront on Rue Saint André in Old Lower Town, wander the Farmer's Market. But buy your maple syrup at JA Moisan Epicier, North America's oldest grocery store.

- Practice your French as you shop.

St. John's, Newfoundland

- Wind your way around the alleys and streets of England's first overseas colony and North America's oldest city.

- For crafts don't miss the Newfoundland & Labrador craft fair in July, September, and November in the St. John's Memorial Stadium. For folk music try the Provincial Folk Festival in the beginning of August at Bannerman Park.

Halifax, Nova Scotia

- Wander the restored, historic central district with boutiques and restaurants.

- Visit Brewery Market on the waterfront in Keith's Brewery building at 1489 Hollis Street. Stop in at the farmer's market there on Friday and Saturday in the summer.

- Micmac Heritage Gallery, in the Barrington Place Shops, sells traditional crafts, such as porcupine quillwork and basketry, and contemporary art by Native artisans.

Fredericton, New Brunswick

- Fredericton, the province's capital on the Saint John River, offers a bit of Micmac Indian history, handicrafts, pewtersmithing, and salmon fishing.

- Tour Aitkens Pewter at 81 Regent Street to watch pewtersmiths at work.

- Visit Boyce Farmer's Market on George Street for crafts and home-made desserts among other things.

- On the weekend before Labor Day attend the Handicraft Show at Mactaquac Park.

- Drive about forty-five minutes from Fredericton to the artist village of Gagetown. Look for Loomcrofters, a weaving studio where you can observe the process and purchase scarves, ties, tartans and other woven goods. The town is home to pottery studios and galleries as well.

Vancouver and Victoria, British Columbia

- With the ocean on one side and the mountains on the other, Vancouver is a scenic shopping city and easy to maneuver.

- Downtown shopping is centered around Robson Square and on Robson Street with a variety of ethnic stores and designer shops.

- Visit the renovated, Victorian Gastown area for galleries, street vendors, and boutiques along with street performers.

- Check out the various museums and their shops in Vancouver: Vancouver Art Gallery at 750 Hornby Street, University of British Columbia Botanical Gardens at 6804 S.W. Marine Drive, Science World at 1455 Quebec Street, Bookmark (the Library store) on 350 W. Georgia Street, and the Vancouver Aquarium.

- Look for the specialty shops at the Lonsdale Quay Market on the North Shore.

- On July 1st join the fun at the Vancouver Folk Festival.

- For quality Northwest Coast Native Indian crafts—carvings, masks, prints, and Cowichan sweaters—stop in at the gift shop at the Vancouver Museums and Planetarium at 1100 Chestnut Street, Images for a Canadian Heritage and Hill's Indian Crafts at 164 and 165 Water Street, respectively. Farther up at 345 Water Street the Inuit Gallery sells carvings, prints, tapestries, jewelry, and sculpture. Leona Lattimer at 1590 West 2nd Avenue specializes in Northwest Coast Indian art, does appraisals, and repairs argillite, a black metamorphic stone used in Indian carvings. Marion Scott Gallery at 671 Howe Street is another reliable source.

> Because I have a "good eye," I enjoy shopping as a creative expression. I don't necessarily have to buy to enjoy the experience.
>
> ♦
>
> *Wendy Wigtail, redecorator*

- For more information on native jewelry and crafts contact the Indian Arts and Crafts Society of B.C. at 540 Burrard Street.

- On Vancouver Island, Victoria is very British and touristy but worth a look, if only for the fabulous Arts of the Raven Gallery at 1015 Douglas Street.

UNITED STATES

Walk any street in any city or country town and you'll find stores worth exploring. If you are visiting the U.S. for the first time, you'll find a staggering amount of consumer goods in traditional department stores, at shopping malls, thrift shops, factory outlets, and at almost any venue you can imagine—from zoo and museum stores to folk festivals and performing arts centers. And don't miss any opportunity to wander into an American supermarket or hardware store. With so much to buy everywhere, I've divided the U.S. into regions with highlights from my favorite cities and states.

Specialties: contemporary and traditional crafts, regional preserves, maple syrup, beers and wines, art, silver, antiques, ethnic folk toys and crafts, Shaker furniture, Amish quilts, Native American crafts, cowboy accessories, electronic gadgetry, and Americana souvenirs.

NORTHEAST & MID-ATLANTIC

Massachusetts

- Boston is loaded with great museums for adults and kids. All of them have well-stocked museum shops.

- Museum of Fine Arts Boston store at 465 Huntington has a large book selection and related museum adaptations and reproductions of jewelry, ceramics, textiles, glass, posters, and prints.

- The shop at the Museum of Science is filled with educational toys, games, science kits, dinosaur models, and souvenirs. On Museum Wharf, look for The Computer Museum and the Children's Museum shops, which appeal to children and sell recycled material to create your own products.

- Touristy but fun, Faneuil Hall Marketplace with Quincy Market offers plenty of shops on the waterfront.

- Newbury Street has upscale boutiques and intriguing stores and cafés. Visit the Society of Arts and Crafts at 175 Newbury Street for quality ceramics, leather, weaving, and other craft items.

- No trip to Boston would be complete without at least a look at the famous Filene's Basement at Downtown Crossing, 426 Washington Street, for bargains on clothing and accessories.

- Drive over to Cambridge for college town shopping, music and book stores, and more. Don't miss Harvard Collections with classy reproductions, and stop in at the Cambridge Artist's Cooperative in Harvard Square.

- Cape Cod, Nantucket, and Martha's Vineyard are nearby shopping and tourist getaways that sport requisite souvenir t-shirts as well as camping and athletic gear, and local contemporary crafts such as kites, jewelry, and ceramics.

> ——— ✦ ✦ ———
>
> Jamaica Plain is a fun neighborhood in Boston, commuting distance by MBTA, quaint Victorian B & Bs, wonderful restaurants and hip stores like Bella Luna and Rhythm and Muse, a book and music store cafe.
>
> ◆
>
> *Bette Ann Libby,*
> *artist and ceramist*

- Re-created as a 1830s New England town, Old Sturbridge Village demonstrates and sells crafts of the period.

- Throughout the Berkshires in western Massachusetts, you'll find numerous college towns, historic villages, and cultural areas with great scenery and fun shopping. If you're driving through, stop at Stockbridge, Lenox, Williamstown, Amherst, and Deerfield.

Vermont

- Vermont is a scenic rural treasure filled with history, green mountains, and local crafts. Whether you ski, hike, canoe, mountain bike, or drive, you'll discover great shopping throughout the state.

- Watch maple sugaring and buy a jug of syrup anywhere you see a road sign. But be aware that tourist prices are higher than in many supermarkets.

- Buy pottery at the Bennington factory in southern Vermont.

- In northern Vermont find good shopping, atmosphere, and talented craftspeople in Burlington, Waitsfield, and Warren.

New York City

- This is the city for everything, almost anytime, day or night.

- Of course, stroll down Fifth Avenue for brand-name specialty stores, bookstores, and more. Find galleries galore and upscale boutiques on Madison Avenue.

- My favorite store is Felissimo's on West 57th near Fifth Avenue for a California/Japanese Zen atmosphere, unique presentation, and merchandise you can't resist.

- Don't miss the department stores, especially Macy's and Bloomingdale's.

- Search museum stores for the best in reproductions, adaptations, and unique gifts: Museum of Modern Art (MoMA), Brooklyn Museum of Art, The Metropolitan Museum of Art and its branch at Rockefeller Center, The Guggenheim Museum and its branch in Soho, American Museum of Natural History, Whitney Museum of American Art, The Jewish Museum, American Craft Museum, The Asia Society, Museum for African Art, The Big Apple Circus, the Metropolitan Opera Guild at Lincoln Center, Pierpont Morgan Library, and Cooper-Hewitt National Design Museum are just a few of the many in NYC.

> ★ ★ ★
>
> For used books, The Strand is a must. Visit the basement for review copies of the latest releases. Be careful though—you could spend your whole day searching through the miles and miles of books that line the walls of this New York treasure.
>
> ◆
>
> *Lisa Bach, editor*

- Wander different neighborhoods and soak up the local culture along with the shopping: Chelsea, SoHo, Greenwich Village, Tribeca, and the Upper West Side.

- Stroll around the ethnic neighborhoods of Chinatown, Little Italy, Harlem, and the Lower East Side. Check out the street stalls along 125th Street in Harlem. Bargain (especially with cash) at the shops and pushcarts on Orchard and Delancey streets on the Lower East Side. For discounts, get a coupon book from the Orchard Street Bargain district office at 261 Broome Street. To fortify you while you shop, don't miss the kosher corned beef sandwich at Katz's Deli on the corner of Houston and Ludlow streets.

- Discover the stores at renovated Grand Central Station for a grand old time.

- Times Square's recent face-lift makes shopping for American pop culture icons like Mickey Mouse and others a fun, crowd-packed outing. Watch your bags.

- Visit the New York Botanical Garden in the Bronx and find an array of specialized garden accessories, gifts, and books in their retail store.

- Climb the WWII aircraft carrier at the Intrepid Sea, Air & Space Museum on the waterfront. The gift store sells replicas and souvenirs.

- Check out Wall Street and its array of narrow shopping streets. While you're down on that end of town, visit the National Museum of the American Indian and Museum of Jewish Heritage museum shops; then relax around Battery Park for the best view of Ellis Island and the Statue of Liberty. Hop a ferry to the Statue and buy a replica there.

Philadelphia
- Philadelphia offers historic sites, museums, neighborhood shopping opportunities, and great Philly cheese steak sandwiches. Buy one at Jim's, Pat's, or Joe's downtown.

- Shop along Market Street and in Reading Terminal Market where you can snack on the best chocolate cookies or purchase a tin.

- Tuesday through Saturday wander the Italian Market, a huge outdoor market in South Philadelphia.

- Find museum stores for kids at Franklin Institute and the Academy of Natural Sciences Museum and adult shops at Philadelphia Museum of Art and the University of Pennsylvania Museum of Archaeology and Anthropology.

- Don't forget your replica Liberty Bell at Independence Hall.

- Visit nearby Pennsylvania Dutch Country, Hershey Park, Gettysburg, and Valley Forge.

- Garden shows abound. Philadelphia boasts the best, but look for shows in New York and Washington, D.C., as well.

Washington, D.C.
- The Smithsonian Institution museums and the many others in the

city could take a lifetime to get through, and they all have shops. Pick a topic and you'll find a museum here. These museum stores also have a superb and extensive book selection.

- My favorite museum stores in the area: The Phillips Collection, Hirshhorn Museum & Sculpture Garden, Corcoran Gallery of Art, and the Renwick Gallery for modern design and contemporary crafts; the National Air & Space Museum for kites and flying toys, models, and science stuff; the National Museum of Natural History for dinosaur things, rocks and minerals, great jewelry and ethnic crafts; the National Museum of American History for educational toys, music CDs, popular culture and Americana souvenirs, and a wide selection of books; Sackler Gallery for Asian products and reproductions; National Museum of African Art for crafts and jewelry: the Textile Museum for scarves, ties, and superb one-of-a kind textiles; and the Building Museum for architectural-designed goods. The National Gallery of Art stands alone for fine art reproductions.

- The Smithsonian's Women's Committee hosts a juried American Craft Show for a few days in April at the Building Museum.

- Don't miss the Smithsonian Festival of American Folklife held annually late June and early July. Each year the festival features a region in the U.S. and folk life in another country. You'll find demonstrations, music, crafts, and more.

- Shopping neighborhoods include: Adams Morgan and Tacoma Park for hip and funky stores, Capitol Hill for Eastern Market craft and flea market finds on Saturday, Georgetown for upscale boutiques and trendy stores, 7th Street for art galleries, and Dupont Circle for gift shops and art galleries.

- A few of my favorite stores and galleries: Politics and Prose Bookstore on Connecticut Avenue, Travel Books and Language Center on Wisconsin Avenue, the Phoenix Gallery on Wisconsin Avenue in Georgetown, Robert Brown Contemporary Art on R Street, Zenith Gallery on 7th Street, and Sansar on Bethesda Avenue in nearby Bethesda, Maryland.

- Downtown near the MCI Center, the Discovery Channel has a flagship store filled with museum exhibits and educational museum store merchandise.

- A tourist arrival and departure point, renovated Union Station has worthwhile shopping and a comfortable environment.

- Visit nearby Bethesda, Maryland, for fun stores, more restaurants than almost anywhere else, less tourists, and a laid-back atmosphere close to Washington.

THE SOUTH

- Wander the states south of the Mason-Dixon line where the shopping venues change with the accents. You'll find hospitality, beauty, Civil War history, highland crafts, a music heartland, and diverse cuisine.

- In North Carolina's Great Smokey Mountains, visit the Museum of the Cherokee Indian and the Qualla Arts & Crafts shop for Indian handicrafts. Ignore the tacky souvenirs elsewhere. Wander High Point, North Carolina, for furniture.

- Visit Charleston, South Carolina's historic district, and Hilton Head's upscale shops.

- Atlanta boasts underground shopping and antique malls. Check out the Lakewood Antiques Market at 2000 Lakewood Way for antiques and collectibles. Stop in at the ACC Craft Fair in mid-March.

- In Florida, shop Miami Beach's young and hip Coconut Grove and the Art Deco district. Fort Lauderdale around Las Olas Boulevard has trendy boutiques and galleries as well as partying college students.

- Find upscale designer shops in Palm Beach, and wander around Boca Raton's Mizner Park. The Morikami Museum in Delray Beach is worth the trip and has a small store with unique Japanese paper crafts and ceramics. The shops at the Kennedy Space Center on Merritt Island and the National Museum of Naval Aviation in Pensacola are a kid's dream. Spend a weekend on a one-stop shopping spree at Miami Beach Convention Center's Indoor Flea Market, held three time a year usually in March, June, and December.

- Big and flashy with oil wells, the Dallas Cowboys, the Alamo, and more, Texas also boasts fine museums in Dallas, Fort Worth, and Houston and fun shopping in San Antonio. Check out the shops in the Dallas Museum of Art, the Amon Carter Museum, and the Kimbell Art Museum in Fort Worth, the Museum of Fine Arts Houston, and the superb Menil Collection Bookstore in Houston.

- Shop while you party in New Orleans. Anytime will do, but for endless (or excessive) fun and games, visit during New Year's Eve, Carnival, or Mardi Gras. Wander the French Quarter and let the buskers entertain you while you look at the local street art. Stock up on hot sauces, kitchen supplies, and cookbooks at the open-air Farmer's Market on Ursulines Avenue. Head for the French Market Community Flea Market, which began operating in 1791, to buy your Mardi Gras masks and preserved alligator heads.

MIDWEST

- The windy but friendly city of Chicago is a great for food, museums, music, and shopping.

- Wander up and down Michigan Avenue, the "Magnificent Mile" of stores.

In the Sarasota area of Florida, I shop at the Ellenton Mall and St. Armand's Circle on Long Boat Key. St. Armand's Circle has the higher-end stores and boutiques. Ellenton (north of Sarasota) is an enormous complex of outlet stores. You can find almost any brand of clothing (Saks, Donna Karan, Carol Little, Geoffrey Beene, Ann Taylor, etc.), china (Mikasa, Lenox), etc. Nothing "craftsy" or unusual—but some good deals. There's also a flea market in Bradenton (also north of Sarasota) that is open weekends. It's fun but crowded.

◆

Betty Weiner, mother

- Museums are everywhere, and their shops have a range of tacky to high-end merchandise. The Art Institute of Chicago has a top-quality collection and a shop to match. Look for fine art, jewelry, textile, and ceramic reproductions along with an extensive selection of art books. Find good ethnic crafts at The Field Museum, toys and souvenirs at the Museum of Science and Industry, and plush animals at the Brookfield Zoo and the Lincoln Park Zoological Society.

- Stroll around neighborhood shopping areas: Gold Coast, Old Town, Lincoln Park, Andersonville, the West Side ethnic areas west of the Loop, the South Side, Chinatown, and the Hyde Park area with the University of Chicago.

- Drive to the suburb of Evanston for a relaxed shopping atmosphere,

Northwestern University, and a few good retro shops.

- Check out the Ashland Avenue Swap-O-Rama on 4100 South Ashland Avenue near White Sox Park for new and used merchandise.

- Look for antiques, toys, collectibles, clothing, and Mexican and African crafts at New Maxwell Street Market on Canal and Roosevelt streets, between Depot Place and Taylor Street. Arrive early for the best finds.

- The Navy Pier, an amusement park and meeting center on Lake Michigan, has tourist shopping and the Chicago Children's Museum nearby.

- Pick up designer crafts at the ACC Craft Fair, usually the last weekend in April.

SOUTHWEST

New Mexico

- Visit the Indian Pueblo Cultural Center at 2401 12th Street, N.W., in Albuquerque for an overview of traditional Native American crafts. Prices tend to be higher here than at the pueblos out of town.

- New Mexico has nineteen Native American communities, eight of which are located near Santa Fe. These communities are Pueblo Indian tribes, and they are referred to as Pueblos. Make time to shop at specific ones and respect their individual customs, which are usually posted. You'll find pottery, weavings, and a variety of other handicrafts. Try Acoma for paintings and white pottery, Zuni for jewelry, San Ildefonso for pottery and clay wash paintings, and Jemez, Santa Clara, and San Juan for pottery.

> She never did decide. She did develop a terrific hankering for a crucifix though. And she bought one from a Santa Fe gift shop during a trip the little family made out West during the Great Depression. Like so many Americasn, she was trying to construct a life that made sense from things she found in gift shops.
>
> ◆
>
> *Kurt Vonnegut,*
> *Slaughterhouse-Five*

- Go slow in Santa Fe, which is 7,000 feet above sea level. It may take you about forty-eight hours to adapt to this high altitude. Avoid alcohol on the first day. One drink is equivalent to three at sea level.

- The sun shines about 300 days a year in Santa Fe. Wear sunglasses, a hat, and apply sunscreen while shopping. If you are older or have a preexisting medical condition, consult a physician before you go.

- Shopping in Santa Fe anytime is an exciting excursion. Canyon Road galleries and the shops in town display an abundance of Native American, Hispanic, and contemporary crafts all year. Mariposa is a favorite of mine for contemporary jewelry and crafts, but explore the entire stretch of shops.

- Contact Robert Gallegos on 30 Alcalde Road for unique wood carvings.

- Collectors often visit Santa Fe in August during Indian Market where 1,200 tribal artisans gather from Mexico, Canada, and the United States in Santa Fe Plaza.

- Wake up early for a broad selection at Indian Market. The collectors have already scouted the scene at 5 A.M. and scooped up the best by early morning, but there's still plenty left.

- Bargaining is fair play, but Native American artists in demand may not budge. The best prices are at the end of the weekend when the artists would rather sell then pack up, and you can make a good deal.

- Visit Taos for a change of atmosphere, great galleries, and local contemporary art. Wander into Bryans Gallery on North Plaza for Native American jewelry and pots, Taos Blue on Bent Street for traditional Acoma pottery, and Salobra Gallery for contemporary, functional, and sculptural glass.

- Stop on the road in the town of Chimayo for Hispanic weavings and woodwork.

- Any shop on the one-street town of Madrid is worth a look.

Arizona
- In Phoenix, wander around Heritage Square to tour museums and shops.

- Visit the Heard Museum Gift Shop for a broad assortment of Native American jewelry and crafts.

- Contact Manfred Susunkewa at 6914 West McKinley Street for wood carvings.

- Downtown Scottsdale is filled with upscale art galleries and shops in a nineteenth-century setting.

- Buy Hopi Indian arts, Kachina dolls, and other crafts and jewelry at the Hopi Cultural Center at Second Mesa. At Third Mesa in Kykotsmovi contact Gary and Elsie Yoyokie for Hopi jewelry.

- For special Nampeyo pottery pieces try James Garcia in Keams Canyon.

- If you are a rock and mineral enthusiast, one of the more unique events in Tucson for the first two weeks every February is the Annual Gem and Mineral Show. It attracts dealers and amateurs. While you're in Tucson, visit the museum store at the Arizona-Sonora Desert Museum.

- If you want to try your hand stringing a few beads, head for The Bead Museum shop in Prescott.

- Visit the Navajo Indian Reservation and shop for weavings and other Navajo crafts at the Navajo Arts and Crafts Enterprise at Window Rock on Highway 264. Or stop by the Hubbell Trading Post in Ganado about thirty miles west of Window Rock.

- For Victorian atmosphere look around Bisbee, an old copper mining town, with galleries, artists, and aging hippies and miners. Enjoy the mix.

Colorado
- In Denver, head to Cherry Creek. There are wonderful shops in the mall but don't miss all of the stores on the surrounding streets, especially Third Avenue. Include a stop at The Tattered Cover, which is one of the largest and best-stocked independent book-stores in the country.

- There are two large outlet shopping centers worth visiting—Castle Rock Factory Shops just outside Denver in Castle Rock and Dillon Factory Stores in Dillon.

- When in Boulder, be sure to walk around downtown at the Pearl Street Mall. An enjoyable area with no street traffic, there are plenty of shops, and during the summer street permformers provide entertainment. One store in particular to visit is the Boulder Arts & Crafts Co-op, at 1421 Pearl Street.

- For Native American crafts, don't miss the Denver Museum of Natural History museum store.

- Whether you're skiing or hiking the Rockies, take time to explore the resorts and towns for western gear and ski clothing.

- Look for great sales on expensive ski clothes and equipment at the end of the ski season in late March.

- Visit Aspen, Vail, and Breckenridge for upscale shops and boutiques with snob appeal.

In July, I always attend the Cherry Creek Arts Festival. Closing off the city streets in downtown Cherry Creek, this annual festival features the nation's most competitive outdoor juried arts show. Artisans from all over the country are present. Every year I find a new treasure to display in my home.

◆

Amy Volin, mother

You'll find good buys at Copper Mountain, Beaver Creek, Snowmass, and Keystone, but nothing in the mountains is cheap.

- On Wednesday and the weekends scavenge 80 acres of the Mile High Flea Market at Interstate 76 and 88th Avenue for new and used goods. From bowling balls and baby clothes to cowboy boots and collectibles you'll find it all here at America's third-largest indoor/outdoor flea market.

Utah
- Park City, a nineteenth-century silver mining town, is the place for art galleries and specialized boutiques.

- Look for collectibles and antiques at the Salt Lake City Antique Collectors' Fair on four weekends a year in April, June, August, and October.

- Find vintage clothing and jewelry, old tools, oak furniture, books, prints, and more at the Salt Palace Convention Center a block from Temple Square downtown in Salt Lake City.

- If you're hiking around Zion National Park, stop over in the town of St. George for a quick look at quaint shops on St. George Boulevard and Main Street.

WEST & NORTHWEST COAST

California
Swap meets and stars, sand and snow, skiing, surfing, sailing, skating, and shopping. The trends start on the West Coast.

- San Francisco is a city with spectacular views and superb shopping. Leave your heart and your money at Union Square, SoMa (South of Market), Chinatown, Fisherman's Wharf, Richmond and Sunset districts, across the Bay Bridge in Berkeley, or over the Golden Gate into arty and now-touristy Sausalito. You choose.

- My favorite museum stores are in the De Young Museum in Golden Gate Park and the San Francisco Museum of Modern Art. The Exploratorium shop has wonderful toys for adults as well as children.

- Don't miss the famous City Lights Bookstore or countless other independent bookstores in the San Francisco area.

- Enjoy a sunny day of shopping on Fourth Street in Berkeley. Stop by Bette's Oceanview Diner—where there is no view of the ocean—for a memorable meal.

- Head up to wine country for spas, mud baths, and wine tastings. Most wineries will ship home whole or mixed cases.

- Go south to Monterey Bay, where John Steinbeck put Cannery Row on the map. Look for fun souvenir shopping in town and at the Monterey Bay Aquarium shops.

- The Outdoor Antique and Collectible Market at Veterans Stadium in Long Beach is held the third Sunday of every month with a special holiday show the first Sunday in November.

- Move on to Los Angeles for a quick stop at L.A.'s largest and oldest open-air food market, Grand Central Market. If you're serious about clothes bargains hit the wholesale Garment District.

- Discover the Art Shop at the L.A. County Museum of Art, and the shops at the Japanese American National Museum and The J. Paul Getty Museum.

- Mingle and shop with Hollywood celebrities in Beverly Hills, Santa Monica, Venice, and at the Rose Bowl Flea Market and Swap Meet in Pasadena. On the second Sunday of each month, dig around for old and new merchandise at the Rose Bowl, one of the largest and best-known markets in the U.S.

- Twice a year, usually in June and November, Santa Monica hosts a juried, contemporary Crafts Market at the Santa Monica Civic Auditorium at 1855 Main Street.

- Take a drive up the coast to shop in Santa Barbara.

- Don't miss these great museum shops in San Diego: Balboa Park is home to the San Diego Museum of Man and the Mingei International Museum and others. Kids will love the Zoological Society of San Diego (San Diego Zoo) and the Ruben H. Fleet Space Theater & Science Center.

Washington
- Between Puget Sound and Lake Washington, Seattle percolates with high tech, grunge music, hip culture, and caffeine.

- Start shopping downtown between 4th and 5th avenues and Olive Way and University Street.

- Head over to Pike Place Market where vendors at the Main and North Arcades sell crafts and gifts.

- Look for upscale designer boutiques in the Belltown area.

- Wander around Pioneer Square and Occidental Park for antique shops and art galleries.

- Kids will enjoy shopping for mementos at the Pacific Science Center while adults search for reproductions and Northwest Coast Indian art at the Seattle Art Museum store.

- If you have the time, do not miss the opportunity or the scenic drive to the most northwest point on the U.S. mainland, Neah Bay. This isolated but beautiful region is home to the Makah Indians. Visit the Makah Cultural & Resource Center. Buy carved wood boxes, masks, totems, jewelry, and argillite carved sculptures, all stunning examples of Northwest Coast Native American art.

SIZE COMPARISION CHART

Children's Clothes

American	3	4	5	6	6X
Continental	98	104	110	116	122
British	18	20	22	24	26

Children's Shoes

American	8	9	10	11	12	13	1	2	3	4.5	5.5	6.5
Continental	24	25	27	28	29	30	32	33	34	36	37	38.5
British	7	8	9	10	11	12	13	1	2	3	4	5.5

Men's Shirts

American	14	14.5	15	15.5	16	16.5	17	17.5	18
Continental	36	37	38	39	41	42	43	44	45
British	14	14.5	15	15.5	16	16.5	17	17.5	18

Men's Shoes

American	7	8	8.5	9	9.5	10	10.5	11	11.5	12	13
Continental	39.5	41	42	42	43	43	44	44.5	45	46	47
British	6	7	7.5	8	8.5	9	9.5	10	10	11	12

Men's Suits and Overcoats

American	32	34	36	38	40	42	44	46	48
Continental	42	44	46	48	50	52	54	56	58
British	32	34	36	38	40	42	44	46	48

Women's Dresses and Suits

American	6	8	10	12	14	16	18
Continental	36	38	40	42	44	46	48
British	8	10	12	14	16	18	20

Women's Hosiery

American	8	8.5	9	9.5	10	10.5
Continental	0	1	2	3	4	5
British	8	8.5	9	9.5	10	10.5

Women's Shoes

American	5	6/6.5	7/7.5	8/8.5	9	10
Continental	36	37	38	39	40	41
British	4	5	6	7	8	9

Socks

American	8.5	9	9.5	10	10.5	11	11.5
Continental	36/37	37/38	38/39	39/40	40/41	41/42	42/43
British	8.5	9	9.5	10	10.5	11	11.5

RESOURCES AND REFERENCES

Books

Bond, Marybeth. *Gutsy Women: Travel Tips and Wisdom for the Road.* San Francisco: Travelers' Tales, 1996.
A pocket guide with travel tips for women on the road.

Cohen, Herb. *You Can Negotiate Anything.* New York: Bantam Books, 1989.
Great advice on negotiating and techniques you can use anywhere, anytime.

Devine, Elizabeth, with Nancy L. Braganti. *The Travelers' Guide to Latin American Customs & Manners.* New York: St. Martin's Press, 1988.
A travel guide with information and tips on customs, everyday behavior, and vocabulary for fifteen Latin American countries.

Gershman, Suzy. *Born to Shop* guides. New York: Macmillian.
An insider's guide to the shopping scene in various destinations with maps, places to dine, hotels, and information on customs. The series includes Hong Kong, France, Paris, Italy, and Mexico.

Gralla, Preston. *The Complete Idiot's Guide to On-line Shopping.* Indianapolis: Alpha Books QUE, 1999.
Everything you need to know to shop on-line.

Grotta, Daniel, and Sally Wiener. *The Green Travel Sourcebook.* New York: John Wiley & Sons, 1992.
A guide for the physically active and socially aware traveler.

Herald, Jacqueline. *World Crafts*. Asheville, North Carolina: Lark Books, 1992.
A coffee-table book that celebrates the world of crafts and craft producers in Asia, Africa, Latin America, and the Caribbean in collaboration with Oxfam trading programs.

Hoff, Al. *Thrift Score*. New York: HarperCollins Publishers, 1997.
A fun read on thrift store shopping as popular culture with hints on scavenging at thrift stores, partying, and decorating with your finds.

King, Trisha, with Deborah Newmark. *Buying Retail is Stupid! USA*. Chicago: Contemporary Publishing Company, 1996.
A coast-to-coast guide on bargain-hunting strategies for factory outlets and catalogs.

Lilienfeld, Robert, with William Rathje. *Use Less Stuff*. New York: Fawcett Books, 1998.
A serious look at consuming less with money- and energy-saving tips.

Sangster, Rob. *Traveler's Tool Kit*. Birmingham, Alabama: Menasha Ridge Press, 1996.
A comprehensive reference book for traveling anywhere.

Weiss, Walter M., with Kurt-Michael Westermann. *The Bazaar Markets and Merchants of the Islamic World* (English ed.). New York: Thames and Hudson, Inc., 1998.
A coffee-table book with lavish color photographs that looks at the history, culture, and products of bazaars in the Islamic world.

Werner, Kitty, ed. *The Official Directory to U.S. Flea Markets* (6th ed.) New York: The Ballantine Publishing Group, 1998.
A bargain hunter's guide with flea market information on every state.

Whitman, John. *The Best European Travel Tips*. New York: HarperPerennial, 1995.
Tips and advice to make European travel easier, safer, and cheaper.

Fair Trade Stores

A Different Approach
824 Chartres Street
New Orleans, LA 70116
504-588-1978

Alternatives of Gainesville
1013 West University Avenue
Gainesville, FL 32601
352-375-7329
352-392-8508

The Black Cat at the White
    Dog Café
3420 Sansom Street
Philadelphia, PA 19104
215-386-6785

Cabin Creek Quilt Cooperative
4208 Malden Drive
Malden, WV 25306
304-925-9499

DZI: The Tibet Collection
117 Carroll Street N.W.
Washington, DC 20012
202-882-0008

The Eco Zone
RR2, Box 2210
Brackney, PA 18812
717-663-2962

Global Exchange
2840 College Avenue
Berkeley, CA 94705
510-548-0370

Los Pastores
Main Street
Post Office Box 118
Los Ojos, NM 87551
505-588-7821

Mountcastle International
    Trading Company
107 Eighth Avenue St. Pete
Beach, FL 33706
813-360-4743

Oceanic Art Museum Gallery/
    The Ethnic Art Institute
    of Micronesia
695 Alamitos Avenue
Long Beach, CA 90802
562-432-4477
www.oceanicmuseum.com

"Oomingmak" Musk Ox
    Producers' Cooperative
604 H Street
Anchorage, AK 99501
907-272-9225

Peace and Justice Store
21 Church Street
Burlington, VT 05401
802-863-8326

PlaNetweavers Treasure Store
1573 Haight Street
San Francisco, CA 94117
415-864-4415

SERRV International Gift Shop
500 Main Street
New Windsor, MD 21776
410-635-8757

Ten Thousand Villages
1609 North 13th
Boise, ID 83702
208-333-0535

Watermark Association
    of Artisans
150 US Highway 158E
Camden, NC 27921
252-338-0853
252-335-1434

International Craft Resources & Retail Stores

Cambodia
Khemera House
P.O. Box 1005
Phnom Penh
855-23-62463

Colombia
Asociacion Mujeres Cabeza
    de Familia
Apartado Aereo 12-54
Cali
57-2-884-2687

France
Boutic Ethic
Boite Postal 11
Le Lion D'amgers 49220
33-241951484

Ghana
Ghana Trade Fair Centre,
    Accra, Kakum National
    Park
Elmina Castle, Cape Coast
233-21-771325

Guatemala
Artensanias Schel
Calle 15, B-17-50
Colonia
San Ignacio de Mixco
Guatemala City
502-2-910-446

Haiti
Gingerbread
Petionville (outside
    Port-au-Prince)
509-577-213

India
People Tree
8, Regal Building
Parliament Street
New Delhi 11001
91-11-373-4877

Self Employed Women's
    Association (SEWA)
SEWA Reception Center
Opposite Lokmanya Tilak

Baug, Bhadra
Ahmedabad 380 001, Gujarat
91-79-550-6477
www.banascraft.org

Japan
Global Village
Noge 1-13-16
Setegaya-Ku
Tokyo 158
81-33-7050233

Kazakstan
Salon Bahyt
56A Abai Street
Almat-Ata
3272-425-777 or 426-400

Sheber Aul Artisan Village
GES 2 Kok-Shoky Village
Kaskelen Area

Kenya
Bambolulu Workshop for
the Handicapped
P.O. Box 83988
Mombasa
254-11-473571

Kyrgyzstan
Kyrgyz Style Artisan Boutique
126 Moskovskaya Street
Bishkek
3312-223-119

Laos
Phaeng Mai Gallery
117 Nongbauathong Tai Village
P.O. Box 1790
Vientiane
856-21-217-341

Mexico
Na Bolom
Vincente Guerrero #33
Barrio del Cerrillo
San Cristóbal de las Casas
Chiapas
52-967 85586

Asociación Mexicana de Arte y
    Cultura Popular (AMACUP)
Río Amazonas 17
Col. Cuauntemoc
Mexico D.F. 06500
52-5-592-7360

Nepal
Mahaguthi
P.O. Box 396
Kathmandu
977-1-521-607

Papua New Guinea
Tami Islands-Malasiga Village
    Woodcarvers
P.O. Box 177
Finschhafen
Morobe Province
675-4747073

Peru
Proart
Berlin 1491
Miraflores, Lima
511-411 1801 Tel/Fax

Philippines
Community Crafts Association
    of the Philippines
Araneta Avenue & Kaliraya St.
Metro Manila
Quezon City 1100
63-2-712-2160

Romania
Astra Museum
Str. Piata Mica Nr. 11
Sibiu, Cod 2400
40-69-218195

Russia
IRIDA gallery
Moscow

South Africa
Durban Art Gallery
City Hall, Second Floor
Smith Street
Durban 4000
27-31-300-6230

Spain
Alternativa 3 Coop V
Pere de Fices, 38
Barcelona
Terrassa 08225
34-3-735-3047
www.citinv.it/equo/

Sweden
Alternativ Handel
Sodra Larmgatan 18
Goteborg 411 16
46-31-7017600

Thailand
Grassroots HQ Company
3/31 Samlan Road, Tambon
    Phrasing
Amphur Muang, Chiang Mai
    50200
66-53-81-4717
www.asiaplus.com/ghq

United Kingdom
Traidcraft Exchange
Kingsway North
Gateshead
Tyne and Wear NE 110NE
44-191-491-0591
www.traidcraft.co.uk

Uzbekistan
Bukhara Artisan Center
    Craft Shop
B.Nakshband Street, 100
Bukhara 705018
3652-24-37-65 Tel/Fax

Meros Handcraft Center Sales
    and Exhibition Hall
State Museum of History,
    Culture and Arts
Registan Square
Samarkand
3662-35-39-18, 35-37-80

Zebiniso Artisan Gallery
(operated by the Business-
    women's Association
    of Bukhara)
Kokuli-khurd Mosque
Mehtar Anbar Street
Bukhara
3652-236-021

Zumrad
41 Afrosiyab Street
Tashkent
152-69-26, 56-81-58

Zimbabwe
Dezign Incorporated
P.O. Box 5266
Harare
263-4-755851

Mail Order Catalogs

With so many choices available the catalogs below were included
for either their unique product mix and presentation, their mission, their reliability, or some combination of these qualities.

African Market
168 2nd Avenue
Suite 409
New York, NY 10003
888-TIMBUKTU (846-2858)
*African clothes, accessories,
and gifts—products that help
promote economic development.*

Alternative Gifts International
9656 Palomar Trail
P.O. Box 2267
Lucerne Valley, CA 92356-2267
800-842-2243
www.altgifts.org
*A nonprofit organization that
sends charitable gifts and grants
to those in need internationally.*

Daily Planet
P.O. Box 64411
St. Paul, MN 55164
800-324-5950
*Fun clothes and accessories
from around the world.*

Essence
104 Challenger Drive
Portland, TN 37148
800-637-7362
*Fashion and African-inspired
clothes and accessories.*

J. Jill
P.O. Box 2006
Tilton, NH 03276
800-642-9989
*Down-to-earth clothes and acces-
sories with ethnic global influences.*

Magellan's
110 West Sola Street
Santa Barbara, CA 93101
800-962-4943
www.magellans.com
Travel gear specialists—supplies,
clothes, and accessories.

Marketplace: Handwork
  of India
1455 Ashland Avenue
Evanston, IL 60201
847-320-4011
800-726-8905
A nonprofit, fair-trade catalog
with handicrafts and clothes
from India.

PBS Home Video
P.O. Box 751089
Charlotte, NC 28275
800-645-4PBS
http://shop.pbs.org/
Public Broadcasting home
video catalog.

SERRV International
500 Main Street
P.O. Box 365
New Windsor, MD 21776-0365
410-635-8757
www.serrv.org
A nonprofit, fair-trade catalog
that promotes social and economic
progress for artisans in developing
countries by marketing their crafts.

Signals
P.O. Box 64428
St. Paul, MN 55164
800-669-9696
A catalog for fans of Public
Television.

Smithsonian Folkways
  Mail Order
955 L'Enfant Plaza, S.W., Suite
  7300 MRC 953
Washington, DC 20560
202-287-7298
800-410-9815
http://www.si.edu/organiza/offi
ces/folklife/folkways/orders.htm
A nonprofit organization offering
archival recordings and folk
music from many nations.

Sundance
3865 West 2400 South
Salt Lake City, UT 84120
800-422-2770
www.sundance.net
Gifts, crafts, and home furnish-
ings that evoke the West and
country living.

The Discovery Channel
  Stores Catalog
750 Hearst Avenue
Berkeley, CA 94710
510-644-1337
800-227-1114
Educational products from
around the world.

The Southwest Indian
   Foundation
P.O. Box 86
Gallup, NM 87302
505-863-4037
www.southwestindian.com
*A Native American foundation
featuring handmade crafts from
various tribes including Zuni,
Navajo, Hopi, Laguna, Acoma,
and Apache that helps support
their philanthropic programs.*

The Tibet Collection
117 Carroll Street, N.W.
Washington, DC 20012
202-882-0008 Phone
202-882-6697 Fax
www.dZi.com
*A fair-trade catalog that markets
handmade clothes, accessories,
folk arts, and gifts from Tibetan
refugees.*

TravelSmith
60 Leveroni Court
Novato, CA 94949
800-950-1600
*Travel gear—clothes, accessories,
luggage, and advice.*

Whispering Pines
43 Ruane Street
Fairfield, CT 06430
800-836-4662
*Gifts, clothes, and home acces-
sories that evoke the cabin spirit.*

Womenswork
Little Big Farm
P.O. Box 543
York, Me 03909
800-639-2709
*Gloves and accessories for
   hard work.*

Museum Stores/Catalogs

Albright-Knox Art Gallery
1285 Elmwood Avenue
Buffalo, NY 14222
716-882-8700 ext. 232

American Museum of
   Natural History
Central Park West at
   79th Street
New York, NY 10024-5192
212-769-5150

Art Institute of Chicago
104 South Michigan Avenue,
   Suite 100
Chicago, IL 60603-6110
312-443-3535 store
800-621-9337 catalog

Brooklyn Museum of Art
200 Eastern Parkway
Brooklyn, NY 11238
718-638-5000 ext. 258

Colonial Williamsburg
   Foundation
P.O. Box 1776
Williamsburg, VA 23187-1776
800-446-9240 catalog

Eiteljorg Museum
500 West Washington St.
Indianapolis, IN 46204-2707
317-636-9378 ext. 139 or 167

Exploratorium Store
3601 Lyon Street
San Francisco, CA 94123
415-561-0390
www.exploratorium.edu/store

Franklin Institute Science
   Museum
222 N. 20th Street
Philadelphia, PA 19103-1194
215-448-1134

Harvard Collections
Harvard University
1350 Massachusetts Avenue
Cambridge, MA 02138
617-496-0700

Heard Museum Gift Shop
22 E. Monte Vista Road
Phoenix, AZ 85004
602-251-0237

Massachusetts Institute
   of Technology
MIT Museum Shop
77 Mass. Avenue N52
Cambridge, MA 02139
617-253-4462 catalog

Monterey Bay Aquarium
886 Cannery Row
Monterey, CA 93940-1085
831-648-4888

Museum of Fine Arts Boston
465 Huntington Avenue
Boston, MA 02115
617-267-9300
800-225-5592 catalog

Museum of Modern Art (MoMA)
11 West 53rd Street
New York, NY 10019
212-708-9400
800-447-6662 catalog

Mystic Seaport Museum Stores
47 Greenmanville Avenue
Mystic, CT 06355
860-572-5385

National Building Museum
401 F. Street, N.W.
Washington, DC 20001
202-272-7706

National Gallery of Art
6th Street and Constitution
   Avenue, N.W.
Washington, DC 20565
202-842-6476
www.nga.gov

National Geographic Society
1145 17th Street N.W.
Washington, DC 20036
202-857-7592
888-225-5647 catalog

National Museum of
   Naval Aviation
P.O. Box 33104
Pensacola, FL 32508-3104
904-456-7037
800-247-6289 catalog

Philadelphia Museum of Art
26th Street and The Parkway
P.O. Box 7646
Philadelphia, PA 19130
215-684-7960

San Francisco Museum
   of Modern Art
Museum Store
151 Third Street
San Francisco, CA 94103
415-357-4035

Smithsonian Institution
Museum Shops & Catalog
Washington, DC 20560
202-287-3303
800-322-0344 catalog
http://www.si.edu/youandsi/
products/start.htm

The Guggenheim Museum
1071 Fifth Avenue
New York, NY 10128
212-423-3622
800-329-6109 catalog

The Metropolitan Museum of Art
1000 Fifth Avenue
New York, NY 10028
212-570-3894
800-468-7386 catalog

The Morikami
4000 Morikami Park Road
Delray Beach, FL 33446
561-495-0233

The Textile Museum
2320 South Street, N.W.
Washington, DC 20008
202-667-0441 ext. 29 shop
         & catalog

Thomas Jefferson Memorial
   Foundation
Monticello Museum Shops
P.O. Box 316
Charlottesville, VA 22902
804-984-9840
800-243-0743 catalog

Winterthur Museum Stores
Route 52
Winterthur, DE 19735
302-888-4822
800-767-0500 catalog

Yale University Art Gallery
201 York St.
P.O. Box 208271
New Haven, CT 06520-0271
203-432-0600

Zoological Society of San Diego
10946 Willow Ct., Bldg. 200
San Diego, CA 92127-2498
619-232-3821 ext. 239

Organizations

Aid To Artisans (ATA)
14 Brick Walk Lane
Farmington, CT 06032
860-677-1649 Phone
860-676-2170 Fax
www.aid2artisans.org
*Offers practical assistance to artisans worldwide in product develop-
ment, production, and marketing. Through training and craft projects provides sustainable economic and social benefits for craftspeople and fosters artistic traditions in an environmental and culturally
sensitive manner. Publishes an informative newsletter.*

American Friends Service Committee
Development Office
1501 Cherry Street
Philadelphia, PA 19102
Fosters sustainable local economies.

Co-op America
1612 K Street, N.W., Suite 600
Washington, DC 20006
800-58-GREEN / 202- 872-5307 Phone
202-331-8166 Fax
*Provides the economic strategies for businesses, deals with social and
environmental problems with programs for small green businesses,
consumer education, socially responsible corporations, and sustainable living. Publishes* National Green Pages, *a directory of socially
responsible businesses.*

The Crafts Center
1001 Connecticut Avenue, N.W., Suite 525
 Washington, DC 20036
202-728-9603 Phone

202-296-2452 Fax
www.craftscenter.org
A membership organization dedicated to improving the lives of low-income artisans by increasing their economic independence and supporting crafts production that respects fair trade and labor practices, cultural traditions, and the environment. Provides market links and clearinghouse of information about and for indigenous artisans. Publishes an informative newsletter.

Fair Trade Federation, Inc.
P.O. Box 3754
Gettysburg, PA 17325
717-334-5583
www.fairtradefederation.com
An association of fair-trade wholesalers, retailers, and producers whose members are committed to providing fair wages and good employment opportunities to economically disadvantaged artisans and farmers worldwide. Directly links low-income producers with consumer markets and educates consumers about the importance of purchasing fairly traded products which support living wages and safe and healthy conditions for workers in the Third World.

Indian Arts & Crafts Association
122 La Veta, N.E., Suite B
Albuquerque, NM 87108-1613
505-265-9149
Provides information and support for Native American artists.

International Colored Gemstone Association
3 East 48th Street, Fifth Floor
New York, NY 10017
212-688-8452 Phone
212-688-9006 Fax
E-mail: ica@gemstone.org

A nonprofit association that promotes gemstone standards and ethics internationally and provides educational information on buying gemstones. Consumers can read shopping tips on their web site: http://gemstone.org/tips.html

Museum Stores Association (MSA)
4100 East Mississippi Avenue, #800
Denver, CO 80246-3048
303-504-9223 Phone
303-504-9585 Fax
Provides museum store support for domestic and international museums.

Oxfam America
26 West Street
Boston, MA 02111-1206
Member organizations work with craft producers in poor countries, paying fair prices. These goods are sold through member trading catalogs.

VSA (formally Very Special Arts)
1300 Connecticut Avenue, N.W.
Washington, DC 20036
www.gallery.vsarts.org
Promotes arts, education, and creative expression of children and adults with disabilities. Acts as resource and showcases art. Offers work for sale on-line and member galleries throughout the U.S.

Resources

Better Business Bureau
1012 14th Street, N.W., 14th Floor
Washington DC 20005-3410
202-393-8000 24-hour phone
202-393-1198 fax

www.dc.bbb.org
Consumer information and tips.

CITES (Convention on International Trade in Endangered Species)
Secretariat
15, chemin des Anémones,
CH-1219 Châtelaine-Genève
Switzerland
(+4122) 979 9139/40 Phone
(+4122) 797 3417 Fax
E-mail: cites@unep.ch
http://www.wcmc.org.uk/CITES/english/index.html
*Obtain documents and international trade information on
endangered species.*

Consumer Information Center (CIC)
Pueblo, Colorado 81009
888-878-3256
http://www.pueblo.gsa.gov/
One-stop shopping for federal consumer publications.

European Tax-free Shopping (ETS)
233 South Wacker Drive, Suite 9700
Chicago, IL 60606
312-382-1100
Information on VAT refunds and tax-free shopping in Europe.

U.S. Customs Service
1300 Pennsylvania Avenue, N.W.
Washington, DC 20229
Brochure Know Before You Go *gives you everything you ever
wanted to know about customs regulations and restrictions.
Available free on-line:*
http://www.customs.ustreas.gov/travel/kbygo.htm

U.S. Fish and Wildlife Service
P.O. Box. 3247
Arlington, VA 22203-3247
703-358-1949
Information on federal wildlife laws, import and export regulations.
Contact for nearest state office.

U.S. State Department
Washington, DC 20520
202-647-6575
www.state.gov
www.state.gov/www/regions_missions.html
Contact for information on security and travel warnings. Links to
embassies and web sites of countries around the world.

Travel Sources

Aid to Artisans (see organization listing above)
860-677-1649

Born to Shop Tours
800-442-6871

Craft World Tours (CWT)
6776CN Warboys
Byron, NY 14422
716-548-2667 Phone
716-548-2821 Fax

Web Sites

Better Business Bureau
BBBOnLine, Inc.
4200 Wilson Boulevard, 8th Floor
Arlington, VA 22203

BBBOnLine Reliability 703-247-9370
BBBOnLine Privacy 703-247-9336
BBBOnLine Privacy Dispute Resolution Intake Center
888-679-3353
www.bbbonline.org
Advice for safe surfing and shopping on-line. Information on filing complaints.

www.cc.cc.ca.us/pfp/index.htm
Potters for Peace (PFP) is a nonprofit network of potters concerned with peace and justice issues. Their on-line catalog helps support pottery cooperatives in Nicaragua.

www.concentric.net/~flieb/
The Enterprising Kitchen is a nonprofit business that provides employment and job training to impoverished women in Chicago's Uptown community.

www.consumerreports.com
Consumer Reports on-line. Free access parts of the site; subscription needed to other parts. Provides advice, ratings, and recommendations, based on independent testing of consumer products and services. No advertising on this site.

www.consumerworld.org
A public service site that gathers useful consumer resources and categorizes them for easy access. Provides buying advice and product reviews. Helps comparison shop for goods and services, files consumer complaints, researches information and scams

www.dZi.com
The Tibet Collection
Clothes and crafts made by Tibetan refugee artisans.

www.ecomall.com
Features links to catalogs that offer environmentally conscious products and links to other eco-friendly information.

www.equalexchange.com
Sells fairly traded gourmet coffee from worker-owned co-ops directly from small-scale farmers in Latin America and Africa.

www.ethicalshopper.com
Shopping source for socially and environmentally responsible products including crafts, hair products, food, furniture, and charitable gifts.

www.eziba.com
Sells global crafts and home furnishings with educational information.

www.fleamarketguide.com
State-by-state directory of flea markets.

www.globalmarketcrafts.com
Socially responsible on-line catalog selling items made by craftspeople using fair-trade practices from developing nations in Central and South America, Africa, and from Native Americans.

www.greenshopping.com
Information, magazine, products, and links to other environmentally friendly goods and services.

www.geocities.com/RainForest/7678
Yard sale stories and tips.

www.peoplink.org
A nonprofit global marketplace selling crafts and accessories.

www.realgoods.com
Sells a wide range of energy and conservation products. Offers publications and educational demonstrations.

www.serrv.org
A nonprofit on-line catalog that promotes social and economic progress of craftspeople in developing countries.

www.shop2give.com
Shop and donate a percentage of your purchase from participating on-line retailers to your favorite charity.

www.thephillipscollection.com
An on-line catalog that sells useful cultural objects and home furnishings with stories about the craft artisans who make them around the world.

www.webcharity.com
Virtual thrift shop and on-line auction site that raises funds through donations to the site and dedicates 100 percent of the sale price to your designated cause and allows tax deductions.

www.womensconsumernet.com
Service that finds the best value on products, services, and information.

www.4charity.com
Web site that donates a percentage of your purchase to your designated charity from linked on-line retailers.

INDEX

INDEX OF
CONTRIBUTORS

———

ACKNOWLEDGMENTS

My sincere thanks go to all those at Travelers' Tales who made this book a reality. To James O'Reilly, Larry Habegger, and Sean O'Reilly, thank you for the idea and the opportunity. My appreciation extends to Susan Brady, whose early guidance and cheerful answers to my many questions began the process, and to Lisa Bach, whose expert editing and organizing skills guided me toward a finished product. The book is a better one for your efforts. Thank you both for your encouragement, suggestions, and patience.

Thank you to all my friends and colleagues who contributed stories and information, especially Nina Smith and Caroline Ramsay Merriam from the Crafts Center and Mary Cockram and Clare Brett Smith from Aid to Artisans. To my brothers Michael and Steven, my cousin Lissa Spiller, and to my friends Rebecca Phillips Abbott, Laura Kaufman, Bette Ann Libby, Florence Lloyd, Peg Nadler, Carl Nash, Judith Katz Nath, Sharon Nelson, Bruce Sklarew, thank you for your supportive voices along the way. Special thanks to Richard Solloway for your ninth-hour rescue to fill in the exotic gaps and to Andrea Boyarsky-Maisel and Terry Lewis for all the introductions and for letting me tag along on your early-morning excursions.

My gratitude to my parents, who are ever present, and to my son Josh knows no bounds. Josh, thank you for reading all the early drafts. Your editing skills, encouragement, and good humor are well beyond your years. Thank you for cheering me on and being a constant joy in my life.

ABOUT THE AUTHOR

———

Kathy Borrus's passion for travel led her to a career as a buyer. She is former assistant director, merchandise manager, and buyer for the Smithsonian Institution Museum Shops, and is currently a specialty retail marketing consultant and free-lance writer. As part of her current consulting work, Kathy advises indigenous populations in developing countries on product development projects. She speaks internationally on merchandising topics, and her writing has appeared in *The Boston Globe*, *The Business of Crafts*, *Art Business News*, and the *Crafts Report*.

Kathy first stepped foot outside of the U.S. during a college year abroad studying in Amsterdam. Since then, roaming the world as a Fearless Shopper, she has traveled to more than forty countries and to five continents. Kathy's two favorite countries in which to shop are Italy and India; to bargain, Morocco; to seek out textiles, Guatemala, Indonesia and India; to discover garnets and glass, the Czech Republic; to hunt for rocks and minerals, Uruguay and Brazil; and to entertain her son in toy stores, Japan. When not traipsing the world in pursuit of a great bargain, Kathy can be found with a good book, on the tennis courts, at art galleries, or on the ski slopes. She revels in being a mom and lives in Washington D.C. with her son.

TRAVELERS' TALES GUIDES

LOOK FOR THESE TITLES IN THE SERIES

FOOTSTEPS: THE SOUL OF TRAVEL
A NEW IMPRINT FROM TRAVELERS' TALES GUIDES

An imprint of Travelers' Tales Guides, the Footsteps series unveils new works by first-time authors, established writers, and reprints of works whose time has come…again. Each book will fire your imagination, disturb your sleep, and feed your soul.

KITE STRINGS OF THE SOUTHERN CROSS
A Woman's Travel Odyssey
By Laurie Gough
ISBN 1-885211-30-9
400 pages, $24.00, Hardcover

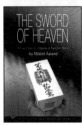

THE SWORD OF HEAVEN
A Five Continent Odyssey to Save the World
By Mikkel Aaland
ISBN 1-885211-44-9
350 pages, $24.00, Hardcover

ᎧPECIAL INTEREST

THE FEARLESS SHOPPER
How to Get the Best Deals on the Planet
By Kathy Borrus
ISBN 1-885211-39-2, 200 pages, $12.95

Check with your local bookstore for
these titles or visit our web site at
www.travelerstales.com

$\mathscr{S}$PECIAL INTEREST

THE GIFT OF BIRDS:
True Encounters with Avian Spirits
Edited by Larry Habegger & Amy Greimann Carlson
ISBN 1-885211-41-4, 275 pages, $17.95

TESTOSTERONE PLANET:
True Stories from a Man's World
Edited by Sean O'Reilly, Larry Habegger & James O'Reilly
ISBN 1-885211-43-0, 300 pages, $17.95

THE PENNY PINCHER'S PASSPORT TO LUXURY TRAVEL
The Art of Cultivating Preferred Customer Status
By Joel L. Widzer
ISBN 1-885211-31-7, 253 pages, $12.95

DANGER!
True Stories of Trouble and Survival
Edited by James O'Reilly, Larry Habegger & Sean O'Reilly
ISBN 1-885211-32-5, 336 pages, $17.95

FAMILY TRAVEL:
The Farther You Go, the Closer You Get
Edited by Laura Manske
ISBN 1-885211-33-3, 368 pages, $17.95

$\mathscr{S}$PECIAL INTEREST

THE GIFT OF TRAVEL:
The Best of Travelers' Tales
Edited by Larry Habegger, James O'Reilly & Sean O'Reilly
ISBN 1-885211-25-2, 240 pages, $14.95

THERE'S NO TOILET PAPER...ON THE ROAD LESS TRAVELED:
The Best of Travel Humor and Misadventure
Edited by Doug Lansky
ISBN 1-885211-27-9, 207 pages, $12.95

A DOG'S WORLD:
True Stories of Man's Best Friend on the Road
Edited by Christine Hunsicker
ISBN 1-885211-23-6, 257 pages, $12.95

$\mathscr{W}$OMEN'S TRAVEL

A WOMAN'S PASSION FOR TRAVEL
More True Stories from A Woman's World
Edited by Marybeth Bond & Pamela Michael
ISBN 1-885211-36-8, 375 pages, $17.95

SAFETY AND SECURITY FOR WOMEN WHO TRAVEL
By Sheila Swan & Peter Laufer
ISBN 1-885211-29-5, 159 pages, $12.95

$\mathcal{W}$OMEN'S TRAVEL

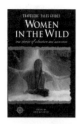

WOMEN IN THE WILD:
True Stories of Adventure and Connection
Edited by Lucy McCauley
ISBN 1-885211-21-X, 307 pages, $17.95

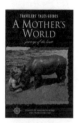

A MOTHER'S WORLD:
Journeys of the Heart
Edited by Marybeth Bond & Pamela Michael
ISBN 1-885211-26-0, 233 pages, $14.95

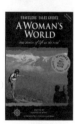

A WOMAN'S WORLD:
True Stories of Life on the Road
Edited by Marybeth Bond
Introduction by Dervla Murphy
ISBN 1-885211-06-6
475 pages, $17.95

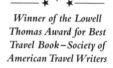

Winner of the Lowell
Thomas Award for Best
Travel Book – Society of
American Travel Writers

GUTSY WOMEN:
Travel Tips and Wisdom for the Road
By Marybeth Bond
ISBN 1-885211-15-5, 123 pages, $7.95

GUTSY MAMAS:
Travel Tips and Wisdom for
Mothers on the Road
By Marybeth Bond
ISBN 1-885211-20-1, 139 pages, $7.95

ℬODY & SOUL

THE ADVENTURE OF FOOD:
True Stories of Eating Everything
Edited by Richard Sterling
ISBN 1-885211-37-6, 375 pages, $17.95

*Small Press Book
Award Winner and
Benjamin Franklin
Award Finalist*

THE ROAD WITHIN:
**True Stories of Transformation
and the Soul**
*Edited by Sean O'Reilly, James O'Reilly
& Tim O'Reilly*
ISBN 1-885211-19-8, 459 pages, $17.95

LOVE & ROMANCE:
True Stories of Passion on the Road
Edited by Judith Babcock Wylie
ISBN 1-885211-18-X, 319 pages, $17.95

*Silver Medal Winner of the
Lowell Thomas Award for
Best Travel Book—Society of
American Travel Writers*

FOOD:
A Taste of the Road
Edited by Richard Sterling
Introduction by Margo True
ISBN 1-885211-09-0
467 pages, $17.95

THE FEARLESS DINER:
**Travel Tips and Wisdom for Eating
around the World**
By Richard Sterling
ISBN 1-885211-22-8, 139 pages, $7.95

$\mathscr{C}$OUNTRY GUIDES

AUSTRALIA
True Stories of Life Down Under
Edited by Larry Habegger & Amy Greimann Carlson
ISBN 1-885211-40-6, 375 pages, $17.95

AMERICA
Edited by Fred Setterberg
ISBN 1-885211-28-7, 550 pages, $19.95

JAPAN
Edited by Donald W. George
& Amy Greimann Carlson
ISBN 1-885211-04-X, 437 pages, $17.95

ITALY
Edited by Anne Calcagno
Introduction by Jan Morris
ISBN 1-885211-16-3, 463 pages, $17.95

INDIA
Edited by James O'Reilly & Larry Habegger
ISBN 1-885211-01-5, 538 pages, $17.95

COUNTRY GUIDES

FRANCE
*Edited by James O'Reilly, Larry Habegger
& Sean O'Reilly*
ISBN 1-885211-02-3, 517 pages, $17.95

MEXICO
Edited by James O'Reilly & Larry Habegger
ISBN 1-885211-00-7, 463 pages, $17.95

──── ★ ★ ★ ────

***Winner of the Lowell
Thomas Award for Best
Travel Book — Society of
American Travel Writers***

THAILAND
*Edited by James O'Reilly
& Larry Habegger*
ISBN 1-885211-05-8
483 pages, $17.95

SPAIN
Edited by Lucy McCauley
ISBN 1-885211-07-4, 495 pages, $17.95

NEPAL
Edited by Rajendra S. Khadka
ISBN 1-885211-14-7, 423 pages, $17.95

$\mathscr{C}$OUNTRY GUIDES

BRAZIL

Edited by Annette Haddad & Scott Doggett
Introduction by Alex Shoumatoff
ISBN 1-885211-11-2
452 pages, $17.95

— ★ ★ ★ —
Benjamin Franklin
Award Winner

$\mathscr{C}$ITY GUIDES

HONG KONG

Edited by James O'Reilly, Larry Habegger & Sean O'Reilly
ISBN 1-885211-03-1, 439 pages, $17.95

PARIS

Edited by James O'Reilly, Larry Habegger & Sean O'Reilly
ISBN 1-885211-10-4, 417 pages, $17.95

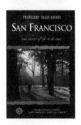

SAN FRANCISCO

Edited by James O'Reilly, Larry Habegger & Sean O'Reilly
ISBN 1-885211-08-2, 491 pages, $17.95

ℛEGIONAL GUIDES

HAWAI'I
True Stories of the Island Spirit
Edited by Rick & Marcie Carroll
ISBN 1-885211-35-X, 416 pages, $17.95

GRAND CANYON
True Stories of Life Below the Rim
Edited by Sean O'Reilly,
James O'Reilly & Larry Habegger
ISBN 1-885211-34-1, 296 pages, $17.95

SUBMIT YOUR OWN TRAVEL TALE

Do you have a tale of your own that you would like to submit to Travelers' Tales? We highly recommend that you first read one or more of our books to get a feel for the kind of story we're looking for. For submission guidelines and a list of titles in the works, send a SASE to:

Travelers' Tales Submission Guidelines
330 Townsend Street, Suite 208, San Francisco, CA 94107

or send email to *guidelines@travelerstales.com*
or visit our Web site at **www.travelerstales.com**

You can send your story to the address above or via email to *submit@travelerstales.com.* On the outside of the envelope, *please indicate what country/topic your story is about*. If your story is selected for one of our titles, we will contact you about rights and payment.

We hope to hear from you. In the meantime, enjoy the stories!